The Long Revolution

Criticism
Culture and Society
Towards 2000
Communications
Television: Technology and Cultural Form
Drama in Performance
Modern Tragedy
Drama from Ibsen to Brecht
The English Novel from Dickens to Lawrence
Orwell
The Country and the City
Politics and Letters (interviews)
Problems in Materialism and Culture
(selected essays)

Fiction
Border Country
Second Generation
The Fight for Manod
The Volunteers
Loyalties
People of the Black Mountains I The Beginning
People of the Black Mountains II The Eggs of the Eagle

The Long Revolution

RAYMOND WILLIAMS

The Hogarth Press

LONDON

Published in 1992 by
The Hogarth Press
20 Vauxhall Bridge Road
London SWIV 2SA

First published by
Chatto & Windus Ltd 1961

A CIP catalogue record for this book is
available from the British Library.

ISBN 0 7012 0898 8

Printed and bound in Great Britain by
Mackays of Chatham PLC, Chatham, Kent

Cover design and illustration by Jeff Fisher

Foreword to the 1961 edition

I HAVE been helped by many people in writing this book, and wish to record my thanks. I am especially grateful to my wife, not only for much general help with the whole text, but for her detailed work in relation to Part Two, Chapter Five. I was greatly helped by my colleague Michael Carritt in discussion of the problems of what we mean by creativity, and for a time the discussion was so close and continuous that it became difficult to separate his ideas from my own; I am sure, in any case, that my account as it stands owes much to him, though I cannot involve him in my errors. I was also helped by Edward Thompson's criticism of an earlier draft of my history of the popular press, and am grateful to him for this as for much else. Other friends, especially Stuart Hall and H. P. Smith, have helped perhaps more than they know. I would also record my general indebtedness to the published works which I list at the end.

Parts of the book have previously appeared in *Partisan Review* (New York), *Nuova Corrente* (Milan), *Monthly Review* (New York), *Universities and Left Review*, and *New Left Review*.

R. W.

Contents

Introduction

THIS book has been planned and written as a continuation of the work begun in my *Culture and Society, 1780–1950*. I described that book as 'an account and an interpretation of our responses in thought and feeling to changes in English society since the late eighteenth century', and this, of course, was its main function, a critical history of ideas and values in this period of decisive change. Yet the method of the book, and in particular its concluding chapter, led to a further intention: from analysing and interpreting the ideas and values I moved to an attempt to reinterpret and extend them, in terms of a still changing society and of my own experience in it.

I did not foresee, when I was working on *Culture and Society*, that by the time it was published an important part of our general social thinking would have developed along lines which included my own themes. The result of this development was not only that the book was very extensively discussed—I have read more than fifty thousand words of comment on it, and taken part in very many verbal discussions—but also that the lines of argument opened up went in many cases considerably beyond the scope of the book itself. I had planned and drafted much of the present book before *Culture and Society* was published, but I have now considerably revised it to take account of the discussion. I have kept, however, to my own ideas of the further work that was necessary, and have limited this book to what in any case I should have written about: questions in the theory of culture, historical analysis of certain cultural institutions and forms, and problems of meaning and action in our contemporary cultural situation. I can work in these general fields only to the limit of my own interests, and do not suppose these to be ideally complete. Indeed I have already risked an extension and variety of themes well beyond the limits of any kind of academic prudence, for what seems to me the good reason that there is no academic subject within which the questions

I am interested in can be followed through; I hope one day there might be, for it was quite obvious from the discussion of *Culture and Society* that the pressure of these questions was not only personal but general.

My title is taken from a sentence in *Culture and Society*, but a further note on it might be useful. It seems to me that we are living through a long revolution, which our best descriptions only in part interpret. It is a genuine revolution, transforming men and institutions; continually extended and deepened by the actions of millions, continually and variously opposed by explicit reaction and by the pressure of habitual forms and ideas. Yet it is a difficult revolution to define, and its uneven action is taking place over so long a period that it is almost impossible not to get lost in its exceptionally complicated process.

The democratic revolution commands our political attention. Here the conflicts are most explicit, and the questions of power involved make it very uneven and confused. Yet in any general view it is impossible to mistake the rising determination, almost everywhere, that people should govern themselves, and make their own decisions, without concession of this right to any particular group, nationality or class. In sixty years of this century the politics of the world have already been changed beyond recognition in any earlier terms. Whether in popular revolution, in the liberation movements of colonial peoples, or in the extension of parliamentary suffrage, the same basic demand is evident. Yet the demand has been and is being very powerfully resisted, not only by the weight of other traditions, but by violence and fraud. If we take the criterion that people should govern themselves (the methods by which they do so being less important than this central fact) it is evident that the democratic revolution is still at a very early stage.

The industrial revolution, backed by immense scientific development, commands our economic attention. Its rate of expansion, in the world as a whole, is already greater than anyone had foreseen, and is indeed too rapid to be easily interpreted. Yet, while its aims and methods have been almost universally accepted, most of the world is still far behind the stage actually reached in the advanced countries, while in the advanced countries the sense of possibility in the transformation of nature is being continually and rapidly extended. Thus the industrial revolution, in its broad sense, is also at a comparatively early stage. Moreover, it is evident that its correlation with the growth of democracy is by no means simple. On the one hand it seems clear that industrial development is a powerful incentive to new kinds of democratic organization. On the other hand the apparent needs of industrial organization, at many levels from the process of accumulating capital to the status of the worker in a very extensive and divided technical system, sometimes delay, sometimes frustrate the aspiration to share in the making of decisions. The complex interaction between the democratic and industrial revolutions is at the centre of our most difficult social thinking.

Yet there remains a third revolution, perhaps the most difficult of all to interpret. We speak of a cultural revolution, and we must certainly see the aspiration to extend the active process of learning, with the skills of literacy and other advanced communication, to all people rather than to limited groups, as comparable in importance to the growth of democracy and the rise of scientific industry. This aspiration has been and is being resisted, sometimes openly, sometimes subtly, but as an aim it has been formally acknowledged, almost universally. Of course, this revolution is at a very early stage. Bare literacy is still unattained by hundreds of millions, while in the advanced countries the sense of possibility, in expanding education and in developing new means of communication, is being revised and extended. Here, as in democracy and industry, what we have done seems little compared with what we are certain to try to do.

Yet at this point it is particularly evident that we cannot understand the process of change in which we are involved if we limit ourselves to thinking of the democratic, industrial and cultural revolutions as separate processes. Our whole way of life, from the shape of our communities to the organization and content of education, and from the structure of the family to the status of art and entertainment, is being profoundly affected by the progress and interaction of democracy and industry, and by the extension of communications. This deeper cultural revolution is a large part of our most significant living experience, and is being interpreted and indeed fought out, in very complex ways, in the world of art and ideas. It is when we try to correlate change of this kind with the changes covered by the disciplines of politics, economics and communications that we discover some of the most difficult but also some of the most human questions.

The scale of the whole process—the struggle for democracy, the development of industry, the extension of communications, and the deep social and personal changes—is indeed too large to know or even imagine. In practice it is reduced to a series of disconnected or local changes, but while this is reasonable, in the ordinary sense, it seems to me that this scaling-down only disguises some of the deepest problems and tensions, which then appear only as scattered symptoms of restlessness and uncertainty. In a country like Britain, in which the long revolution is at a relatively advanced stage, it seems customary for each generation to announce the completion of the revolution, and to be bewildered and angry when the new young generation asserts that the revolution has after all not occurred. We are quite clearly in this situation in 1960, when the objectives for which many generations worked have been quite generally achieved, yet when the society has never been more radically criticized, not only by particular writers and thinkers, in articulate ways, but also more generally and in ways often so inarticulate and confused that old descriptions, such as cynicism, apathy, pointlessness, are usually the best we can find to acknowledge them. We seem severely hindered, in such a situation, by the very practice of scaling-down. Thus certain expectations are shaped and defined, as universal suffrage, a particular standard of living, a given school-leaving age and level of education. These are adequate as incentives to effort, and anyone who knows their history knows that their achievement did not simply evolve, but had to be worked and struggled for, over generations. But it is characteristic of the history of what I see as the long revolution that such aims, once achieved, are quite quickly absorbed, and either new expectations are commonly defined, or in their absence there is a mood of both stagnation and restlessness. For a long time now we have been hearing from every kind of ruling group that people are never satisfied, never even grateful. Indeed this thrust of demand has been so deeply learned, and is so deeply feared, that one can see, on all sides, a ruling philosophy of delayed and graded concessions, for, as has been said, today's concession is to-morrow's springboard. Ruling groups have their own reasons for not wishing to recognize the true scale of the revolution, but elsewhere it is a genuine crisis of consciousness, and anybody concerned with his own life and the life of his society, in this process of general change, must obviously do what he can to try to resolve and clarify. My own view is that we must keep trying to grasp the process as a whole, to see it in new ways as a long revolution, if we are to understand either the theoretical crisis, or our actual history, or the reality of our immediate condition and the terms of change.

A very large part of our intellectual life, to say nothing of our social practice, is, however, devoted to criticizing the long revolution, in this or that aspect, by many powerful selective techniques. But as the revolution itself extends, until nobody can escape it, this whole drift seems increasingly irrelevant. In naming the great process of change the long revolution, I am trying to learn assent to it, an adequate assent of mind and spirit. I find increasingly that the values and meanings I need are all in this process of change. If it is pointed out, in traditional terms, that democracy, industry, and extended communication are all means rather than ends, I reply that this, precisely, is their revolutionary character, and that to realize and accept this requires new ways of thinking and feeling, new conceptions of relationships, which we must try to explore. This book is a record of such an attempt.

In my first part I begin from an examination of the nature of creative activity, which I see now as the necessary basis for extending the account of the relation between communication and community which I tried to establish in *Culture and Society*. I then go back to examining certain theoretical problems in the definition and analysis of culture, and work a practical example. Following a lead from the discussion of communication, I then try to analyse the concepts of 'the individual' and 'society' that we ordinarily use, and to describe certain typical relationships of this kind. I then extend this argument to a discussion of some of the existing concepts of our own society, and discuss some of the processes of social and cultural change.

My second part is an account and analysis of the development of certain of our major cultural institutions, from education to the press, and is completed by a series of essays on the relation between certain forms in art and the general development of the society. I think much of this is useful simply as information brought together in the light of a common process, though I do not doubt that my factual accounts will have to be revised as research continues. The critical essays are experimental and arguable, but attempt to develop the kind of inquiry represented by my chapter on 'The Industrial Novel' in *Culture and Society*.

My third and concluding part returns to the theme of the long revolution, which I have outlined in this introduction, by attempting a description of our contemporary culture and society in terms of what I see as a pattern of change. Briefly I attempt to assess the progress of the long revolution in Britain, and to consider its next stages. I do not confine myself to British society because of any lack of interest in what is happening elsewhere, but because the kind of evidence I am interested in is only really available where one lives. I think, however, that it could be added that Britain was very early in entering this revolution, and that our society consequently offers very rich material for the consideration of some of its general problems. It is true also that the present crisis in British society is sufficiently interesting in itself, and of commanding importance to those of us involved in it, to make this attempt to take bearings useful.

With this book and *Culture and Society*, and with my novel *Border Country* which I believe to have, in its particular and quite different way, an essential relevance to the two general books, I have completed a body of work which I set myself to do ten years ago. Other work will necessarily follow from this, but it feels like the completion of a particular stage in one's life, and while this need not interest anybody else, it is perhaps worth recording.

PART ONE

ONE

The Creative Mind

No word in English carries a more consistently positive reference than 'creative', and obviously we should be glad of this, when we think of the values it seeks to express and the activities it offers to describe. Yet, clearly, the very width of the reference involves not only difficulties of meaning, but also, through habit, a kind of unthinking repetition which at times makes the word seem useless. I propose to examine the significance of the 'creative' idea: first, by reviewing its history; second, by comparing its development as a term in the arts with some important recent scientific work on perception and communication; third, by looking at it as a possible key term in our contemporary discussion of culture—a discussion which centres on the relations between art and learning and the whole complex of our activities that we call our society.

I

The history of the 'creative' idea is in many ways difficult to trace. It seems to me to begin, essentially, in the thought of the Renaissance, but, when we look at these sources, we find its originators referring the idea to classical thought, as if unaware of the new emphasis they seem to be making. In any past writing, only part of the original meaning is recoverable, for the meaning as a whole has come to us through many minds, and even when we have distinguished their influence we find that the original significance is, with its context, still partly withheld. Yet as I read the authors, in particular Aristotle and Plato, on whom these Renaissance thinkers relied, I see a distinction, an altered significance, which seems of fundamental importance. The activity being described is a common activity, but its description, essentially, has altered.

We speak now of the artist's activity as 'creation', but the word used by Plato and Aristotle is the very different 'imitation'. The general meaning of the Greek word *mimesis* is either 'doing what another has done', or 'making something like something else'. In actual use it included the activities of the dancer, the singer, the musician, the painter, the sculptor, the actor, the dramatist, and the common quality in these activities was seen as 'the representation of something else': 'imitation'. Aristotle wrote:

> The general origin of poetry was due to two causes, each of them part of human nature. Imitation is natural to man from childhood, one of his advantages over the lower animals being this, that he is the most imitative creature in the world, and learns at first by imitation. And it is also natural for all to delight in works of imitation. The truth of this second point is shown by experience: though the objects themselves may be painful to see, we delight to view the most realistic representations of them in art, the forms for example of the lowest animals and of dead bodies. The explanation is to be found in a further fact: to be learning something is the greatest of pleasures not only to the philosopher but also to the rest of mankind, however small their capacity for it; the reason of the delight in seeing the picture is that one is at the same time learning —gathering the meaning of things.

It seems clear from this, as from the whole of his main argument, that Aristotle considers art primarily as a representation of some hitherto-existing reality. The artist imitates this, and by his imitation, which is akin to our first process of learning, we gather the meaning of the thing that is imitated.

Plato, similarly, described the artist as an 'imitator' of a pre-existing reality. God was the creator of things; workmen the artificers of things; artists the imitators of things. Thus, Plato and Aristotle agree on the fact of imitation, but go on to draw different conclusions from it. For Plato, although in the *Ion* he describes the poet as divinely inspired, the act of imitation is at two removes from reality (the Idea, then the material thing, then the imitation) and the famous discussion in the *Republic*, proposing the censorship of poets, emphasizes the dangers of the influence of these 'mere imitators' on the weaker parts of the mind.

4

> The art of imitation is the worthless mistress of a worthless friend, and the parent of a worthless progeny. . . . The imitative poet . . . resembles the painter in producing things that are worthless when tried by the standard of truth, and he resembles him also in this, that he holds intercourse with a part of the soul which is like himself, and not with the best part. . . . He excites and feeds this worthless part of the soul, and thus destroys the rational part.

Aristotle, on the other hand, not only emphasizes imitation as part of the normal learning process, but introduces a new principle, that of 'the universal':

> The poet's function is to describe, not the thing that has happened, but a kind of thing that might happen, i.e. what is possible as being probable or necessary. . . . Hence poetry is something more philosophic and of graver import than history, since its statements are of the nature rather of universals, whereas those of history are singulars. By a universal statement I mean one as to what such or such a kind of man will probably or necessarily say or do—which is the aim of poetry though it affixes proper names to the characters; by a singular statement, one as to what, say, Alcibiades did or had done to him.

Thus while Plato emphasizes the dangers of fiction, as the imitation not even of ultimate reality but of mere appearances, Aristotle develops his concept of imitation as a form of learning towards its definition as the highest form of learning, in that it shows, through its universal statements, the permanent and the necessary.

The immense intellectual tradition which flowed from Plato and Aristotle came to include not only these two opposing valuations, but an extraordinary series of modifications, transvaluations, developments, and interpretations. Thus Platonism came to include a theory of art directly opposed to that of the *Republic*, arguing that the divinely inspired poet was able to teach the highest reality because he penetrated mere appearance, and embodied in his work the divine Idea. Aristotle's idea of universals, which in context reads primarily as the embodiment of general truths about human nature, became identified, in many minds, as the same doctrine: the universals were the divine Ideas, and the poet

5

embodied them. Still, however, even after these developments, the process of art was 'imitation' and not 'creation'.

From the excitement and confusion of Renaissance theory four doctrines of art emerged. The first defined art as an imitation of the hidden reality, thus making it a form of revelation; this was particularly useful to some Christian thinkers, who could then see art as an allegory of the mind of God. This developed into the idea of art as an esoteric activity, and a high valuation of works of an allegorical or symbolic kind. The second doctrine, from much the same source but less affected by Christian thinking, saw art as a perpetual imitation and embodiment of the 'Idea of Beauty'. This came to include, in practice, the idea of imitating, not slavishly yet seriously, earlier works of art in which this Idea of Beauty was embodied (this is the major tradition which became known as classicism). The third doctrine, developing some of the emphases of Aristotle, saw art as the 'idealization of nature'; that is to say, showing things not as they are but as they ought to be. This, while based on the same source as allegiance to the 'Idea of Beauty', moved not towards classicism, but towards an important tradition of exemplary, moralizing and didactic works. The fourth doctrine, from which the 'creative' emphasis primarily springs, saw nature as God's art (Tasso) and saw art as a form of energy which vies with nature. As Castelvetro put it:

> Art is not a thing different from nature, nor can it pass beyond the limits of nature; it sets out with the same purpose as that of nature.

This purpose is a distinct form of creation. Nature is God's creation; art is man's creation. 'There are two creators', Tasso wrote, 'God and the poet.'

In any particular Renaissance work one is likely to find the four doctrines that I have here distinguished, not as alternatives, but frequently involved with each other, as the extreme ambiguity and vagueness of the terms makes easily possible. But in the more important writers the tendency towards a distinctly humanist theory of art is quite marked. For some centuries yet, the idea of art as creation, in a kind of rivalry with God, would seem blasphemous. Yet, entangled as it was with both actual and false reliance on Plato and

Aristotle, complicated as it was by different kinds of Christian tradition, the emergence of this idea can be seen as part of the new thinking of the Renaissance, and at the head of a line which leads down to our day. In the English tradition, its classical statement is that of Sidney. All other 'arts' and 'sciences' (astronomy, mathematics, music, philosophy, law, history, grammar, rhetoric, medicine, metaphysics) are, Sidney argues, tied to nature.

Onely the Poet, disdayning to be tied to any such subjection, lifted up with the vigor of his owne invention, dooth growe in effect another nature, in making things either better then Nature bringeth forth, or, quite a newe, formes such as never were in Nature, as the Heroes, Demigods, Cyclops, Chimeras, Furies, and such like: so as hee goeth hand in hand with Nature, not inclosed within the narrow warrant of her guifts, but freely ranging onely within the Zodiack of his owne wit.

Nature never set forth the earth in so rich tapistry as divers poets have done, neither with plesant rivers, fruitful trees, sweet smelling flowers, nor whatsoever els may make the too much loved earth more lovely. Her world is brasen, the Poets only deliver a golden. But let those things alone and goe to man, for whom as the other things are, so it seemeth in him her uttermost cunning is imployed, and knowe whether shee have brought foorth so true a lover as Theagenes, so constant a friend as Pylades, so valiant a man as Orlando, so right a Prince as Xenophon's Cyrus, so excellent a man every way as Virgils Aeneas. Neither let this be jestingly conceived, because the works of the one be essentiall, the other, in imitation or fiction; for any understanding knoweth the skil of the Artificer standeth in that Idea or foreconceite of the work, and not in the work it selfe. And that the Poet hath that Idea is manifest, by delivering them forth in such excellencie as hee hath imagined them. Which delivering forth also is not wholie imaginative, as we are wont to say by them that build Castles in the ayre; but so farre substantially it worketh, not onely to make a Cyrus, which had been but a particular excellencie, as Nature might have done, but to bestow a Cyrus upon the worlde, to make many Cyrus's, if they wil learne aright why and how that Maker made him.

Neyther let it be deemed too sawcie a comparison to ballance the highest poynt of mans wit with the efficacie of Nature: but rather give right honour to the heavenly Maker of that maker, who, having made man to his owne likenes, set him beyond and over all the workes of that second nature, which in nothing hee sheweth so much as in Poetrie, when with the force of a divine breath he bringeth things forth far surpassing her doings, with no small argument to the incredulous of that first accursed fall of Adam, sith our erected wit maketh us know what perfection is, and yet our infected will keepeth us from reaching it.

The strands of many traditions can be seen in this, but the decisive novelty (it is not Sidney's, but of his period) is clear. This is the doctrine of man the creator, who 'with the force of a divine breath' brings forth 'things far surpassing' nature. Sidney glances back at one part of Plato's teaching, to find this force given by God to one kind of man, the poet. But the claim occurs within a larger movement of thought, in which man is asserting his right to break out of the order of nature: to see the rest of nature as subordinate to his creative will. For Sidney, poetry can be supernatural because it is an energy of the soul which in discovering God is able to create beyond natural limits. But another way of making the same claim is to assert a purely human creativity, the powers of the emergent mind. When imitation, the learning of reality, becomes creation, man making new reality, a critical stage in art and thought has been reached.

II

As we follow the historical argument, we find a growing complexity, as the implications of this claim are realized. In Marvell's famous verse in *The Garden*, we are still with Sidney, but the point is interestingly put:

> The mind, that ocean where each kind
> Does straight its own resemblance find;
> Yet it creates, transcending these,
> Far other worlds, and other seas,
> Annihilating all that's made
> To a green thought in a green shade.

This 'creation' is still, as the whole poem makes clear, an

energy of the soul which is an approach to God. But it assumes, as a contrast with this, an order of natural seeing, 'where each kind does straight its own resemblance find'. Sidney also had assumed this, but had claimed that only the poet could go beyond it. In Marvell this is a creative activity of the human mind as such. It is this emphasis that we must bear in mind as we watch the extraordinary flowering of the creative idea in the development of what we now call Romantic thought. The attachment of 'creative' to the work of the artist remains the easiest to trace. Donne spoke of poetry as 'a counterfeit Creation'. Mallet, in 1728, spoke of the 'companion of the Muse, Creative Power, Imagination'. By the end of the eighteenth century, this emphasis, with its key-word, 'imagination', was becoming paramount. The main line runs as an emphasis on 'creative imagination' as a general human faculty, which is seen at its highest in the poet. This is the basis of Shelley's *Defence of Poetry*, which like Sidney's *Apologie* contains many strands of traditional thought, but is most significant in relation to developing ideas of perception and imagination:

> Man is an instrument over which a series of external and internal impressions are driven, like the alternations of an ever-changing wind over an Aeolian lyre, which move it by their motion to ever-changing melody. But there is a principle within the human being, and perhaps within all sentient beings, which acts otherwise than in the lyre, and produces not melody, alone, but harmony, by an internal adjustment of the sounds or motions thus excited to the impressions which excite them. It is as if the lyre could accommodate its chords to the motions of that which strikes them, in a determined proportion of sound.

This, of course, is still 'imitation', with the addition of the organizing principle—what Shelley calls 'synthesis'—as the creative human act. The child and the savage imitate external objects, and

> language and gesture, together with plastic or pictorial imitation, become the image of the combined effect of those objects, and of his apprehension of them.

9

To be a poet is to carry to its highest form this general activity:

> to apprehend . . . the good which exists . . . in the relation subsisting first between existence and perception, and secondly between perception and expression.

The poet does this through the use of a language which is

> vitally metaphorical; that is, it marks the before unapprehended relations of things and perpetuates their apprehension.

The 'authors of revolutions in opinion' act similarly, for

> their words unveil the permanent analogy of things by images which participate in the life of truth.

A poem is

> the creation of actions according to the unchangeable forms of human nature, as existing in the mind of the creator, which is itself the image of all other minds.

Here Shelley returns to the emphasis of Sidney, which in other parts of his argument he had perhaps been moving beyond. He returns again, but with altered emphasis, in his most famous definition:

> All things exist as they are perceived; at least in relation to the percipient. 'The mind is its own place, and of itself can make a Heaven of Hell, a Hell of Heaven.' But poetry defeats the curse which binds us to be subjected to the accident of surrounding impressions. And whether it spreads its own figured curtain, or withdraws life's dark veil from before the scene of things, it equally creates for us a being within our being. It makes us the inhabitants of a world to which the familiar world is chaos. It reproduces the common Universe of which we are portions or percipients, and it purges from our inward sight the film of familiarity which obscures from us the wonder of our being. It compels us to feel that which we perceive, and to imagine that which we know. It creates anew the universe, after it has been annihilated in our minds by the recurrence of impressions blunted by reiteration. It justifies that bold and true word of Tasso: Non Merita nome di creatore, se

non Iddio ed il Poeta (none merits the name of creator, except God and the poet).

It is an eloquent argument, and remains important, but it fluctuates between *imitative and creative ideas of perception*, seeming to reserve real creation to secondary association, and it tends towards a denial of general human creativity, and its special reservation to the poet. It was, typically, Coleridge, in one of those extraordinary flashes of intelligence, who extended the idea of creation to all perception:

> The primary IMAGINATION I hold to be the living Power and prime Agent of all human perception, and as a repetition in the finite mind of the eternal act of creation.

With this startling hypothesis, of which only later shall we see the full significance, the transformation of 'imitative' into 'creative' theories reaches its next critical stage.

III

We must now turn aside to notice an effect of the 'creative' theory, as it existed before Coleridge. The claim that art represented a 'superior reality', essentially higher than that accessible to other human faculties, was, naturally enough, contested. The basis of the opposition goes back to Plato. What the new thinkers called creation Plato had called falsehood. Art was fiction, and as such inferior to reality. The persistence of this attitude needs no emphasis. It is a commonplace of modern thought, as anyone who says he prefers biographies to novels 'because at least they are true' will affirm. What I want to observe is that the claim of art to 'superior reality' and its contemptuous description as 'inferior fiction' have been, in modern thought, counterparts. If you rely on the theory of art as imitation, this is inevitable, at a certain stage. Even in a culture in which it is deeply accepted that there is a 'reality' beyond 'appearances', it is by no means certain that the artist's singular ability to reach and depict this will be accepted. If a religion is the medium of belief in a 'higher reality', the artist's singularity will certainly not be conceded, although his role in depicting such a reality, in the accepted terms of the religion, will often be stressed. In such a case, however, this will not be a special kind of 'creative' act. The belief in artistic creation as the medium of a superior reality seems most likely to be held in a period of transition from a primarily religious to a primarily humanist culture, for it embodies elements of both ways of thinking: that there is a reality beyond ordinary human vision, and yet that man has supreme creative powers. But, in such a transition, the latter claim will be made on general grounds, thus tending to challenge the artist's singularity. Moreover, there will be elements in the assertion of human powers which will tend to devalue 'imagination', or at least to make it ambiguous. The growth of scepticism, which will be part of the movement from a primarily religious culture, will extend into this province, putting increasing emphasis upon the possibility of delusion or the idle construction of 'mere romance'. Historically, this has been the general development, for the artist's claim that he is a creator of superior reality has been counterpointed, from the beginning, by a stress on the possible delusions of imagination and the misleading elements of fiction and romance.

From the hundreds of possible examples, a famous passage from Shakespeare may be taken, for its ambiguity:

T: More strange than true. I never may believe
These antique fables, nor these fairy toys.
Lovers and madmen have such seething brains,
Such shaping fantasies, that apprehend
More than cool reason ever comprehends.
The lunatic, the lover and the poet
Are of imagination all compact.
One sees more devils than vast hell can hold;
That is the madman. The lover, all as frantic,
Sees Helen's beauty in a brow of Egypt.
The poet's eye, in a fine frenzy rolling,
Doth glance from heaven to earth, from earth to heaven,
And as imagination bodies forth
The forms of things unknown, the poet's pen
Turns them to shapes, and gives to airy nothing

A local habitation, and a name.
Such tricks hath strong imagination
That if it would but apprehend some joy
It comprehends some bringer of that joy.
Or in the night, imagining some fear,
How easy is a bush supposed a bear.
H: But all the story of the night told over,
And all their minds transfigured so together,
More witnesseth than fancy's images,
And grows to something of great constancy.

The lines about the poet are frequently quoted, in the 'creative' tradition to which they obviously belong, but it is less often observed that the context of the description is a general description of delusion. The valuation seems to veer, even in the writing, and perhaps fairly represents a continuing line of belief: that delusion, or illusion, is common, but that there is a special category of illusion, used by artists, which is valuable.

Almost every possible variation of position, in this confused debate, has in fact been taken up. In practice, since the beginning of the eighteenth century, we have seen an alternation, but only of emphasis, between a naïve realism—'describing things as they really are', and the varying kinds of romanticism, from 'describing things as they ought to be, as they ideally are' to the simple 'superior reality' claim, as here in Shelley:

He will watch from dawn to gloom
The lake-reflected sun illume
The yellow bees in the ivy bloom,
Nor heed nor see, what things they be;
But from these create he can
Forms more real than living man,
Nurslings of immortality.

Two strong emphases, nearer our own time, have been widely made. The growing belief in a simple kind of materialism, usually accompanied by an explicit denial of any kind of supernatural reality, any reality beyond man's reach, has made room for art in terms of its 'reflection of reality' (imitation) or, more subtly, its 'organization of reality'—the artist selects, organizes (Shelley's 'synthesis') and thus gives meaning and value. The new psychology, on the other hand, particularly in Freud and Jung, has repeated, in a different form, the claim that there is a reality beyond man's reach: the 'unconscious'. Or rather, beyond man's ordinary reach, and here might be the entry, either for a new science or for a new definition of art. For Freud, the material of art was 'phantasy', which he contrasted with 'reality'. The artist is one who from a certain psychological disposition

> turns away from reality and transfers all his interest, and all his libido too, on to the creation of his wishes in the life of phantasy. . . . But the way back to reality is found by the artist thus: he is not the only one who has a life of phantasy; the intermediate world of phantasy is sanctioned by general human consent. . . . But to those who are not artists the gratification that can be drawn from the springs of phantasy is very limited. . . . A true artist has more at his disposal. First of all he understands how to elaborate his day-dreams, so that they lose that personal note which grates upon strange ears. . . . He knows too how to modify them sufficiently so that their origin in prohibited sources is not easily detected. Further, he possesses the mysterious ability to mould his particular material until it expresses the ideas of his phantasy faithfully, and then he knows how to attach to this reflection of his phantasy-life so strong a stream of pleasure that, for a time at least, the repressions are outbalanced and dispelled by it. When he can do all this he opens out to others the way back to the comfort and consolation of their own unconscious sources of pleasure, and so reaps their gratitude and admiration. . . .

The 'gratitude and admiration', it will be noted, are the 'reality' to which the artist finds his way back.

A development of this position is found in Herbert Read, who starts from Freud's account of the mind:

> If we picture the regions of the mind as three superimposed strata (we have already noted how inadequate such a picture must be), then continuing our metaphor we can imagine in certain rare cases a phenomenon comparable to a 'fault' in geology, as a result

of which in one part of the mind the layers become discontinuous, and exposed to each other at unusual levels. . . . Some such hypothesis is necessary to explain that access, that lyrical intuition, which is known as inspiration and which in all ages has been the rare possession of those few individuals we recognize as artists of genius.

In Jung, on the other hand, there is a distinction between two kinds of artistic creation, one 'psychological', drawn from the materials of consciousness raised to intensity, the other 'visionary', drawn from 'timeless depths . . . the hinterland of man's mind'. He further distinguishes the private personality of the artist and the nature of his activity as an artist, which latter he sees as 'an impersonal creative process'. The creative activity is a general human process, of which the artist is, in his art, the impersonal embodiment, taking us back to

that level of experience at which it is man who lives, and not the individual.

Thus, the 'creative' idea has undergone a further development, the ordinarily inaccessible reality being placed within man himself, with the artist as a specially gifted person who is able to penetrate to this region. But the association with 'phantasy', especially in Freud, links with the ordinary realist position, in which it is assumed that the material of art is different from and inferior to 'reality'. This has been countered, from the realist side in art, either with the reassertion that the material of art is ordinary reality, but that the artist, in imitating it, is doing something valuable—imitating, recording, and teaching; or with the claim that art is a special kind of exploration and organization of reality, the artist being primarily an 'emotional' explorer, whereas the scientist, by contrast, is a 'rational' explorer. The extreme positions have emerged as, on the one hand, that the material of art is a special kind of abnormal experience, devalued as 'phantasy' or valued as 'inspiration'; on the other hand, that the material is 'ordinary everyday reality', which the artist imitates or organizes. The linguistic curiosity, in this often angry debate, is that by all schools, and from all assumptions, art and the artist are referred to as 'creative'. It would be a brave man who would say, after even the briefest review of the long inquiry into the nature of art, that he is sure, once the habit is checked, what 'creative' quite means. It is at this point that we can turn to recent work on perception, as a process of the brain and the nervous system. It seems to me, certainly, that it enables us to take a decisive step forward, in the necessary clarification.

IV

The brain of each one of us does literally create his or her own world.

This startling sentence, from Professor J. Z. Young's *Doubt and Certainty in Science—a Biologist's Reflections on the Brain*, introduces clearly enough a new stage in the discussion. In the traditional discussion, the 'creative' emphasis had rested clearly enough on an implied opposite, which was natural seeing. A Platonist would express this as:

Man — natural seeing — Appearances.
Artist — exceptional seeing — Reality.

A Romantic would express it as:

Man — natural seeing — Reality.
Artist — exceptional seeing — Superior Reality.

A typical modern account would be:

Man — natural seeing — Reality.
Artist — exceptional seeing — Art.

There are indeed almost innumerable variations of expression of this relationship, for the word 'reality' can be used in so many ways, but at the centre of all of them is the common assumption: that there is an ordinary everyday kind of perception, and that this can exceptionally be transcended by a certain kind of man or a certain kind of activity. Most versions, furthermore, would describe the product of the everyday perception as 'reality'—the things in themselves as they really are—so that the product of the artist's perception must be seen as in any of a number of ways an alteration (organization, idealization, transcendence) of this 'reality' that is shared by all other men. This way of thinking is so deeply built into our language and intellectual tradition that the necessary revaluation, in terms of what we now know about perception, is exceptionally difficult. The challenge in Young's sentence is the use of the word 'create' to describe not merely the artist's activity, but the activity of every human mind.

The central fact of this new account of the activity of our brains is that each one of us *has to learn to see*. The growth of every human being is a slow process of learning what Young calls 'the rules of seeing', without which we could not in any ordinary sense see the world around us. There is no reality of familiar shapes, colours, and sounds, to which we merely open our eyes. The information that we receive through our senses from the material world around us has to be interpreted, according to certain human rules, before what we ordinarily call 'reality' forms. The human brain has to perform this 'creative' activity before we can, as normal human beings, see at all:

> The visual receiving system in its untrained state has only very limited powers. We are perhaps deceived by the fact that the eye is a sort of camera. Contrary to what we might suppose, the eyes and brain do not simply record in a sort of photographic manner the pictures that pass in front of us. The brain is not by any means a simple recording system like a film. . . . Many of our affairs are conducted on the assumption that our sense organs provide us with an accurate record, independent of ourselves. What we are now beginning to realize is that much of this is an illusion, that we have to learn to see the world as we do.

That is Young's account, and he goes on:

> In some sense we literally create the world we speak about. . . . The point to grasp is that we cannot speak simply as if there is a world around us of which our senses give true information. In trying to speak about what the world is like we must remember all the time that what we see and what we say depends on what we have learned; we ourselves come into the process.

Or, as Sir Russell Brain puts it:

> The sensory qualities of normal perception, such as colours, sounds, smells and touches are generated by the brain of the percipient and are unlike those external events which constitute the states of objects by which they are caused.

17

The philosophical implications of this view are both far-reaching and difficult, but there can be little doubt that henceforth we must start from the position that reality *as we experience it* is in this sense a human creation; that all our experience is a human version of the world we inhabit. This version has two main sources: the human brain as it has evolved, and the interpretations carried by our cultures. Man's version of the world he inhabits has a central biological function: it is a form of interaction with his environment which allows him to maintain his life and to achieve greater control over the environment in which this must be done. We 'see' in certain ways—that is, we interpret sensory information according to certain rules—as a way of living. But these ways—these rules and interpretations—are, as a whole, neither fixed nor constant. We can learn new rules and new interpretations, as a result of which we shall literally see in new ways. There are thus two senses in which we can speak of this activity as 'creative'. The evolution of the human brain, and then the particular interpretations carried by particular cultures, give us certain 'rules' or 'models', without which no human being can 'see' in the ordinary sense, at all. In each individual, the learning of these rules, through inheritance and culture, is a kind of creation, in that the distinctively human world, the ordinary 'reality' that his culture defines, forms only as the rules are learned. Particular cultures carry particular versions of reality, which they can be said to create, in the sense that cultures carrying different rules (though on a common basis of the evolved human brain) create their own worlds which their bearers ordinarily experience. But, further, there is not only variation between cultures, but the individuals who bear these particular cultural rules are capable of altering and extending them, bringing in new or modified rules by which an extended or different reality can be experienced. Thus, new areas of reality can be 'revealed' or 'created', and these need not be limited to any one individual, but can, in certain interesting ways, be communicated, thus adding to the set of rules carried by the particular culture.

The effect of this new knowledge seems to me to be of the greatest importance, but I know from my own attempts to absorb it that it is so difficult to grasp, in any substantial sense, that its application must meet with all kinds of resistance and confusion. The formulation of the knowledge (for any detailed account of which the original accounts must be turned to) is in itself an effort towards a new interpretation, a new rule, which is very difficult either to learn or to communicate. Yet, if we have followed the 'creative' idea thus far, we are perhaps in an exceptionally favourable position to understand the nature of this effort, and to clarify it.

v

The theories of 'imitation' and of 'creation' can best be seen as attempts to define the relationship between two named areas of fact—'reality' and 'art'. We have seen how various these definitions can be, but nevertheless we must observe, finally, that virtually the whole body of the theory of art contains, and starts from, this assumed opposition between two distinct kinds of thing. Art is the imitation of reality, and this may be valued as a form of learning or record, or dismissed as mere fiction—second-hand reproduction—or falsehood. Art is creation, and this may be valued as revelation or transcendence, or dismissed as mere fancy or phantasy. In all of these positions, the assumption of a fundamental duality is clear. High theory and low prejudice share this position equally. Plato or a Puritan or a modern Practical Man can dismiss art as inferior. Aristotle or a Renaissance theorist or a modern Romantic or aesthete can praise art as superior. Yet the long and often bitter dialogue between these contrasted positions leads now, not to a taking of sides, but to a rejection of the premises which both parties share. The contrast between art and reality can be seen, finally, as a false meaning.

Sophisticated modern thinking about art, in a century which has seen a great variety and confusion of styles, has evolved a position which can be stated as follows. One kind of art, which we call representational or realistic or naturalistic, offers an ordinary description or reproduction of reality, in the most common and objective terms. Another kind, less easily labelled but sometimes called romantic, offers not merely a representation of reality, but this representation modified by the artist's subjective emotional reactions to it—reality has been organized, selected, idealized, caricatured, by the artist's personal vision. A third kind, most commonly called abstract, is neither the reproduction of reality nor the subjective modification of reality, but the direct expression of purely 'aesthetic' experience, the representation in art, not of reality, but of the artist's vision. Some such classification as this was obviously necessary, as an attempt to come to terms with the observable difference in modern artistic methods. But again we can now see that it is basically inadequate, because again it is based on the assumed duality: the separation of art and reality, or of man and the world he observes.

The crucial importance of what we now know about perception is that it opens the way to ending this duality, and thus transforming our thinking about art. The new facts about perception make it impossible for us to assume that there is any reality experienced by man into which man's own observations and interpretations do not enter. Thus the assumptions of naïve realism—seeing the things as they really are, quite apart from our reactions to them—become impossible. Yet equally, the facts of perception in no way lead us to a late form of idealism; they do not require us to suppose that there is no kind of reality outside the human mind; they point rather to the insistence that all human experience is an interpretation of the non-human reality. But this, again, is not the duality of subject and object—the assumption on which almost all theories of art are based. We have to think, rather, of human experience as both objective and subjective, in one inseparable process. As Caudwell put it:

Body and environment are in constant determining relations. Perception is not the decoding of tappings on the skin. It is a determining relation between neural and environmental electrons. Every part of the body not only affects the other parts but is also in determining relations with the rest of reality. It is determined by it and determines it, this interchange producing development—the constantly changing series of interlocking events. . . . Of this multitude of relations . . . we distinguish a certain group, changing as the world changes, not with it or separately from it but in mutually determining interaction with it. This selection, rich, highly organized and recent, we call the consciousness, or our ego. We do not select it out. In the process of development it separates out, as life separated out, as suns and planets and the elements separated out from the process of becoming. Separated out, and still changing, it is consciousness, it is *us* in so far as we regard ourselves as conscious egos. But in separating out, it does not completely separate out, any more than any element did. It remains like them, in determining relation with the rest of the Universe, and the study of the organization of this developed structure, of its inner relations and the relations of the system with all other systems in the Universe, is psychology.

The difficulty of this conception hardly needs stressing, and to grasp it in any substantial way needs long effort. Yet it is interesting to see that we have approached this conception, not only through the science of perception, but also through some of our traditional thinking about art as 'creation'. Coleridge, as I have noted earlier, was very near to it, when he wrote of 'the primary imagination' as

the living Power and prime Agent of all human perception . . . a repetition in the finite mind of the eternal act of creation.

Yet the pull of earlier thinking limited even this, in the movement towards personifying this process (a Power, an Agent), and in the implied opposition of the 'finite mind' and a personified 'Creation'. We can look at this again in Young's conclusion, as a biologist:

Our short experience of time and existence does not warrant us in postulating any creation or beginning at all. To do so is our crude way of talking about things, in terms of the model that speaks of the basic reality of life as an I, with a beginning and an end. Biological discovery has shown that this assumption of a sudden beginning for each of us is not true. Our organization, the most essential and enduring thing about us, does not begin from nothing, but is passed on continually. . . . Perhaps instead of focusing on beginning as the act of creation we should do exactly the opposite and centre our speech on continuity. The sense in which we do see creation is in the building of organization that goes on in the life of each individual, especially, in the case of men, in our brains. . . . There appear to be two general laws of the universe: first, that of association, of binding, the tendency for randomly distributed processes to become linked together to form larger units; second is the law that such unity is not permanent, but sooner or later dissolves, providing fresh randomness. This certainly seems to be a general principle in biology and we have seen how it usefully describes the progress of the growth of our brains and of the whole organization of our species, by alternation of aggregation and disaggregation. Each species remains in balance with its surroundings by alternate periods of development and death, followed by replacement by a new version of the organization. This is the means by which life maintains, as it were, communication with the non-living world. . . . There is a rhythmic building by alternation of organization and disorder, a continuous process of 'creation'.

Thus man shares with all living creatures this fundamental process, but in fact has evolved in such a way that his 'building of organization' is a continual process of learning and relearning, as compared with the relatively fixed instinct-mechanisms of animals. It is man's nature, and the history of his evolution, to be continually learning by the processes described. Since this continuing organization and reorganization of consciousness is, for man, the organization and reorganization of reality—the consciousness a way of learning to control his environment—it is clear that there is a real sense in which man can be called a creator.

All living forms have communication systems of a kind, but again, in man, the process of learning and relearning, which is made possible by social organization and tradition, has led to a number of communication-systems of great complexity and power. Gesture, language, music, mathematics are all systems of this kind. We can think of them as separate systems, yet to understand their nature, in any depth, we must see them in their context of the whole process of social learning. At one level we can oppose art to science, or emotion to reason, yet the activities described by these names are in fact deeply related parts of the whole human process. We cannot refer science to the object, and art to the subject, for the view of human activity we are seeking to grasp rejects this duality of subject and object: the consciousness is part of the reality, and the reality is part of the consciousness, in the whole process of our living organization. Coleridge spoke of 'substantial knowledge' as

> that intuition of things which arises when we possess ourselves as one with the whole.

This realization, the capacity for 'substantial knowledge', is the highest form of human organization, though the process it succeeds in grasping is the common form of our ordinary living. At a less organized level, we fall back on what Coleridge called 'abstract knowledge', when we

> think of ourselves as separated beings, and place nature in antithesis to the mind, as object to subject, thing to thought, death to life.

The antithesis of nature to the mind, 'as object to subject', we now know to be false, yet so much of our thinking is based on it that to grasp the substantial unity, the sense of a whole process, is to begin a long and difficult revolution in the mind. Yet it is certain that theories of art which begin from the separated categories of 'artist' and 'reality' are, from now on, irrelevant. We have to retrace our steps and look for new definitions.

VI

We learn to see a thing by learning to describe it; this is the normal process of perception, which can only be seen as complete when we have interpreted the incoming sensory information either by a known configuration or rule, or by some new configuration which we can try to learn as a new rule. The process of interpretation is neither arbitrary nor abstract; it is a central and necessary vital function, by which we seek so to understand our environment that we can live more successfully in it. But to say that we see by learning to describe is in fact to relate seeing to communication in a fundamental way. We have many ways of describing, both by learned rules—conventional descriptions—and by certain kinds of response, in gesture, language, image, which we often literally feel ourselves creating as we struggle to describe certain new information for which the conventional descriptions are inadequate. This vital descriptive effort—which is not merely a subsequent effort to describe something known, but literally a way of seeing new things and new relationships—has often been observed, by artists, yet it is not the activity of artists alone. The same effort is made, not only by scientists and thinkers, but also, and necessarily, by everyone. The history of a language is a very good example of this, for the ways in which a language changes, to amend old descriptions or accommodate new ones, are truly social, in the most ordinary business of living. It is not in this activity that the special function of the arts, or the special nature of the artist, can be discerned. A vital imaginative life, and the deep effort to describe new experience, are found in many others besides artists, and the communication of new descriptions and new meanings is carried out in many ways—in art, thought, science, and in the ordinary social process. What we call an art is one of a number of ways of describing and communicating, and most arts, quite clearly, are developments of ways commonly used—as dance from gesture, poetry from speech. Yet description is a function of communication, and we can best understand the arts if we look at this vital relationship, in which experience has to be described to be realized (this description being, in fact, putting the experience into a communicable form) and has then, because this is the biological purpose of the description, to be shared with another organism. The distinction of the arts is that in different ways they command very powerful means of this sharing; although again, in most arts, these means are developments from general communication.

Rhythm, as the most obvious of these means, may be taken as an example. We are only beginning to investigate this on any scientific basis, but it seems clear from what we already know that rhythm is a way of transmitting a description of experience, in such a way that the experience is re-created in the person receiving it, not merely as an 'abstraction' or an 'emotion' but as a physical effect on the organism—on the blood, on the breathing, on the physical patterns of the brain. We use rhythm for many ordinary purposes, but the arts (I would say all the arts, though in the visual arts this would be more difficult to prove) comprise highly developed and exceptionally powerful rhythmic means, by which the communication of experience is actually achieved. Man has made and is making these rhythms, as he has also 'made' colours. The dance of the body, the movement of the voice, the sounds of instruments are, like colours, forms, patterns, means of transmitting his experience in so powerful a way that the experience can be literally lived by others. This has been felt, again and again, in actual experience of the arts, and we are now beginning to see how and why it is more than a 'way of speaking'; it is a physical experience as real as any other.

Thus the arts are certain intense forms of general communication, but at this stage we encounter a further difficulty. For, of course, the speaking voice, the dancing body, the sculpture, the picture are, in their turn, 'objects' which have to be interpreted and received. The sensory information which comes to us from a painting is no more 'like' that painting than the sensory information which comes to us from a stone or a tree. The painting, like other visual 'objects', has itself to be interpreted and described before, in any normal sense, it is seen. We realize, from this, the necessary social basis of any art, for nobody can see (not understand, but *see*) the artist's actual work unless he and the artist can come to share the complex details and means of a learned communication system. But of course there are many possible levels of communication, from absolute failure (which within a given culture would hardly ever occur) through partial failure and misinterpretation to something like full reception. We may, as we put it, see the painting but not feel it. Something is coming through, but not at a significant level. This may be anybody's fault (the artist's as often as the spectator's) but to stray into the usual recriminations is less useful than to realize the nature and difficulty of what is being attempted: the substantial communication of experience from one organism to another. Art cannot exist unless a working communication can be reached, and this communication is an activity in which both artist and spectator participate. When art communicates, a human experience is actively offered and actively received. Below this activity threshold there can be no art.

The nature of the artist's activity, in this process, may be further defined. The artist shares with other men what is usually called the 'creative imagination': that is to say, the capacity to find and organize new descriptions of experience. Other men share with the artist the capacity to transmit these descriptions, which are only in the full sense descriptions when they are in a communicable form. The special nature of the artist's work is his use of a learned skill in a particular kind of transmission of experience. His command of this skill is his art (we remember that the traditional meaning of 'art' was, precisely, 'skill'). But the purpose of the skill is similar to the purpose of all general human skills of communication: the transmission of valued experience. Thus the artist's impulse, like every human impulse to communicate, is the felt importance of his experience; but the artist's activity is the actual work of transmission. There can be no separation, in this view, between 'content' and 'form', because finding the form is literally finding the content— this is what is meant by the activity we have called 'describing'. It is, in the first instance, to every man, a matter of urgent personal importance to 'describe' his experience, because this is literally a remaking of himself, a creative change in his personal organization, to include and control the experience. This struggle to remake ourselves—to change our personal organization so that we may live in a proper relation to our environment—is in fact often painful. Many neurologists would now say that the stage before description is achieved, the state of our actual organization before new sensory experience is comprehended, the effort to respond adequately while the new experience is still disorganized and disturbing, is biologically identical with what we call 'physical pain'. The creative agony, sometimes thought of as hyperbole, is literally true. Further, the impulse to communicate is a learned human response to disturbance of any kind. For the individual, of course, the struggle is to communicate successfully by describing adequately. The state often noticed in artists, when the struggle for adequate description—an actual manipulation of words or paint—seems primarily of personal importance, without regard to its effect on others, is to be understood in this sense. For unless the description is adequate, there can be no relevant communication. To think merely of making contact with others, rather than of making contact with this precise experience, is irrelevant and distracting. Genuine communication depends on this absorbed attention to precise description, but of course it does not follow that the description is for its own sake; the attention, rather, is a condition of relevant communication.

We respond to disturbance not only by remaking ourselves, but, if we can, by changing the environment. Indeed these are parts of a single process, as consciousness and reality interpenetrate. The artist's way of remaking himself is, as in man generally, by work, which is remaking the environment and, in learning to work, remaking himself. This is so in the arts of language, sound, and movement, where the artist's transmission of experience is intended to alter existing real relationships. It can be seen more simply in an art like that of the sculptor, where an object is worked on, in what seems a whole process of modelling experience and yet discovering the experience by the act of modelling. The artist works on the material until it is 'right', but when the material is right he also is right: the art-work has been made and the artist has remade himself, in a continuous process. In abstraction we can say that he has worked on the material until it retransmits, to himself, his experience; or that he has discovered, by working on the material, a new kind of experience, which he has in effect learned from it. But, difficult though it may be to hold in the mind, the actual process is neither of these. It is neither subject working on object, nor object on subject: it is, rather, a dynamic interaction, which in fact is a whole and continuous process. The man makes the shape, and the shape remakes the man, but these are merely alternative descriptions of one process, well known by artists and in fact central to man himself. The excitement and pain of the effort are followed by the delight and rest of completion, and this is not only how the artist lives and works, but how men live and work, in a long process, ending and beginning again.

VII

The true importance of our new understanding of perception and communication is that it verifies the creative activity of art in terms of a general human creativity. The word 'creative' was turned to because of the tradition, yet the forces which made the tradition led also to use of the 'creative' idea in other fields. We must now note one effect of this on the definition of art.

J. Z. Young writes:

> The creative artist is an observer whose brain works in new ways, making it possible for him to convey information to others about matters that were not a subject for communication before. It is by search for means of communication that we sharpen our powers of observation. The discoveries of the artist and scientist are exactly alike in this respect.

And again:

> The painter has his own way of communicating his observations. Original painters find new ways of doing this, new art-forms. These literally enlarge the vision both of the artist himself and of those who look at his paintings. Artists have discovered new aspects of space with one symbolism, just as physicists have with another.

Now this is a very useful and acceptable argument, so far as it goes, but there is a problem in the description of valuable art as 'new', once we stop thinking about art in general and turn to actual works. It is quite common for philosophers and scientists to restrict their discussion of art, perhaps unconsciously, to great and original works: a restriction that can hardly be observed by the critic, who has to live with art of all kinds. The best aesthetic definitions can seem quite unreal as we turn back to the latest novel, the new book of poems, the current play or film, the ordinary exhibition. And if this is true of the usual run of art, it is even more true of the really bad art, of which we all see sufficient examples. The makers of all kinds of art claim the 'creative' description, quite reasonably, though it is obvious that only a few of them 'convey information . . . about matters that were not a subject for communication before'. It is customary to evade this difficulty by saying that works which do not fit the definition are 'not art', 'not really art', or 'the products of poetasters'. But will this do? Almost all art works are the result of the same general activity, the same *kinds* of skill, as produced *Lear*, Blake's *Sunflower* or van der Weyden's *Pieta*. The disparity in value is not evidence of a fundamentally different practice and intention, especially since we find not only great art and bad art, but a range of infinite gradations between these, with no obvious line where a difference in kind can be drawn. The fact is, I think, that aesthetic theory, even when profoundly enriched by new knowledge about perception and communication, has normally retained two traditional ideas of what it is to be 'creative'. It has retained, in a curious way, the idea that the artist is specially inspired, which offers an easy but false solution to the problem of quality in art: 'we mean by art the work of those who are artists, that is specially inspired, and not the work of those who though they write, paint and compose are not artists, in that they are not inspired'. This sounds very silly, spelled out, but we have all learned it, in effect. Secondly, the idea of 'revelation', the discovery of a 'superior reality', has been similarly retained, and of course leads us to believe that the work of the artist is to make new discoveries about the world ('creative' equals 'new'). Yet this is a really disabling idea, in that it forces the exclusion of a large amount of art, which it is clearly our business to understand. By returning the ideas to their place in the tradition, we can become conscious enough of them to reject them, and when we have done so, we shall find that it is possible, as a part of our ordinary account of perception and communication, to describe all art, and not merely selected examples.

It is characteristic of aesthetic theory that it tacitly excludes communication, as a social fact. Yet communication is the crux of art, for any adequate description of experience must be more than simple transmission; it must also include reception and response. However successfully an artist may have embodied his experience in a form capable of transmission, it can be received by no other person without the further 'creative activity' of all perception: the information transmitted by the work has to be interpreted, described, and taken into the organization of the spectator. It is not a question of 'inspired' or 'uninspired' transmission to a passive audience. It is, at every level, an offering of experience, which may then be accepted, rejected, or ignored. Any art-work that we are conscious of having seen at all we have in the simple sense received, but in every spectator's mind there is a further and crucial stage. The experience reaches the spectator in some sense, but exactly how, and with what effects?

In certain cases, the artist's experience, described by his work in a given medium, will be accepted by the spectator in the sense that the means will be interpreted in the spectator's mind, in the artist's terms, in such a way that the experience literally becomes part of him. Such experience, accessible through these means, is what Young refers to as the 'literal enlargement' of vision, but 'enlargement' is not perhaps the best word. Sometimes indeed it is a kind of extension, a new way of seeing. But some experience of art, including great art, is not 'new' in this sense. Our experience includes the apparently different quality of 'recognition': that this, literally, is what we have always known. Now there need be no difficulty in this, if we look at the history of art. In many societies it has been the function of art to embody what we can call the common meanings of the society. The artist is not describing new experiences, but embodying known experiences. There is great danger in the assumption that art serves only on the frontiers of knowledge. It serves on these frontiers, particularly in disturbed and rapidly changing societies. Yet it serves, also, at the very centre of societies. It is often through the art that the society expresses its sense of being a society. The artist, in this case, is not the lonely explorer, but the voice of his community. Even in our own complex society, certain artists seem near the centre of common experience while others seem out on the frontiers, and it would be wrong to assume that this difference is the difference between 'mediocre art' and 'great art'. Not all 'strange' art, by any means, is found valuable, nor is all 'familiar' art found valueless.

It seems better to speak of art in terms of the organization of experience, especially in its effect on a spectator or an audience. If people have lived together, and come to share a certain kind of organization by which their minds have been trained to activity, we shall find that the processes of organization are in fact institutions, of which art is usually one. Young points out how the central building of a community, from mound to cathedral, is in fact a means of communication: it both organizes and *continues to express* a common meaning by which its people live. The discovery of a means of communication is the discovery of a common meaning, and the artist's function, in many societies, is to be skilled in the means by which this meaning can continue to be experienced and activated. The human bodies which carry the meanings die, but either the lasting monument, or the inherited and traditional artistic skills, embodied in the making of certain images, patterns, rhythms, survive to continue the process of organization. It has to be a continual re-creation of meaning, by the society as a whole and by every individual in it. Even the skills themselves are not commodities to be passively inherited, but processes that have to be learned, as part of any individual artist's growth: the means and the meaning, in a whole process, have to find this personal verification. Yet, the common experience which the meanings interpret will itself be changing, either slowly and hardly noticeably or at a variety of rates to one so rapid that the fact of change is a matter of general consciousness. The relationships between men and their environment change, yet consciousness of these relationships has to be achieved by descriptions capable of being communicated. The organization of received meanings has to be made compatible with possible new meanings that are emerging, and this is a process of great complexity. It is not just a matter of 'a society' changing, but of real changes in the personal organization of all its members. Moreover, though the members share an area of common meaning, the actual process of organization, in each individual, is necessarily personal. According to his position within the complex of real relationships in the society, and according to an important degree of inherited individuality (the result of a particular selection from the great complex of variable factors in human inheritance) the individual will learn in his own way by interaction with the changing organization of his society. Thus we see a series of unique individuals, in real relationships, learning and contributing to a changing pattern. It is in this context that we must understand both change and failure in art.

The individual artist may either re-create common meanings, in the quite literal sense that he builds his personal organization in their terms, or he may create new meanings, in the sense that to organize his actual experience he has to find new descriptions. For the individual artist, in his actual work, these processes will be similar, for in either case he is engaged in a substantial effort to make a particular form of experience so active in himself that he can communicate it to others. Yet, in the process of communication, the exact degree of relation between his personal meanings and the common meanings will be of vital importance. Where the relation is very close, he will be able to draw in a direct way on practised means of communication, with which his audience will be familiar. So far from this being simply 'conventional' art, with the implication that it is less likely to be valuable, it is probable that most great art has been made in these conditions. For the artist, in such a case, is not simply 'copying' the common meanings; the meanings are his own, in a deep realization, and yet the conditions for their communication are powerfully available. At the opposite extreme, where the relation between common and personal meanings is distant, the struggle to find means of communication will obviously be long and hard.

In practice, the process of change in art is normally one of extension of meanings, or modification of means. Beyond a certain point, a new meaning could hardly be communicated at all, or perhaps even described; the pressure would simply break up the artist's organization. The 'creative' act, of any artist, is in any case the process of making a meaning active, by communicating an organized experience to others. We have to see the process as one of many meanings being offered, by particular means, and only some of these meanings being received. Often, the art of a society changes without awareness of discontinuity: an effective number of individual offerings are taken up and composed into new common meanings, and there is no effective residue of rejected meanings to constitute challenge and tension. In our own time, clearly, we have change of such complexity, due not only to the rapidity of change in common experience but to the great extension and diversification of communities, that for a time at least discontinuity seems central, and we are primarily aware of art as the series of individual offerings, the making of common meanings being almost lost. It is in such a period that we develop theories of art which while rightly stressing the individual offering neglect the reality of communication. A tension between artist and audience is assumed as inevitable, and one form of this tension is described in terms of the artist's function to describe 'new' experience. In fact, however, even in this complex situation, a substantial number of the offered meanings are composed into new common meanings, though after initial disturbance and with a time-lag that again makes us conscious of the fact of change. This is an ordinary process of growth, and of course, whether the meaning is new or not (in the sense of having never been previously described) it can be felt as new (in the sense of being freshly and personally experienced). But to maintain growth, a significant area of common description and response must be maintained, and one of the functions of art, like other communication systems, is to recharge this area, with our own living energy. Much new art does this, and also the art of earlier periods and of other places, which we have preserved for just this reason, as a means of re-creation of a sense of common experience. (How we use this older art we shall see later, in discussing the nature of tradition.) At the same time, other new art succeeds in describing and communicating new experience, and in doing so may lead us to new kinds of response and activity. Here also, art from earlier periods and other places may succeed in communicating descriptions and responses that are new to us. Yet, whether it is communicating known forms of organization or moving us to new forms, art comes to us as part of our actual growth, not entering a 'special area' of the mind, but acting on and interacting with our whole personal and social organization. The distinction of value, in actual works of art, is always, in the first instance, in the actual power to communicate. Since the meaning and the means cannot be separated, it is on the artist's actual ability to live the experience that successful communication depends. By living the experience we mean that, whether or not it has been previously recorded, the artist has literally made it part of himself, so deeply that his whole energy is available to describe it and transmit it to others. Bad art is then the failure or relative failure of this kind of personal organization, which we know now to be more than a figure of speech but an actual process by which we live. Our actual human organization is for the purpose of communicating, and in art as in other kinds of communication—most notably sexual relationship, which is our fundamental communicating process, in which life is offered and accepted—the ability to communicate is not a matter of abstract qualities, such as feeling, intelligence, or will, but is rooted in certain whole patterns of organization: success or failure is a matter of the whole self. The various communication systems which human beings have developed make personal organization ever more varied and complex. The special attachments of particular individuals to certain kinds of communication, the selection of certain classes of means which they value highly and in which they are capable of becoming highly skilled, are forms of growth within the great range of genetic variety and social inheritance and experience. We cannot say that art is a substitute for other kinds of communication, since when successful it evidently communicates experience which is not apparently communicable in other ways. We must see art, rather, as an extension of our capacity for organization: a vital faculty which allows particular areas of reality to be described and communicated.

To succeed in art is to convey an experience to others in such a form that the experience is actively re-created—not 'contemplated', not 'examined', not passively received, but by response to the means, actually lived through, by those to whom it is offered. At this stage, a number of art-works already fail, fundamentally because the artist's experience is insufficiently organized and in consequence he cannot discover the means by which the experience could be shared. There are absolute failures, in this sense, but there are also many partial failures or partial successes, in which certain parts of the experience come through, and can be shared as a lived reality, while other parts reach us with diminished or insignificant strength. We can often see, in the cases of failure, how the process of organization, which is also description, breaks down. We see the relapse to mere imitation of other works, in general pattern or in details of the pattern, and the failure is not that the methods of the other works are intrinsically inadequate, but that they are incongruous with this particular experience; active description has become mechanical repetition. Such failure is common, but hardly less so than a kind less often noticed theoretically, where the effort towards new descriptions is obvious, yet communication fails. It has often been said that audiences must be patient, if they are to learn an artist's 'new language', but this, while true, must not carry the implication that every new language can be learned, given time. To suppose this is to forget that for members of the audience, as for artists, communication is a way of living: to receive and live an artist's experience is no casual activity, but an actual living change. We depend for our growth on new descriptions being offered, but whether we accept them depends on our capacity to grow in such ways, and it is clear that some offered ways will be impossible to us, others actively rejected. Successful communication depends on the organization of audiences as well as artists, and while it is right that we should hold ourselves open to learn, it is necessary to remember that any response is part of a way of living, and that the selection of responses is a condition of any organization. In some cases we will be literally unable to receive what is offered; we simply cannot see the world, cannot respond to experience, in that way. Often, again, the power of the work will move us, yet still, later, we will reject it. For the experience has to be fitted into our whole organization, and in some cases, after a process of comparison that may be prolonged over years, acceptance will not be possible. Again, an apparent failure may eventually succeed, or will be valued by some while rejected by others. If we think of the real process of communication, we can find something better than the popular (and sentimental) formula: artist's new language, initial resistance, eventual acceptance. For the history of art shows not only this sequence, but three other sequences: artist's new language, initial acceptance, continued acceptance; artist's new language, initial acceptance, eventual rejection; artist's new language, initial resistance, eventual rejection. And indeed this range is what we should expect, for communication is a process between real individuals, who are all learning. Because of the range of these individuals, communication will always be uneven, and when it is a matter of new descriptions this unevenness will be very marked. Whether the new descriptions will become a new general way of seeing will depend on the direction of the common experience. In favourable cases, a work that virtually failed initially may become very successful, as the movement of common experience finds its terms valuable. In unfavourable cases, the work will simply be forgotten, however new and valuable it seemed to some people at the time. It is the same with the art of common meanings, for here again, while the meanings still satisfy the art will be preserved to recharge them, but when the meanings really fail the art loses its power to move us, unless, as quite often happens, we take it and reinterpret it according to meanings of our own.

We must remember, finally, that our increasing consciousness of the importance of art has led us to a complicated process of recording and preserving, which has in effect changed its status. By recording and preserving, in our many techniques, we gain control over some of the inherent problems of communication, in particular that of unevenness. Communication is no longer, in most cases, a single act. The transmission is recorded or stored, and we value certain communication-systems precisely because they are capable of this kind of permanence. The offering of experience is preserved, for long consideration, and communication can take place over a gap of a hundred generations. Because of the complexity of growth, it is obviously wise to keep alive as many offerings as possible, for we can never be sure in advance what may eventually be taken up, and this habit of storing experience has been central in man's whole organization. However, we only use such stores, as we use new art, by the active process already described. Like new ways of seeing, old ways must be actively learned.

VIII

To see art as a particular process in the general human process of creative discovery and communication is at once a redefinition of the status of art and the finding of means to link it with our ordinary social life. The traditional definition of art as 'creative' was profoundly important, as an emphasis, but when this was extended to a contrast between art and ordinary experience the consequences were very damaging. In modern industrial societies, particularly, it came to be felt that art would be lost unless it was given this special status, but the height of the claim ran parallel with a widespread practical rejection and exclusion. So powerful has been the tendency to exclude art from serious practical concerns, that, in a natural mood of defence, the claim that art is special and extraordinary has been urgent and even desperate; even to question this produces reactions of extreme violence, from those who are convinced that they are the sole defenders of art in a hostile world. The suggestion that art and culture are ordinary provokes quite hysterical denials, although, with every claim that they are essentially extraordinary, the exclusion and hostility that are complained of are in practice reinforced. The solution is not to pull art down to the level of other social activity as this is habitually conceived. The emphasis that matters is that there are, essentially, no 'ordinary' activities, if by 'ordinary' we mean the absence of creative interpretation and effort. Art is ratified, in the end, by the fact of creativity in all our living. Everything we see and do, the whole structure of our relationships and institutions, depends, finally, on an effort of learning, description and communication. We create our human world as we have thought of art being created. Art is a major means of precisely this creation. Thus the distinction of art from ordinary living, and the dismissal of art as unpractical or secondary (a 'leisure-time activity'), are alternative formulations of the same error. If all reality must be learned by the effort to describe successfully, we cannot isolate 'reality' and set art in opposition to it, for dignity or indignity. If all activity depends on responses learned by the sharing of descriptions, we cannot set 'art' on one side of a line and 'work' on the other; we cannot submit to be divided into 'Aesthetic Man' and 'Economic Man'.

The arts, like other ways of describing and communicating, are learned human skills, which must be known and practised in a community before their great power in conveying experience can be used and developed. Human community grows by the discovery of common meanings and common means of communication. Over an active range, the patterns created by the brain and the patterns materialized by a community continually interact. The individual creative description is part of the general process which creates conventions and institutions, through which the meanings that are valued by the community are shared and made active. This is the true significance of our modern definition of culture, which insists on this community of process.

Communication is the process of making unique experience into common experience, and it is, above all, the claim to live; for what we basically say, in any kind of communication, is: 'I am living in this way because this is my experience'. The ability to live in a particular way depends, ultimately, on acceptance of this experience by others, in successful communication. Thus our descriptions of our experience come to compose a network of relationships, and all our communication systems, including the arts, are literally parts of our social organization. The selection and interpretation involved in our descriptions embody our attitudes, needs and interests, which we seek to validate by making them clear to others. At the same time the descriptions we receive from others embody their attitudes, needs and interests, and the long process of comparison and interaction is our vital associative life. Since our way of seeing things is literally our way of living, the process of communication is in fact the process of community: the sharing of common meanings, and thence common activities and purposes; the offering, reception and comparison of new meanings, leading to the tensions and achievements of growth and change.

It is of the utmost importance to realize this sense of communication as a whole social process. If we have done so, we can then usefully look at particular kinds and means of communication, which have, as it were, separated out, but not separated out altogether. The fatally wrong approach, to any such study, is from the assumption of separate orders, as when we ordinarily assume that political institutions and conventions are of a different and separate order from artistic institutions and conventions. Politics and art, together with science, religion, family life and the other categories we speak of as absolutes, belong in a whole world of active and interacting relationships, which is our common associative life. If we begin from the whole texture, we can go on to study particular activities and their bearings on other kinds. Yet we begin, normally, from the categories themselves, and this has led again and again to a very damaging suppression of relationships. Each kind of activity in fact suffers, if it is wholly abstracted and separated. Politics, for example, has gravely suffered by its separation from ordinary relationships, and we have seen the same process in economics, science, religion, and education. The abstraction of art has been its promotion or relegation to an area of special experience (emotion, beauty, phantasy, the imagination, the unconscious), which art in practice has never confined itself to, ranging in fact from the most ordinary daily activities to exceptional crises and intensities, and using a range of means from the words of the street and common popular stories to strange systems and images which it has yet been able to make common property. It has been the purpose of this review of creative activity to allow us to acknowledge this, which is the real history of art and yet which we are kept from by definitions and formulas that were stages in its interpretation but that we must now move beyond. A further consequence of this sense of creative activity is that we are helped, by what it shows of communication and community, to review the nature of our whole common life: the terms of this review are the terms of the definition of culture. When we have grasped the fundamental relation between meanings arrived at by creative interpretation and description, and meanings embodied by conventions and institutions, we are in a position to reconcile the meanings of culture as 'creative activity' and 'a whole way of life', and this reconciliation is then a real extension of our powers to understand ourselves and our societies.

TWO

The Analysis of Culture

I

THERE are three general categories in the definition of culture. There is, first, the 'ideal', in which culture is a state or process of human perfection, in terms of certain absolute or universal values. The analysis of culture, if such a definition is accepted, is essentially the discovery and description, in lives and works, of those values which can be seen to compose a timeless order, or to have permanent reference to the universal human condition. Then, second, there is the 'documentary', in which culture is the body of intellectual and imaginative work, in which, in a detailed way, human thought and experience are variously recorded. The analysis of culture, from such a definition, is the activity of criticism, by which the nature of the thought and experience, the details of the language, form and convention in which these are active, are described and valued. Such criticism can range from a process very similar to the 'ideal' analysis, the discovery of 'the best that has been thought and written in the world', through a process which, while interested in tradition, takes as its primary emphasis the particular work being studied (its clarification and valuation being the principal end in view) to a kind of historical criticism which, after analysis of particular works, seeks to relate them to the particular traditions and societies in which they appeared. Finally, third, there is the 'social' definition of culture, in which culture is a description of a particular way of life, which expresses certain meanings and values not only in art and learning but also in institutions and ordinary behaviour. The analysis of culture, from such a definition, is the clarification of the meanings and values implicit and explicit in a particular way of life, a particular culture. Such analysis will include the historical criticism already referred to, in which intellectual and imaginative works are analysed in relation to particular traditions and societies, but will also include analysis of elements in the way of life that to followers of the other definitions are not 'culture' at all; the organization of production, the structure of the family, the structure of institutions which express or govern social relationships, the characteristic forms through which members of the society communicate. Again, such analysis ranges from an 'ideal' emphasis, the discovery of certain absolute or universal, or at least higher and lower, meanings and values, through the 'documentary' emphasis, in which clarification of a particular way of life is the main end in view, to an emphasis which, from studying particular meanings and values, seeks not so much to compare these, as a way of establishing a scale, but by studying their modes of change to discover certain general 'laws' or 'trends', by which social and cultural development as a whole can be better understood.

It seems to me that there is value in each of these kinds of definition. For it certainly seems necessary to look for meanings and values, the record of creative human activity, not only in art and intellectual work, but also in institutions and forms of behaviour. At the same time, the degree to which we depend, in our knowledge of many past societies and past stages of our own, on the body of intellectual and imaginative work which has retained its major communicative power, makes the description of culture in these terms, if not complete, at least reasonable. It can indeed be argued that since we have 'society' for the broader description, we can properly restrict 'culture' to this more limited reference. Yet there are elements in the 'ideal' definition which also seem to me valuable, and which encourage the retention of the broad reference. I find it very difficult, after the many comparative studies now on record, to identify the process of human perfection with the discovery of 'absolute' values, as these have been ordinarily defined. I accept the criticism that these are normally an extension of the values of a particular tradition or society. Yet, if we call the process, not human perfection, which implies a known ideal towards which we can move, but human evolution, to mean a process of general growth of man as a kind, we are able to recognize areas of fact which the other definitions might exclude. For it seems to me to be true that meanings and values, discovered in particular societies and by particular individuals, and kept alive by social inheritance and by embodiment in particular kinds of work, have proved to be universal in the sense that when they are learned, in any particular situation, they can contribute radically to the growth of man's powers to enrich his life, to regulate his society, and to control his environment. We are most aware of these elements in the form of particular techniques, in medicine, production, and communications, but it is clear not only that these depend on more purely intellectual disciplines, which had to be wrought out in the creative handling of experience, but also that these disciplines in themselves, together with certain basic ethical assumptions and certain major art forms, have proved similarly capable of being gathered into a general tradition which seems to represent, through many variations and conflicts, a line of common growth. It seems reasonable to speak of this tradition as a general human culture, while adding that it can only become active within particular societies, being shaped, as it does so, by more local and temporary systems.

The variations of meaning and reference, in the use of culture as a term, must be seen, I am arguing, not simply as a disadvantage, which prevents any kind of neat and exclusive definition, but as a genuine complexity, corresponding to real elements in experience. There is a significant reference in each of the three main kinds of definition, and, if this is so, it is the relations between them that should claim our attention. It seems to me that any adequate theory of culture must include the three areas of fact to which the definitions point, and conversely that any particular definition, within any of the categories, which would exclude reference to the others, is inadequate. Thus an 'ideal' definition which attempts to abstract the process it describes from its detailed embodiment and shaping by particular societies—regarding man's ideal development as something separate from and even opposed to his 'animal nature' or the satisfaction of material needs—seems to me unacceptable. A 'documentary' definition which sees value only in the written and painted records, and marks this

43

area off from the rest of man's life in society, is equally unacceptable. Again, a 'social' definition, which treats either the general process or the body of art and learning as a mere by-product, a passive reflection of the real interests of the society, seems to me equally wrong. However difficult it may be in practice, we have to try to see the process as a whole, and to relate our particular studies, if not explicitly at least by ultimate reference, to the actual and complex organization.

We can take one example, from analytic method, to illustrate this. If we take a particular work of art, say the *Antigone* of Sophocles, we can analyse it in ideal terms—the discovery of certain absolute values, or in documentary terms—the communication of certain values by certain artistic means. Much will be gained from either analysis, for the first will point to the absolute value of reverence for the dead; the second will point to the expression of certain basic human tensions through the particular dramatic form of chorus and double *kommos*, and the specific intensity of the verse. Yet it is clear that neither analysis is complete. The reverence, as an absolute value, is limited in the play by the terms of a particular kinship system and its conventional obligations—Antigone would do this for a brother but not for a husband. Similarly, the dramatic form, the metres of the verse, not only have an artistic tradition behind them, the work of many men, but can be seen to have been shaped, not only by the demands of the experience, but by the particular social forms through which the dramatic tradition developed. We can accept such extensions of our original analysis, but we cannot go on to accept that, because of the extensions, the value of reverence, or the dramatic form and the specific verse, have meaning only in the contexts to which we have assigned them. The learning of reverence, through such intense examples, passes beyond its context into the general growth of human consciousness. The dramatic form passes beyond its context, and becomes an element in a major and general dramatic tradition, in quite different societies. The play itself, a specific communication, survives the society and the religion which helped to shape it, and can be re-created to speak directly to unimagined audiences. Thus, while we could not abstract the ideal value or the specific document, neither could we reduce these to explanation within the local terms of a particular culture. If we study real relations, in any actual analysis, we reach the point where we see that we are studying a general organization in a particular example, and in this general organization there is no element that we can abstract and separate from the rest. It was certainly an error to suppose that values or art-works could be adequately studied without reference to the particular society within which they were expressed, but it is equally an error to suppose that the social explanation is determining, or that the values and works are mere by-products. We have got into the habit, since we realized how deeply works or values could be determined by the whole situation in which they are expressed, of asking about these relationships in a standard form: 'what is the relation of this art to this society?' But 'society', in this question, is a specious whole. If the art is part of the society, there is no solid whole, outside it, to which, by the form of our question, we concede priority. The art is there, as an activity, with the production, the trading, the politics, the raising of families. To study the relations adequately we must study them actively, seeing all the activities as particular and contemporary forms of human energy. If we take any one of these activities, we can see how many of the others are reflected in it, in various ways according to the nature of the whole organization. It seems likely, also, that the very fact that we can distinguish any particular activity, as serving certain specific ends, suggests that without this activity the whole of the human organization at that place and time could not have been realized. Thus art, while clearly related to the other activities, can be seen as expressing certain elements in the organization which, within that organization's terms, could only have been expressed in this way. It is then not a question of relating the art to the society, but of studying all the activities and their interrelations, without any concession of priority to any one of them we may choose to abstract. If we find, as often, that a particular activity came radically to change the whole organization, we can still not say that it is to this activity that all the others must be related; we can only study the varying ways in which, within the changing organization, the particular activities and their interrelations were affected. Further, since the particular activities will be serving varying and sometimes conflicting ends, the sort of change we must look for will rarely be of a simple kind: elements of persistence, adjustment, unconscious assimilation, active resistance, alternative effort, will all normally be present, in particular activities and in the whole organization.

The analysis of culture, in the documentary sense, is of great importance because it can yield specific evidence about the whole organization within which it was expressed. We cannot say that we know a particular form or period of society, and that we will see how its art and theory relate to it, for until we know these, we cannot really claim to know the society. This is a problem of method, and is mentioned here because a good deal of history has in fact been written on the assumption that the bases of the society, its political, economic, and 'social' arrangements, form the central core of facts, after which the art and theory can be adduced, for marginal illustration or 'correlation'. There has been a neat reversal of this procedure in the histories of literature, art, science, and philosophy, when these are described as developing by their own laws, and then something called the 'background' (what in general history was the central core) is sketched in. Obviously it is necessary, in exposition, to select certain activities for emphasis, and it is entirely reasonable to trace particular lines of development in temporary isolation. But the history of a culture, slowly built up from such particular work, can only be written when the active relations are restored, and the activities seen in a genuine parity. Cultural history must be more than the sum of the particular histories, for it is with the relations between them, the particular forms of the whole organization, that it is especially concerned. I would then define the theory of culture as the study of relationships between elements in a whole way of life. The analysis of culture is the attempt to discover the nature of the organization which is the complex of these relationships. Analysis of particular works or institutions is, in this context, analysis of their essential kind of organization, the relationships which works or institutions embody as parts of the organization as a whole. A key-word, in such analysis, is pattern: it is with the discovery of patterns of a characteristic kind that any useful cultural analysis begins, and it is with the relationships between these patterns, which sometimes reveal unexpected identities and correspondences in hitherto separately considered activities, sometimes again reveal discontinuities of an unexpected kind, that general cultural analysis is concerned.

It is only in our own time and place that we can expect to know, in any substantial way, the general organization. We can learn a great deal of the life of other places and times, but certain elements, it seems to me, will always be irrecoverable. Even those that can be recovered are recovered in abstraction, and this is of crucial importance. We learn each element as a precipitate, but in the living experience of the time every element was in solution, an inseparable part of a complex whole. The most difficult thing to get hold of, in studying any past period, is this felt sense of the quality of life at a particular place and time: a sense of the ways in which the particular activities combined into a way of thinking and living. We can go some way in restoring the outlines of a particular organization of life; we can even recover what Fromm calls the 'social character' or Benedict the 'pattern of culture'. The social character—a valued system of behaviour and attitudes—is taught, formally and informally; it is both an ideal and a mode. The 'pattern of culture' is a selection and configuration of interests and activities, and a particular valuation of them, producing a distinct organization, a 'way of life'. Yet even these, as we recover them, are usually abstract. Possibly, however, we can gain the sense of a further common element, which is neither the character nor the pattern, but as it were the actual experience through which these were lived. This is potentially of very great importance, and I think the fact is that we are most conscious of such contact in the arts of a period. It can happen that when we have measured these against the external characteristics of the period, and then allowed for individual variations, there is still some important common element that we cannot easily place. I think we can best understand this if we think of any similar analysis of a way of life that we ourselves share. For we find here a particular sense of life, a particular community of experience hardly needing expression, through which the characteristics of our way of life that an external analyst could describe are in some way passed, giving them a particular and characteristic colour. We are usually most aware of this when we notice the contrasts between generations, who never talk quite 'the same language', or when we read an account of our lives by someone from outside the community, or watch the small differences in style, of speech or behaviour, in someone who has learned our ways yet was not bred in them. Almost any formal description would be too crude to express this nevertheless quite distinct sense of a particular and native style. And if this is so, in a way of life we know intimately, it will surely be so when we ourselves are in the position of the visitor, the learner, the guest from a different generation: the position, in fact, that we are all in, when we study any past period. Though it can be turned to trivial account, the fact of such a characteristic is neither trivial nor marginal; it feels quite central.

The term I would suggest to describe it is *structure of feeling*: it is as firm and definite as 'structure' suggests, yet it operates in the most delicate and least tangible parts of our activity. In one sense, this structure of feeling is the culture of a period: it is the particular living result of all the elements in the general organization. And it is in this respect that the arts of a period, taking these to include characteristic approaches and tones in argument, are of major importance. For here, if anywhere, this characteristic is likely to be expressed; often not consciously, but by the fact that here, in the only examples we have of recorded communication that outlives its bearers, the actual living sense, the deep community that makes the communication possible, is naturally drawn upon. I do not mean that the structure of feeling, any more than the social character, is possessed in the same way by the many individuals in the community. But I think it is a very deep and very wide possession, in all actual communities, precisely because it is on it that communication depends. And what is particularly interesting is that it does not seem to be, in any formal sense, learned. One generation may train its successor, with reasonable success, in the social character or the general cultural pattern, but the new generation will have its own structure of feeling, which will not appear to have come 'from' anywhere. For here, most distinctly, the changing organization is enacted in the organism: the new generation responds in its own ways to the unique world it is inheriting, taking up many continuities, that can be traced, and reproducing many aspects of the organization, which can be separately described, yet feeling its whole life in certain ways differently, and shaping its creative response into a new structure of feeling.

Once the carriers of such a structure die, the nearest we can get to this vital element is in the documentary culture, from poems to buildings and dress-fashions, and it is this relation that gives significance to the definition of culture in documentary terms. This in no way means that the documents are autonomous. It is simply that, as previously argued, the significance of an activity must be sought in terms of the whole organization, which is more than the sum of its separable parts. What we are looking for, always, is the actual life that the whole organization is there to express. The significance of documentary culture is that, more clearly than anything else, it expresses that life to us in direct terms, when the living witnesses are silent. At the same time, if we reflect on the nature of a structure of feeling, and see how it can fail to be fully understood even by living people in close contact with it, with ample material at their disposal, including the contemporary arts, we shall not suppose that we can ever do more than make an approach, an approximation, using any channels.

We need to distinguish three levels of culture, even in its most general definition. There is the lived culture of a particular time and place, only fully accessible to those living in that time and place. There is the recorded culture, of every kind, from art to the most everyday facts: the culture of a period. There is also, as the factor connecting lived culture and period cultures, the culture of the selective tradition.

When it is no longer being lived, but in a narrower way survives in its records, the culture of a period can be very carefully studied, until we feel that we have reasonably clear ideas of its cultural work, its social character, its general patterns of activity and value, and in part of its structure of feeling. Yet the survival is governed, not by the period itself, but by new periods, which gradually compose a tradition. Even most specialists in a period know only a part of even its records. One can say with confidence, for example, that nobody really knows the nineteenth-century novel; nobody has read, or could have read, all its examples, over the whole range from printed volumes to penny serials. The real specialist may know some hundreds; the ordinary specialist somewhat less; educated readers a decreasing number: though all will have clear ideas on the subject. A selective process, of a quite drastic kind, is at once evident, and this is true of every field of activity. Equally, of course, no nineteenth-century reader would have read all the novels; no individual in the society would have known more than a selection of its facts. But everyone living in the period would have had something which, I have argued, no later individual can wholly recover: that sense of the life within which the novels were written, and which we now approach through our selection. Theoretically, a period is recorded; in practice, this record is absorbed into a selective tradition; and both are different from the culture as lived.

It is very important to try to understand the operation of a selective tradition. To some extent, the selection begins within the period itself; from the whole body of activities, certain things are selected for value and emphasis. In general this selection will reflect the organization of the period as a whole, though this does not mean that the values and emphases will later be confirmed. We see this clearly enough in the case of past periods, but we never really believe it about our own. We can take an example from the novels of the last decade. Nobody has read all the English novels of the nineteen-fifties; the fastest reader, giving twenty hours a day to this activity alone, could not do it. Yet it is clear, in print and in education, not only that certain general characteristics of the novel in this period have been set down, but also that a reasonably agreed short list has been made, of what seem to be the best and most relevant works. If we take the list as containing perhaps thirty titles (already a very drastic selection indeed) we may suppose that in fifty years the specialist in the novel of the 1950s will know these thirty, and the general reader will know perhaps five or six. Yet we can surely be quite certain that, once the 1950s have passed, another selective process will be begun. As well as reducing the number of works, this new process will also alter, in some cases drastically, the expressed valuations. It is true that when fifty years have passed it is likely that reasonably permanent valuations will have been arrived at, though these may continue to fluctuate. Yet to any of us who had lived this long process through, it would remain true that elements important to us had been neglected. We should say not only 'I don't understand why these young people don't read X any more; a fine writer, no doubt about it', but also 'No, that isn't really what it was like; it is your version'. Since any period includes at least three generations, we are always seeing examples of this, and one complicating factor is that none of us stay still, even in our most significant period: many of the adjustments we should not protest against, many of the omissions, distortions and reinterpretations we should accept or not even notice, because we had been part of the change which brought them about. But then, when living witnesses had gone, a further change would occur. The lived culture would not only have been fined down to selected documents; it would be used, in its reduced form, partly as a contribution (inevitably quite small) to the general line of human growth; partly for historical reconstruction; partly, again, as a way of having done with us, of naming and placing a particular stage of the past. The selective tradition thus creates, at one level, a general human culture; at another level, the historical record of a particular society; at a third level, most difficult to accept and assess, a rejection of considerable areas of what was once a living culture.

Within a given society, selection will be governed by many kinds of special interest, including class interests.

Just as the actual social situation will largely govern contemporary selection, so the development of the society, the process of historical change, will largely determine the selective tradition. The traditional culture of a society will always tend to correspond to its *contemporary* system of interests and values, for it is not an absolute body of work but a continual selection and interpretation. In theory, and to a limited extent in practice, those institutions which are formally concerned with keeping the tradition alive (in particular the institutions of education and scholarship) are committed to the tradition as a whole, and not to some selection from it according to contemporary interests. The importance of this commitment is very great, because we see again and again, in the workings of a selective tradition, reversals and re-discoveries, returns to work apparently abandoned as dead, and clearly this is only possible if there are institutions whose business it is to keep large areas of past culture, if not alive, at least available. It is natural and inevitable that the selective tradition should follow the lines of growth of a society, but because such growth is complex and continuous, the relevance of past work, in any future situation, is unforeseeable. There is a natural pressure on academic institutions to follow the lines of growth of a society, but a wise society, while ensuring this kind of relevance, will encourage the institutions to give sufficient resources to the ordinary work of preservation, and to resist the criticism, which any particular period may make with great confidence, that much of this activity is irrelevant and useless. It is often an obstacle to the growth of a society that so many academic institutions are, to an important extent, self-perpetuating and resistant to change. The changes have to be made, in new institutions if necessary, but if we properly understand the process of the selective tradition, and look at it over a sufficiently long period to get a real sense of historical change and fluctuation, the corresponding value of such perpetuation will be appreciated.

In a society as a whole, and in all its particular activities, the cultural tradition can be seen as a continual selection and re-selection of ancestors. Particular lines will be drawn, often for as long as a century, and then suddenly, with some new stage in growth, these will be cancelled or weakened, and new lines drawn. In the analysis of contemporary culture, the existing state of the selective tradition is of vital importance, for it is often true that some change in this tradition—establishing new lines with the past, breaking or re-drawing existing lines—is a radical kind of *contemporary* change. We tend to underestimate the extent to which the cultural tradition is not only a selection but also an interpretation. We see most past work through our own experience, without even making the effort to see it in something like its original terms. What analysis can do is not so much to reverse this, returning a work to its period, as to make the interpretation conscious, by showing historical alternatives; to relate the interpretation to the particular contemporary values on which it rests; and, by exploring the real patterns of the work, confront us with the real nature of the choices we are making. We shall find, in some cases, that we are keeping the work alive because it is a genuine contribution to cultural growth. We shall find, in other cases, that we are using the work in a particular way for our own reasons, and it is better to know this than to surrender to the mysticism of the 'great valuer, Time'. To put on to Time, the abstraction, the responsibility for our own active choices is to suppress a central part of our experience. The more actively all cultural work can be related, either to the whole organization within which it was expressed, or to the contemporary organization within which it is used, the more clearly shall we see its true values. Thus 'documentary' analysis will lead out to 'social' analysis, whether in a lived culture, a past period, or in the selective tradition which is itself a social organization. And the discovery of permanent contributions will lead to the same kind of general analysis, if we accept the process at this level, not as human perfection (a movement towards determined values), but as a part of man's general evolution, to which many individuals and groups contribute. Every element that we analyse will be in this sense active: that it will be seen in certain real relations, at many different levels. In describing these relations, the real cultural process will emerge.

Any theoretical account of the analysis of culture must submit to be tested in the course of actual analysis. I propose to take one period, the 1840s in England, and to examine, in the context of its culture, the theoretical methods and concepts I have been discussing.

The first and most striking fact, as we begin to study the 1840s in a direct way, is the degree to which the selective tradition has worked on it. A simple example is in the field of newspapers, for it is customary to think of *The Times* as the characteristic paper of the period, and to draw our ideas of early Victorian journalism from its practice. Certainly *The Times* was the leading daily paper, but the most widely read newspapers in this decade were the Sunday papers, *Dispatch*, *Chronicle*, *Lloyd's Weekly* and *News of the World*. These had what we can now recognize as a distinctly 'Sunday paper' selection of news: *Bell's Penny Dispatch* (1842) is sub-titled *Sporting and Police Gazette, and Newspaper of Romance*, and a characteristic headline is 'Daring Conspiracy and Attempted Violation', illustrated by a large woodcut and backed by a detailed story. The total circulation of newspapers of this kind, at the end of the decade, was about 275,000, as compared with a total of 60,000 for the daily papers. If we are examining the actual culture of the period, we must begin from this fact, rather than from the isolation of *The Times* which its continuing importance in a tradition of high politics has brought about.

In the case of literature, the working of the selective tradition is similarly obvious. We think of the period as that of Dickens, Thackeray, Charlotte and Emily Brontë, at the upper levels of the novel, and of Elizabeth Gaskell, Kingsley, Disraeli, in a subsidiary range. We know also, as 'period' authors, Lytton, Marryat, Reade. Dickens, of course, was very widely read at the time. *Pickwick*, to take one example, had sold 40,000 copies a number in periodical publication, and later examples climbed to 70,000 and above. Yet if we look at the other most widely read writers of the period, we find the following list, in order of popularity, given by W. H. Smith's bookstalls, opened in 1848: Lytton,

Marryat, G. P. R. James, James Grant, Miss Sinclair, Haliburton, Mrs Trollope, Lever, Mrs Gaskell, Jane Austen. The two most popular series of cheap novels, the Parlour and Railway Libraries (1847 and 1849), included as their leading authors G. P. R. James (47 titles), Lytton (19), Mrs Marsh (16), Marryat (15), Ainsworth (14), Mrs Gore (10), Grant (8), Grattan (8), Maxwell (7), Mrs Trollope (7), Emma Robinson (6), Mayne Reid (6), W. Carleton (6), Jane Austen (6), Mrs Grey (6). A list of titles from these authors gives an idea of the range: *Agincourt, Last Days of Pompeii, Midshipman Easy, Tower of London, Romance of War, Heiress of Bruges, Stories from Waterloo, Refugee in America, Scalp Hunters, Rody the Rover, Pride and Prejudice, The Little Wife*. In 1851 *The Times* commented:

> Every addition to the stock was positively made on the assumption
> that persons of the better class who constitute the larger portion of
> railway readers lose their accustomed taste the moment they enter
> the station.

However this may be, it is clear that the fiction mentioned was not merely the reading of the degraded poor, but that, at least for railway journeys, this was the taste of 'persons of the better class'. If we take the whole range of readers, we must include an author not yet mentioned, G. W. M. Reynolds, of whom *The Bookseller* at his death said that he was 'the most popular writer of our time', having previously said that he had written more and sold in far greater numbers than Dickens. Reynolds was at his height in the new popular periodicals of the 1840s, the *London Journal* and his own *Reynolds' Miscellany*, in which appeared such typical works as *Mysteries of the Inquisition* and *Mysteries of the Court of London*. We must add to this list of the reading of the period what has been described as a 'huge trade' in pornographic books, illegally produced and distributed from the 'filthy cellars of Holywell Street'. We must also add the works of Carlyle, Ruskin, Macaulay, Mill, Thomas Arnold, Pugin, and of Tennyson, Browning, Clough, Matthew Arnold and Rossetti, as selections from a great body of philosophical, historical, religious and poetic writing. The operation of the selective tradition, to compose what we now think of as the characteristic work of the period, hardly needs stressing.

Already, from looking at the documents, we are necessarily led out to the social history of the period. We come to see certain crucial changes in cultural institutions: the effective establishment of a popular Sunday press as the most successful element in journalism; the growth of new kinds of periodical, combining sensational and romantic fiction with recipes, household hints, and advice to correspondents, as opposed to the more sober 'popular education' journals of the previous decade (the *Penny Magazine* ceased publication in 1845, the year in which the new-type *London Journal* began); the coming of cheap fiction, at one level with the 'penny dreadful', from 1841, at another with half-crown and shilling Parlour and Railway Libraries; important changes in the theatre, with the ending of the monopoly of the Patent Theatres in 1843, the development of minor theatres and, from 1849, the rise of the music-halls. Moreover, these changes at the institutional level, in distribution, relate to a variety of causes that take us far out into the whole history of the period. Thus, technical changes (in newspapers, developed steam-printing and rotary presses; in books, ink-blocking on cloth) provided part of the basis of the printed expansion. The railway boom led to new reading needs and, more centrally, to new points of distribution. Yet the kind of people who made use of these technical opportunities must equally attract our attention. There is an important increase, in this decade, in the entry of pure speculators into these profitable businesses: Lloyd and Bell, in newspapers and periodicals, combining (as did Reynolds more seriously) a generalized radicalism with a sharp commercial instinct; or, in the theatre, the essential beginning of the ownership of theatres by men not directly concerned with the drama, but finding commercial opportunity in building and letting to actor-managers and companies, a method that has had a profound effect on English theatrical development. Again, a large part of the impetus to cheap periodical publishing was the desire to control the development of working-class opinion, and in this the observable shift from popular educational journals to family magazines (the latter the immediate ancestors of the women's magazines of our own time) is significant. Respectable schemes of moral and domestic improvement became deeply entangled with the teaching and implication of particular social values, in the interests of the existing class society. These changes, in a wide field, are necessary parts of the real cultural process that we must examine.

As we move into this wider field, we see, of course, that the selective tradition operates here as in the documents. The institutional developments just noted, representing a critical phase in the commercial organization of popular culture, interest us primarily because they relate to a subsequent major trend. So also do developments of a different kind, in the same field; the beginnings of public museums (a limited Bill in 1845), public libraries (limited provisions in 1850), and public parks (allowed from the rates in 1847). The fierce controversy surrounding these innovations (from the charges of extravagance to the anxious pleas that the working people must be 'civilized') tends to drop away, in our minds, according to subsequent interpretations. The complexity we have to grasp, in the field of cultural institutions, is that this decade brought crucial developments in the commercial exploitation of culture, in its valuable popular expansion, and in enlightened public provision. This is the reality that various strands of the selective tradition tend to reduce, seeking always a single line of development.

This is true also of the general political and social history of the period. As I see it, it is dominated by seven features. There is the crucial Free Trade victory in the Repeal of the Corn Laws, in 1846. There is the virtual re-creation of a new-style Tory Party, under Disraeli, with some influence from the ideas of Young England. There is the Chartist movement, among other things a major stage in the development of working-class political consciousness. There is the factory legislation, culminating in the Ten Hours Bill of 1847. There is the complicated story of the punitive Poor Law and the attempts to amend its operation in 1844 and 1847, and, linked with this by Chadwick, the fight for the Public Health Act of 1848. There is the important re-involvement of the churches, in different ways, in social conflict. There is the major expansion in heavy industries and in capital investment, notably in the railways. Other factors might easily be added, but already from these we can observe two points in analysis. First, that these 'factors' compose a single story, though one of great complexity and conflict: several of them are obviously linked, and none of them, in the real life of the period, can be considered in isolation. Second, that each is subject to highly selective interpretation, according to subsequent directions and commitments. The case of Chartism is the most obvious example. Few would now regard it as dangerous and wicked, as it was widely regarded at the time: too many of its principles have been subsequently built into the 'British way of life' for it to be easy openly to agree with Macaulay, for example, that universal suffrage is 'incompatible with the very existence of civilization'. Yet other selective images of the movement remain powerful: that, like the General Strike of 1926, it was a tragic example of 'the wrong way to get change', the right way being the actually succeeding phase; or, again, that it was muddled and even ridiculous, with its oddly mixed supporters and its monster petitions which were simply disregarded. But the fact is that we have no adequate history of Chartism; we have substitutes for such a history, in one or other of the partial versions thrown up by the selective tradition. We see from this, also, the importance of our theoretical observation on one aspect of the working of the selective tradition: that it is not only affected, even governed, by subsequent main lines of growth, but also changes, as it were retrospectively, in terms of subsequent change. The attention now given to the growth of working-class movements in the nineteenth century would have seemed absurd in 1880, and is governed, now, less by the material itself than by the knowledge of the fruition of these movements, or commitment to them. The stress on economic history has a similar basis of retrospective change.

In the case of literature, the working of the selective tradition needs separate examination. To a considerable extent it is true that the work we now know from the 1840s is the best work of the period: that repeated reading, in a variety of situations, has sifted the good from the less good and bad. Yet there are other factors. Mrs Gaskell and probably Disraeli survive by this criterion, but in both their cases there are other affecting elements: in Mrs Gaskell the documentary interest that is useful to a social history preoccupied by this period; in Disraeli, the fact of his subsequent fame in politics. Kingsley's novels, in my view, would not have survived on literary merit at all, but again they have some documentary interest, and his contribution to intellectual history, in Christian Socialism, has been thought important. Thackeray, Dickens, and Charlotte Brontë survive on strict literary merit, but we see that their best works have carried inferior works that in other authors would have vanished. Emily Brontë would now be said by many critics to be the finest novelist of the decade, but *Wuthering Heights*, for a long time, was carried by the fame of Charlotte, and its major importance, now, is related to changes in twentieth-century literature, moving towards the theme and language of *Wuthering Heights* and away from the main fictional tradition of the decade in which it was written. In verse, we read Tennyson and Browning for their intrinsic interest, though their reputations have violently fluctuated, but I do not think we should read many of Matthew Arnold's 1849 poems if he had not subsequently acquired a reputation of a different kind. We read Carlyle, Ruskin, and Mill because, in spite of obvious faults, they are major writers and additionally belong to living intellectual traditions. But, where we read Thomas Arnold, it is because of his educational importance; where we read Pugin, we have had to remake his significance, with our own emphasis on the relations between art and society; where we read Macaulay, we read perhaps with less interest, not because his ability seems less, but because his way of thinking seems increasingly irrelevant. Thus the selective tradition, which we can be certain will continue to change, is in part the emphasis of works of general value, in part the use of past work in terms of our own growth. That part of the tradition which relates to this period is different from the period itself, just as the period culture, consciously studied, is necessarily different from the culture as lived.

The work of conscious reconstruction, and of the selective tradition, tends to specialization of different classes of activity, and we must look now at the area of relations between these, to see if our theoretical description of such relations is valid. We have already seen one important class of relationships, in the field of cultural institutions. Such factors in the society as the class situation (particularly the range of middle-class attitudes to the dissident working-class), the technical expansion which followed from the growth of an industrial economy, and the kinds of ownership and distribution natural to such an economy, can be seen to have affected such institutions as the press, book publishing, and the theatre, and the form of these institutions, with the purposes they expressed, had observable effects on some cultural work: new styles in journalism, changes in the novel because of serial publication, some adaptation of material in terms of the new publics being reached. With this kind of interrelation we are reasonably familiar, but it is not the only kind.

A second kind, in which, knowing the society, we look for its direct reflection in cultural work, is, in this period, quite clear. Of the seven general features listed, from the political and social history of the 1840s, all are extensively reflected in contemporary literature, particularly in the novel. If we read only *Mary Barton, Sybil, Coningsby, Dombey and Son, Yeast, Alton Locke, Past and Present*, we move directly into the world of Chartism, factory legislation, the Poor Law, the railways, the involvement of the churches (the decade produced several novels of the crisis of religious belief and affiliation), and the politics of Free Trade and Young England. The interrelation is important, but again it is not the only kind, and indeed, if we limit relationships to this direct description and discussion, we shall find it difficult to estimate even these.

The further area of relations, that we must now examine, is that described and interpreted by such concepts as the social character and the structure of feeling. The dominant social character of the period can be briefly outlined. There is the belief in the value of work, and this is seen in relation to individual effort, with a strong attachment to success

60

gained in these terms. A class society is assumed, but social position is increasingly defined by actual status rather than by birth. The poor are seen as the victims of their own failings, and it is strongly held that the best among them will climb out of their class. A punitive Poor Law is necessary in order to stimulate effort; if a man could fall back on relief, without grave hardship in the form of separation from his family, minimum sustenance, and such work as stonebreaking or oakum-picking, he would not make the necessary effort to provide for himself. In this and a wider field, suffering is in one sense ennobling, in that it teaches humility and courage, and leads to the hard dedication to duty. Thrift, sobriety, and piety are the principal virtues, and the family is their central institution. The sanctity of marriage is absolute, and adultery and fornication are unpardonable. Duty includes helping the weak provided that the help is not of such a kind as to confirm the weakness: condoning sexual error, and comforting the poor, are weaknesses by this definition. Training to the prevailing virtues must be necessarily severe, but there is an obligation to see that the institutions for such training are strengthened.

This can be fairly called the dominant social character of the period, if we look at its characteristic legislation, the terms in which this was argued, the majority content of public writing and speaking, and the characters of the men most admired. Yet, of course, as a social character, it varied considerably in success of transmission, and was subject to many personal variations. The more serious difficulty arises as we look more closely at the period and realize that alternative social characters were in fact active, and that these affected, in important ways, the whole life of the time. A social character is the abstract of a dominant group, and there can be no doubt that the character described—a developed form of the morality of the industrial and commercial middle class—was at this time the most powerful. At the same time, there were other social characters with substantial bases in the society. The aristocratic character was visibly weakening, but its variations—that birth mattered more than money; that work was not the sole social value and that civilization involved play; that sobriety and chastity, at least in young men, were not cardinal virtues but might even be a sign of meanness or dullness—are still alive in the period, all in practice, some in theory. In attitudes to the poor, this character is ambiguous: it includes a stress on charity, as part of one's station, very different from punitive rehabilitation, but also a brutality, a willingness to cut down troublemakers, a natural habit of repression, which again differ from the middle-class attitude. The 1840s are very interesting in this respect, for they show the interaction of different social characters: Tory charity against Whig rehabilitation; brutality and repression against positive civilization through institution. Some of the best criticism of the Whig Poor Law came from Tories with a conscious aristocratic ideal, as most notably in Young England. Brutality and repression are ready, in crisis, but as compared with the twenties and thirties, are being steadily abandoned in favour of positive legislation. Play may be frowned on by the social character, but the decade shows a large increase in light entertainment, from cheap novels to the music-halls. Not only is the dominant social character different, in many ways, from the life lived in its shadow, but alternative social characters lead to the real conflicts of the time. This is a central difficulty of the social character concept, for in stressing a dominant abstraction it seriously underestimates the historical process of change and conflict, which are found even when, as in the 1840s, such a social character is very strong. For we must add another alternative, of major importance: the developing social character of the working class, different in important respects from its competitors. As the victims of repression and punitive rehabilitation, of the gospel of success and the pride of birth, of the real nature of work and the exposure to suffering, working-class people were beginning to formulate alternative ideals. They had important allies from the interaction of the other systems, and could be a major force either in the Corn Laws repeal or in the Factory legislation, when these were sponsored by different sections of the ruling class. But the 1840s show an important development of independent aims, though these are to be realized, mainly, through alliance with other groups. Thus Chartism is an ideal beyond the terms of any dominant group in the society, and is more than an expression of democratic aspirations; is also an assertion of an individual dignity transcending class. The Ten Hours Bill, in working-class minds, was more than a good piece of paternal legislation on work; it was also the claim to leisure, and hence again to a wider life. At the same time, in their own developing organizations, the most radical criticism of all was being made: the refusal of a society based either on birth or on individual success, the conception of a society based on mutual aid and co-operation.

We can then distinguish three social characters operative in the period, and it is with the study of relations between them that we enter the reality of the whole life. All contribute to the growth of the society: the aristocratic ideals tempering the harshness of middle-class ideals at their worst; working-class ideals entering into a fruitful and decisive combination with middle-class ideals at their best. The middle-class social character remains dominant, and both aristocrats and working people, in many respects, come to terms with it. But equally, the middle-class social character as it entered the forties is in many respects modified as the forties end. The values of work and self-help, of social position by status rather than birth, of the sanctity of marriage and the emphasis on thrift, sobriety and charity, are still dominant. But punitive rehabilitation, and the attitudes to weakness and suffering on which it rests, have been, while not rejected, joined by a major ideal of public service, in which the effort towards civilization is actively promoted by a genuine altruism and the making of positive institutions.

This is one level of change, and such analysis is necessary if we are to explore the reality of the social character. In some respects, the structure of feeling corresponds to the dominant social character, but it is also an expression of the interaction described. Again, however, the structure of feeling is not uniform throughout the society; it is primarily evident in the dominant productive group. At this level, however, it is different from any of the distinguishable social characters, for it has to deal not only with the public ideals but with their omissions and consequences, as lived. If we look at the fiction of the forties, we shall see this clearly.

The popular fiction of the periodicals, so carefully studied by Dalziel, is very interesting in this context. At first sight we find what we expect: the unshakeable assumptions of a class society, but with the stress on wealth rather than birth (aristocrats, indeed, being often personally vicious); the conviction that the poor are so by their own faults—their stupidity and depravity stressed, their mutual help ignored; the absolute sanctity of marriage, the manipulation of plot to bring sexual offenders to actual suffering; the fight against weakness, however terrible, as one of the main creators of humble virtue. All this, often consciously didactic, is the direct expression of the dominant social character, and the assumptions tend to be shared by the pious 'improving' fiction (cf. Mrs Tonna's *Helen Fleetwood*) and by the sensational fiction which the improvers condemned. But then we are reminded of the extent to which popular fiction retains older systems of value, often through stereotyped conventions of character. The 'fashionable novel' of high life only became unfashionable late in the decade. The typical hero is sometimes the successful exponent of self-help, but often he is an older type, the cultivated gentleman, the soldier governed by a code of honour, even the man who finds pleasure a blessing and work a curse. To the earlier hero, loss of income and the need to work were misfortunes to be endured; to have a safe fortune was undoubtedly best. The new attitude to work came in only slowly, for understandable reasons. (Ordinary middle-class life was still thought too plain and dull for a really interesting novel). Further, heroes of either kind are capable of strong overt emotion; they can burst into public tears, or even swoon, as strong men used to do but were soon to do no more. Heroines have more continuity: they are weak, dependent, and shown as glad to be so, and of course they are beautiful and chaste. One interesting factor, obviously related to a continuing general attitude in the period, is that schools, almost without exception, are shown as terrible: not only are they places of temptation and wickedness, mean, cruel and educationally ridiculous, but also they are inferior to the home and family, as a way of bringing up children. This is perhaps the last period in which a majority of English public opinion believed that home education was the ideal. From the sixteenth century, this belief had been gaining ground, and its complete reversal, with the new public-school ethos after Arnold, is of considerable general importance. But the new attitude does not appear in fiction until *Tom Brown's Schooldays* in 1857.

In the popular fiction of the forties, then, we find many marks of older ways of feeling, as well as faithful reproduction of certain standard feelings of the approved social character. We find also, in an interesting way, the interaction between these and actual experience. The crucial point, in this period, is in the field of success and money. The confident assertions of the social character, that success followed effort, and that wealth was the mark of respect, had to contend, if only unconsciously, with a practical world in which things were not so simple. The confidence of this fiction is often only superficial. What comes through with great force is a pervasive atmosphere of instability and debt. A normal element, in these stories, is the loss of fortune, and this is hardly ever presented in terms consistent with the social character: that success or failure corresponded to personal quality. Debt and ruin haunt this apparently confident world, and in a majority of cases simply happen to the characters, as a result of a process outside them. At one level, the assumptions of the social character are maintained: if you lose your fortune, you get out of the way—you cannot embarrass yourself or your friends by staying. But this ruthless code is ordinarily confined to subsidiary characters: the parents of hero or heroine. For the people who matter, some other expedient is necessary. It is found, over the whole range of fiction, by two devices: the unexpected legacy, and the Empire. These devices are extremely interesting, both at the level of magic and at the level of developing attitudes necessary to the society.

Magic is indeed necessary, to postpone the conflict between the ethic and the experience. It is widely used in sexual situations, where hero or heroine is tied to an unloved wife or husband, while the true lover waits in the wings. Solutions involving infidelity or breaking the marriage are normally unthinkable, and so a formula is evolved, for standard use: the unsuitable partner is not merely unloved, but alcoholic or insane; at a given point, and after the required amount of resigned suffering, there is a convenient, often spectacular death, in which the unloving partner shows great qualities of care, duty, and piety; and then, of course, the real love can be consummated. In money, the process is similar: legacies, at the crucial moment, turn up from almost anywhere, and fortunes are restored. Nobody has to go against the principle that money is central to success, but equally very few have to be bound by the ethic preached to the poor: that the deserving prosper by effort. This element of cheating marks one crucial point of difference between the social character and the actual structure of feeling.

The use of the Empire is similar but more complex. Of course there were actual legacies, and these eventually changed the self-help ethic, in its simplest form: the magic, at this stage, lay in their timing. But the Empire was a more universally available escape-route: black sheep could be lost in it; ruined or misunderstood heroes could go out and return with fortunes; the weak of every kind could be transferred to it, to make a new life. Often indeed, the Empire is the source of the unexpected legacy, and the two devices are joined. It is clear that the use of the Empire relates to real factors in the society. At a simple level, going out to the new lands could be seen as self-help and enterprise of the purest kinds. Also, in the new lands, there was a great need for labourers, and emigration as a solution to working-class problems was being widely urged, often by the most humane critics of the existing system. In 1840, 90,000 people a year were emigrating, and in 1850 three times as many. In a different way, in terms of capital and trade, the Empire had been one of the levers of industrialization, and was to prove one major way of keeping the capitalist system viable. These factors are reflected in fiction, though not to the same extent as later in the century, when Imperialism had become a conscious policy. Meanwhile, alongside this reflection of real factors, there was the use as magic: characters whose destinies could not be worked out within the system as given were simply put on the boat, a simpler way of resolving the conflict between ethic and experience than any radical questioning of the ethic. This method had the additional advantage that it was consonant with another main element of the structure of feeling: that there could be no general solution to the social problems of the time; there could be only individual solutions, the rescue by legacy or emigration, the resolution by some timely change of heart.

Now the fascinating thing about the structure of feeling as described is that it is present in almost all the novels we now read as literature, as well as in the now disregarded popular fiction. This is true of the reflections and of the magic. Disraeli seems daring in dramatizing the two-nation problem in the love of an aristocrat and a Chartist girl, but Sybil, following the pattern of almost all poor heroines in such situations in the periodicals, is discovered in the end to be 'really' a dispossessed aristocrat. (The uniting of the two nations is in fact, in Disraeli, the combination of agricultural and industrial property, a very sanguine political forecast, and the same pattern is followed in *Coningsby*, where the young aristocrat marries the Lancashire manufacturer's daughter, and is elected for an industrial constituency.) Mrs Gaskell, though refusing the popular fiction that the poor suffered by their own faults, succeeds in *Mary Barton* in compromising working-class organization with murder, and steers all her loved characters to Canada. Kingsley, in *Alton Locke*, sends his Chartist hero to America. And these are the humane critics, in many ways dissenting from the social character, but remaining bound by the structure of feeling.

The same correspondence is evident in novels less concerned with the problems of the society. The novels of Charlotte and Anne Brontë are, in terms of plot and structure of feeling, virtually identical with many stories in the periodicals: the governess-heroine, the insane wife or alcoholic husband, the resolution through resignation, duty, and magic. Dickens, similarly, uses the situations, the feelings, and the magic of periodical fiction again and again.

This connection between the popular structure of feeling and that used in the literature of the time is of major importance in the analysis of culture. It is here, at a level even more important than that of institutions, that the real relations within the whole culture are made clear: relations that can easily be neglected when only the best writing survives, or when this is studied outside its social context. Yet the connection must be carefully defined. Often it is simply that in the good novel the ordinary situations and feelings are worked through to their maximum intensity. In other cases, though the framework is retained, one element of the experience floods through the work, in such a way as to make it relevant in its own right, outside the conventional terms. This is true of Elizabeth Gaskell, in the early parts of *Mary Barton*; of Charlotte Brontë, taking lonely personal desire to an intensity that really questions the conventions by which it is opposed; of Dickens, certainly, in that the conventional figure of the orphan, or the child exposed by loss of fortune, comes to transcend the system to which he refers, and to embody many of the deepest feelings in the real experience of the time. These are the creative elements, though the connection with the ordinary structure of feeling is still clear. The orphan, the exposed child, the lonely governess, the girl from a poor family: these are the figures which express the deepest response to the reality of the way of life. In the ordinary fiction, they were conventional figures; in the literature they emerge carrying an irresistible authenticity, not merely as exemplars of the accidents of the social system, but as expressions of a *general* judgement of the human quality of the whole way of life. Here, in the 1840s, is the first body of fiction (apart from occasional earlier examples, in Godwin and perhaps Richardson) expressing, even through the conventional forms, a radical human dissent. At the level of social character, the society might be confident of its assumptions and its future, but these lonely exposed figures seem to us, at least, the personal and social reality of the system which in part the social character rationalized. Man alone, afraid, a victim: this is the enduring experience. The magic solutions will be grasped at, in many cases, in the end, but the intensity of the central experience is on record and survives them. And it is at this point that we find the link with a novel like *Wuthering Heights*, which rejects so much more of the conventional structure. Here, at a peak of intensity, the complicated barriers of a system of relationships are broken through, finally, by an absolute human commitment. The commitment is realized through death, and the essential tragedy, embodied elsewhere in individual figures who may, by magic, be rescued from it, becomes the form of the whole work. The creative elements in the other fiction are raised to a wholeness which takes the work right outside the ordinary structure of feeling, and teaches a new feeling.

Art reflects its society and works a social character through to its reality in experience. But also, art creates, by new perceptions and responses, elements which the society, as such, is not able to realize. If we compare art with its society, we find a series of real relationships showing its deep and central connections with the rest of the general life. We find description, discussion, exposition through plot and experience of the social character. We find also, in certain characteristic forms and devices, evidence of the deadlocks and unsolved problems of the society: often admitted to consciousness for the first time in this way. Part of this evidence will show a false consciousness, designed to prevent any substantial recognition; part again a deep desire, as yet uncharted, to move beyond this. As George Eliot wrote, recording this latter feeling, in 1848:

> The day will come when there will be a temple of white marble, where sweet incense and anthems shall rise to the memory of every man and woman who has had a deep *Ahnung*, a presentiment, a yearning, or a clear vision of the time when this miserable reign of Mammon shall end—when men shall be no longer 'like the fishes of the sea'—society no more like a face one half of which —the side of profession, of lip-faith—is fair and God-like, the other half—the side of deeds and institutions—with a hard old wrinkled skin puckered into the sneer of a Mephistopheles.

Much of the art, much of the magic, of the 1840s, expressed this desire. And at this point we find ourselves moving into a process which cannot be the simple comparison of art and society, but which must start from the recognition that all the acts of men compose a general reality within which both art and what we ordinarily call society are comprised. We do not now compare the art with the society; we compare both with the whole complex of human actions and feelings.

We find some art expressing feelings which the society, in its general character, could not express. These may be the creative responses which bring new feelings to light. They may be also the simple record of omissions: the nourishment or attempted nourishment of human needs unsatisfied. An element in the 1840s that we have not yet noted shows this kind of evidence clearly. The characteristic verse of Tennyson and Arnold in the decade, from *Morte d'Arthur* and *Ulysses* to *The Forsaken Merman*, is a late phase of that part of the Romantic movement which sought to express, through other places and other times, a richness not evident in ordinary contemporary life. That this poetry is weaker than that of Coleridge and Keats, which it formally resembles, seems to mark a further and perhaps disastrous moving away from the energies of the actual life; yet the impulse is characteristic, and in strength and weakness indicates experience that study of the society alone could not adduce. Then again we can link with this the general romanticizing of the past, at a serious level in Carlyle, at a popular level in the form of the historical novel, again a Romantic creation and at a high level of production and popularity in the early 1840s, beginning to fade in the later years. Linking the weak romanticism of exotic colour and richness with the strong romanticism of the vision of a fuller human life is the sense of omission, from the bleak reality and dominant ideals of the period, of certain basic human needs. The magic and tinsel of illegitimate theatre and music-hall, the ornate furnishing, the Gothicism in architecture, belong in the same category. And 1848, the last year of the Chartists, is also the first year of the Pre-Raphaelite Brotherhood. It is not that we cannot relate this art to the rest of the general life, but that we see it, by its very contrast with the main features of the society, as an element of the general human organization which found expression in this specific way, and which must be set in parity with the other elements, if we are to analyse the culture as a whole.

Finally, as we look at the whole period, we recognize that its creative activities are to be found, not only in art but, following the main lines of the society, in industry and engineering, and, questioning the society, in new kinds of social institution. We cannot understand any period of the Industrial Revolution if we fail to recognize the real miracle that was being worked, by human skill and effort. Again and again, even by critics of the society, the excitement of this extraordinary release of man's powers was acknowledged and shared. The society could not have been acceptable to anybody, without that. 'These are our poems', Carlyle said in 1842, looking at one of the new locomotives, and this element, now so easily overlooked, is central to the whole culture.

In a quite different way, in new institutions, the slow creation of different images of community, different forms of relationship, by the newly-organizing workers and by middle-class reformers, marks a reaching-out of the mind of comparable importance. We cannot understand even the creative part of a culture without reference to activities of this kind, in industry and institutions, which are as strong and as valuable an expression of direct human feeling as the major art and thought.

To make a complete analysis of the culture of the 1840s would go far beyond the scope and intention of this chapter. I have simply looked at this fascinating decade as a way of considering what any such analysis involves. I have only indicated the ways in which it might begin, but I think it is clear that analysis of the kind described is feasible, and that the exploration of relations between apparently separate elements of the way of life can be illuminating. In any event, as we follow the analysis through, and as we see the ways in which it could be continued, we can decide for ourselves the extent to which the main theoretical approach, and the theoretical distinctions which follow from it, are valid.

THREE

Individuals and Societies

W E are seeking to define and consider one central
principle: that of the essential relation, the true
interaction, between patterns learned and created in
the mind and patterns communicated and made active in
relationships, conventions, and institutions. Culture is our
name for this process and its results, and then within this
process we discover problems that have been the subject of
traditional debate and that we may look at again in this new
way. Among such problems, that of the relationship between
an individual and his society is evident and crucial. It has
been discussed through the whole series of systems of thinking that compose our tradition, and it is still widely discussed, from current experience, since it seems to be agreed
that precisely this issue is at the centre of the conflicts of our
time. Yet of course we approach the experience through the
descriptions we have learned: in a more or less conscious
way if we know parts of the vast body of accumulated theory
in the matter; still, in effect, if we know none of the theory
directly, yet find it embedded in the very language and forms
of relationship through which we are bound to live. When
we examine actual relationships, we start from the descriptions we have learned. When we speak of 'the individual' and
of 'society', we are using descriptions which embody particular interpretations of the experience to which they refer:
interpretations which gained currency at a particular point
in history, yet which have now virtually established themselves in our minds as absolutes. By a special effort, we may
become conscious of 'the individual' and 'society' as 'no
more than descriptions', yet still so much actual experience
and behaviour is tied to them that the realization can seem
merely academic. There are times, however, when there is so
high a tension between experience and description that we
are forced to examine the descriptions, and to seek beyond

72

them for new descriptions, not so much as a matter of theory but as literally a problem of behaviour. It has seemed to me for some years that our ways of thinking about 'the individual and society' are inadequate, confusing, and at times sterile. In thinking about culture, rather than directly about this issue as named, I have found my own descriptions of this kind of experience changing quite radically. I want to see if it is possible, from what I have said about the creative mind and about culture, to reconsider this traditional debate. I propose to review the main descriptions historically, to examine the effect on them of recent work in a number of disciplines, and to offer some amendments and possible new descriptions.

I

We can conveniently begin the historical examination at the point where 'individual' emerged as the description we now have. It is always difficult to date an experience by dating a concept, but when a word appears—either a new word or a new sense of a word—a particular stage has been reached that is the nearest we can get to a consciousness of change. 'Individual' meant 'inseparable', in medieval thinking, and its main use was in the context of theological argument about the nature of the Holy Trinity. The effort was to explain how a being could be thought of as existing in his own nature yet existing by this nature as part of an indivisible whole. The logical problem extended to other fields of experience, and 'individual' became a term used to indicate a member of some group, kind, or species. The complexity of the term is at once apparent in this history, for it is the unit that is being defined, yet defined in terms of its membership of a class. The separable entity is being defined by a word that has meant 'inseparable': an identity—a particular name—is conferred by a realization of identity—the fact of common status. The crucial history of the modern description is a change in emphasis which enabled us to think of 'the individual' as a kind of absolute, without immediate reference, by the very structure of the term, to the group of which he is a member. And this change, so far as we can now trace it in the imperfectly recorded history of the word

73

itself, seems to have taken place in England in the late sixteenth and early seventeenth centuries. Slowly, and with
many ambiguities, since that time, we have learned to think
of 'the individual in his own right', where previously to describe an individual was to give an example of the group of
which he was a member, and so to offer a particular description of that group and of the relationships within it.

This semantic change, in itself very difficult to trace,
seems clearer in its context of an actual change in relationships, in our long and uneven growth from the medieval
world. In describing this we are of course reducing a whole
area of complicated experience to a few simple patterns, but
our sense of the general change is within these limits probably accurate. The basis of the new sense of 'individual' can
be interestingly explored in the history of the idea of the
individual soul, and we are probably right to see in the
controversies of the Reformation an extension of ideas
inherent in the Christian tradition, by which it was possible
to pass from seeing the soul's destiny within an ordered
structure, of God and the Church, to seeing this destiny as
in a different way personal: a man's direct and individual
relationship with God. In either way of thinking, the problem
of personal destiny was real, but at one extreme this could
be seen as an example of common destiny, important primarily as indicating this common destiny, while at the other
extreme it was the individual destiny, in its own right, which
claimed primary attention. One destiny was apprehended
through the complicated structure of relationships of a total
order; the other through one direct relationship, between the
individual and his God. When we speak of the 'individualism'
of Protestant thinking, we do not mean that the fact of a
personal destiny is more real than in previous systems, but
that the relationships within which the destiny is realized are
differently defined. A change in the conception of relationships—crudely from man-church-God to man-God—is
recorded by the new sense of what it is to be 'an individual'.

There is a similar and related change in the conception of
man's individual 'position' in life. To speak of a position
implies relationships, and we are still very conscious of this.
But there is an evident change, between medieval and modern

thinking, in this difficult conception of 'man in society'. Most accounts of medieval society stress the way in which a man was defined by his position in the social order: an 'individual' in the old sense, defined by his membership of a group. As Erich Fromm has put it: 'a person was identical with his role in society; he was a peasant, an artisan, a knight, and not *an individual* who *happened* to have this or that occupation'. We can see that this must to a large extent have been true, in a rigid society in which the possibility of 'becoming something else' was comparatively very limited. As mobility increased, and at least some men could change their status, the idea of being an individual in a sense separable from one's social role obviously gained in strength. The growth of capitalism, and the great social changes associated with it, encouraged certain men to see 'the individual' as a source of economic activity, by his 'free enterprise'. It was less a matter of performing a certain function within a fixed order than of initiating certain kinds of activity, choosing particular directions. The social and geographical mobility to which in some cases these changes gave rise led to a re-definition of the individual—'what I am'—by extension to 'what I want to be' and 'what by my own efforts I have become'. Yet this is still a definition of an individual in his social or economic role, and we can all observe that this kind of definition has persisted into our own times. I think, among many examples, of the magistrate's question to William Morris in the dock, in 1885:

Mr Saunders: What are you?
Prisoner: I am an artist, and a literary man, pretty well known,
             I think, throughout Europe.

The curtness of the question, and yet Morris's immediate understanding of it, stick in my mind, for I know my own reaction, that the only answer to 'what are you?' is 'a man', yet with the certainty that the answer would be considered insolent, as I consider the question insolent. And in rejecting the question 'what are you?', thinking of the more acceptable question 'who are you?' and then 'what is your work?', I am living out this particular history, in which we have become increasingly conscious of individual existence as a thing separable from, more important than, an occupation, a social function, a social rank. I can think of some people who would have answered the magistrate's question with the proud 'an Englishman', and indeed that kind of consciousness is a stage in the development. We have at our command, now, a number of ways of defining our existence, in terms of nationality, class, occupation and so on, in which we in fact offer a personal description in terms of membership of a group. Yet for most of us, when all these terms have been used, an area of conscious and valued existence remains, which in this mode of description could not be expressed at all. It is in relation to this area of existence that the problem of 'the individual and society' takes shape.

Thus we can trace our concept of 'the individual' to that complex of change which we analyse in its separable aspects as the Renaissance, the Reformation, the beginnings of capitalist economy. In essence it is the abstraction of the individual from the complex of relationships by which he had hitherto been normally defined. The counterpart of this process was a similar abstraction of 'society', which had earlier indicated an actual relationship—'the society of his fellows'—but which in the late sixteenth century began to develop the more general modern sense of 'the system of common life'—society as a thing in itself. 'Community' reached the same stage of development in the seventeenth century, and 'State' had reached this stage rather earlier, having added to its two earlier meanings—the condition of the common life, as now in 'state of the nation'; the signs of a condition or status, as in 'the King's state'—the sense of the 'apparatus' of the common life, its framework or set order. Thus we see the terms of relationship separating out, until 'individual' on the one hand, 'society', 'community', and 'state' on the other, could be conceived as abstractions and absolutes.

The major tradition of subsequent social thinking has depended on these descriptions. In England, from Hobbes to the Utilitarians, a variety of systems share a common starting-point: man as a bare human being, 'the individual', is the logical starting-point of psychology, ethics, and politics. It is rare, in this tradition, to start from the fact that man is born into relationships. The abstraction of the bare human being, as a separate substance, is ordinarily taken for granted. In other systems of thinking, the community would be the axiom, and individual man the derivative. Here individual man is the axiom, and society the derivative. Hobbes virtually drops all middle terms between separate individuals and the State, and, seeing the individuals as naturally selfish, sees society as a rational construction to restrain the destructive elements in individuals and to enforce co-operation. Locke sees the rational and co-operative elements as natural, but similarly postulates separate individuals who create society by consent or contract, for the protection of their individual interests. The whole Liberal tradition, following from this, begins with the individual and his rights and, judging society as an arrangement to ensure these abstract rights, argues normally for only the necessary minimum of government. It is clear that much human good resulted from this emphasis, in the actual liberation of men from arbitrary and oppressive systems. Yet it rested on descriptions which, while corresponding to the experience of man breaking out from obsolete social forms, came to conflict with experience of the difficulties of new kinds of organization.

While the abstract individual was idealized in this tradition, an alternative tradition, sharing some but not all of its terms, moved in the direction of the idealization of society. Rousseau, arguing that 'we begin properly to become men only after we have become citizens', saw the community as the source of values and hence as 'a moral person'. Hegel, beginning from the similar emphasis that man becomes an individual through society and civilization, saw the State as the organ of the highest human values—an embodiment of what Matthew Arnold called 'our best self'. Yet both Rousseau and Hegel, with differences of emphasis, saw the importance of actual communities and forms of association as the necessary mediating element between individuals and the large Society. It is from this line of thinking that an important revision of the descriptions has followed. We preserve, from the early Liberalism, the absolutes of 'individual' and 'society', but we add to these, as mediating terms, 'community' and 'association', to describe local and face-to-face relationships through which the great abstractions of Individual and Society operate in detail. A particular and crucial addition was the concept of 'class', which is quite different from the static concepts of 'order' and 'rank' because it includes this kind of middle term between 'the individual' and 'society'—the individual relates to his society through his class. Yet 'class' carries an emphasis different from 'community' or 'association', because it is not a face-to-face grouping but, like 'society' itself, an abstraction. Marx argued that by their common membership of a particular class, men will think and act in certain common ways even though they do not belong to the same actual communities, and that the processes of 'society' are in fact best understood in terms of the interaction of these classes. Thus, in the nineteenth century, while the abstract descriptions of 'individual' and 'society' retained their force, a number of new descriptions were made and emphasized, their general import being the indication of particular kinds of relationship. It is on this whole range—rising, as we have seen, from a complex of historical changes and rival intellectual traditions—that certain twentieth-century disciplines have acted.

II

The influence of Freud, as an analyst of personal and social behaviour, has been very great, and has reinforced one part of the tradition that we have been examining. For Freudian theory assumes a basic division between the individual and society, and hence basic division between the individual and such mediating forms as 'community', or 'class', which are seen simply as social agents which operate on the individual. Man, the 'bare human being', has certain fundamental drives which are also fundamentally anti-social. Some of these society must restrain; others it must refine and divert into socially acceptable or valuable channels. Society is a mechanism of restraint and diversion, and civilization is the product, through 'sublimation', of suppressed natural impulses. Man as a bare human being is thus fundamentally alienated from society, and the best that can be hoped for is a reasonably adjusted balance between the conflicting needs of individual and society, the process of sublimation being the mechanism of balance, and breakdown being due to faulty adjustment of this kind.

Yet if Freud's account of the individual and society is, in its basic terms, merely an item in an old tradition, his actual inquiries led to a highly significant emphasis on relationships. Indeed he introduced, in a wholly new way, a new mediating term, the family, and thus remarkably extended the study of actual social growth. It was not that the family, as a first form of association, had not always been available as a concept, but that Freud's emphasis on the radical importance, in all human behaviour, of the patterns of relationship established in infancy, transformed its significance. Freud's descriptions are contained and limited by his theoretical separation of 'the individual' and 'society', yet in different hands they have been differently developed. In dogmatic Freudianism very little of interest to the study of social relationships has emerged, since such relationships are always construed as of secondary importance. In other hands, the possibility of linking our deeply personal relationships with the whole network of social relationships has been interestingly explored. The work of Fromm seems particularly useful, since he has developed one new mediating description, that of the 'social character'. This offers to describe the process by which social behaviour becomes part of an individual personality: not by regular processes of restraint and diversion, as in Freud, but by a shaping process which can include many kinds of relationship. The 'social character' is a selective response to experience, a learned system of feeling and acting, in a majority of the community into which the child is born. The family is then the community's agent in creating this desired social character in individuals. If it is successful, the individual's social activity will be at one with his personal desires, for the social character 'internalizes external necessities and thus harnesses human energy for the task of a given economic and social system'. The individual, in such a case, comes to 'act according to what is necessary for him from a practical standpoint, and also to give him satisfaction for his activity psychologically'. Instead of a permanent human nature, which society restrains or modifies, individual psychology is then a matter of 'the particular kind of relatedness of the individual towards the world'. This relatedness can correspond with the current social character, or can diverge from it.

In this we can see Freud playing the role of Hobbes, and Fromm that of Locke: in both cases with a greatly refined description of the actual process of relationship between an individual and society. Fromm has advanced considerably in showing how 'society' can become truly embodied in individuals, so that we need not think of them as separate and absolute but always in terms of relationships. The real problem arises, however, when we ask what is the source of the individual character that can diverge from the social character, or, more accurately, what kinds of relationship affect the individual character that are not forms of social relationship? If 'social character' is reserved to a particular construction which may or may not adequately interpret the real relationships which the individual forms, then its function is clearer, and the possibility of variant individual response has an obvious theoretical basis. Yet it is then a question whether 'social character' is a finally useful term, since it seems only a partial explanation of how relationships (society) create psychology (the individual).

The concept of 'social character' is similar to the anthropological concept of a 'pattern of culture'. Comparative studies of different societies have added to our historical evidence to show how various are the learned systems of behaviour and attitudes which groups of human beings adopt. Each of these systems, while it lasts, is the form of a society, a pattern of culture to which most of its individual members are successfully trained. Comparison of the systems has done much to transform traditional arguments about the individual and society, for it has shown how various are the feelings and forms of behaviour that bring individual and common satisfaction. Instead of asking the relationship between an ideally identified individual, with a standard equipment of desires and attitudes, and an ideally identified society, with standard purposes, it has been possible to look at real and changing relationships, with an amount of detail that has broken up the standard prescriptions. Yet, in extending the evidence, it has made theoretical inquiry more difficult. Perhaps the main result has been an enormous strengthening of the tradition which emphasized the extent to which individual personality is formed by social processes, even at very deep levels. This has been wholly valuable, as a way of correcting the false emphasis on the abstract 'individual', which we can now see to be a product of a particular social and historical situation rather than a correct reading of the general human condition. Yet this is not, rightly interpreted, a denial of the importance of individuals. As Benedict argues:

> No culture yet observed has been able to eradicate the differences in the temperaments of the persons who compose it. It is always a give-and-take. The problem of the individual is not clarified by stressing the antagonism between culture and the individual, but by stressing their mutual reinforcement. This *rapport* is so close that it is not possible to discuss patterns of culture without considering specifically their relation to individual psychology.

A 'pattern of culture', like a 'social character', is a selective response to experience, a learned system of feeling and acting, in a particular society. Benedict argues that this pattern will be 'congenial' to a majority of the members of the society, and that therefore they can be trained to it, in such a way that by becoming members of the society they will adequately express their individuality. But to others, the pattern will not be 'congenial', and these will either not conform, or conform at a possibly heavy price to their individual desires. It is difficult to know what weight to put on 'congenial': the variations Benedict actually describes—different reactions to frustration and grief—look very like what others would call 'learned responses', although the problem then arises that these are 'learned' and yet are different from those the particular society teaches and approves. If they are not learned but innate, we are back to 'human nature', to be understood now not as a single thing, but as comprising an innate range of temperaments: the relation between the individual and society thus becomes a kind of lottery, in which an individual of particular temperament draws a winning or losing card in the society in which he happens to be born. We do not yet know nearly enough to prove or disprove this hypothesis, but it represents one attempted solution in a direction rather different from the general trend in social psychology. Another anthropologist, Linton, finds it

> safe to conclude that innate, biologically determined factors cannot be used to account for personality configurations as wholes or for the various response patterns included within such configurations. They operate simply as one among several sets of factors responsible for the formation of these.

Linton goes on to describe, in the now familiar way, the creation of mature individuals by learned culture patterns, and emphasizes

> the fact that most human behaviour is taught in the form of organized configurations rather than simply developed by the individual on the basis of experience.

Included in this teaching, as parts of a whole pattern, are some elements serving 'to meet individual needs' and others 'to satisfy social necessities'. But the carrier of these patterns is simply acting as a 'unit in the social organism', and he has other resources which constitute his individuality. The social function of this individuality is that, in the changing world in which the society lives, the individual, by using his own resources, can help to change the pattern, in order to meet new problems.

Yet what, precisely, is the process of this individuation? The ordinary emphases of social psychology show how far we have moved, at one level of our thinking, from the idea that the individual in some way *precedes* his society—the society being a secondary creation through restraint or contract. Most social psychologists now stress the way in which awareness of oneself as a separate individual has to be learned by the infant: 'the infant has no idea of himself as a separate individual'. As G. H. Mead has put it:

> The self, as that which can be object to itself, is essentially a social structure, and it arises in social experience.

This definition implies different levels of individuality. We can distinguish between the primary individual organism and the 'self' which is socially created. This is useful, but it is only by using very difficult terms that we can clarify the distinction, since the word 'individual' ordinarily and naturally includes these theoretically separable elements. Perhaps the most useful stress is that which describes the social process of making 'selves' in terms of individuation: the conscious differences between individuals arise in the social process. To begin with, individuals have varying innate potentialities, and thus receive social influence in varying ways. Further, even if there is a common 'social character' or 'culture pattern', each individual's social history, his actual network of relationships, is in fact unique. These are the basic individualizing factors, but again, as the unique potentialities and the unique history interact, the very fact of the growth of self-consciousness produces a distinct organization, capable both of self-scrutiny and self-direction. This 'autonomous' self grows within a social process which radically influences it, but the degree of gained autonomy makes possible the observed next stage, in which the individual can help to change or modify the social process that has influenced and is influencing him.

To this vital description must be added another distinction, greatly stressed in recent sociology. The abstraction implicit in 'society' can make it difficult for us to recognize theoretically what in practice we see quite clearly: that even in a very simple society it is hardly ever one single 'social character' or 'culture pattern' that the individual encounters. In complex societies like our own, the variations encountered are so marked that we can speak of them as alternative systems within 'a society'. This is obviously very important. If the analysis of 'the individual' has returned an abstraction to its actual processes of growth, so analysis of 'society' has returned an abstraction to the actual complex of real relationships. Instead of thinking of 'society' as a single and uniform object, we look at actual groups and the relationships between them. Since these relationships can be not only those of co-operation but also of tension and conflict, the individual with his sense of particular directions finds material in the alternative directions of his society making it possible for him to express variant growth in social terms.

The recognition of 'groups' within a society is thus a considerable step forward. But of course it is possible merely to shift the ground of the abstraction, making the group in its turn a uniform absolute. Even in the simplest group, there are, as in 'society', relations of tension and conflict as well as of co-operation. This is as true of a face-to-face group like a family or a village as of a common-interest group like a trade union or a social class. Each of these will have its distinct 'social character' or 'culture pattern', to which it will seek to train its members. Yet enclosing this will be the constant interaction of particular individuals, and in such groups, as in 'society', new directions will emerge. Again, since the group will be in real relations with other groups, the processes of training and amendment within the group will be part of the processes of training and amendment of the larger 'society'. A group may be a convenient mark on the scale, but it is only a mark, and the fact of continuity, over the whole scale, is fundamental.

III

We have briefly traced, first the traditional discussion of 'the individual and society', second the main directions of certain contemporary disciplines. We must now turn again to experience, and to the fact that we normally find ourselves, in thinking about 'the individual and society', limited in practice to a very simple model: that of the individual's conformity or nonconformity, and of the society's attitude to either of these courses. We have a number of names for conformity, which enable us to approve it as 'responsible' and 'law-abiding', or to condemn it as 'timidly conventional' or 'servile'. We have also a number of names for nonconformity and some of these, such as 'independence' and 'the free spirit' are approving, while others, such as 'lawlessness' and 'eccentricity' are damning. Some of us move to one side or other of these lines, and try to make a consistent position. More commonly we make a virtue out of either, as it seems to us at the moment. Such valuations may be real, but while they depend, ultimately, on the simple model—conformity or nonconformity—they are relatively very weak. I want to try to get past this model, and by examining some actual relationships between individuals and their societies extend our practical vocabulary for discussing this issue.

We can take first the description *member*. In its modern sense this is a useful way of describing an individual's positive identification with the society in which he lives. The member of a society feels himself to belong to it, in an essential way: its values are his values, its purposes his purposes, to such an extent that he is proud to describe himself in its terms. He is of course conscious of himself as *a* member—an individual within the society to which he belongs—but it is of the essence of membership that the individual, so far from feeling that the society is opposed to him, looks upon it as the natural means by which his own purposes will be forwarded. If change is necessary, he will contribute to its discussion and coming into effect, for he is confident of the values, attitudes and institutions of the society, accepts the ways in which its life is conducted, and sees even conflicts and tensions within the society as soluble by reference to these fundamental ways and values, in such a manner that the essential unity of the society will be preserved.

This experience of membership is probably much more common than is normally allowed theoretically. It is true that in many modern societies it has become much more difficult, and indeed it is when it significantly breaks down that the *problem* of 'the individual and society' is most apparent. Yet that membership can be real seems certain, and to omit its significance is to falsify the whole subsequent argument.

But if we have identified the member, we must go on to identify other relationships which apparently resemble it, and which have, by displacement, led to criticism of it. Existentialist thinkers have made an important distinction between the 'authentic self' and the 'unauthentic self', and their ordinary description of the 'unauthentic self' has been of a man who is 'the creature' of his heredity, his environment and his society. Thus Kierkegaard argues that society presses us to be 'objective' and 'typical', and that we must break through this to our own existence. Jaspers sees modern society as offering the 'unauthentic self' as a whole version of man; we are the creatures of heredity, environment and society until some basic experience (suffering, guilt, death) enables us to break through these offered versions to an authentic realization of our true existence. Nietzsche, similarly, sees the acceptance of social typification as Philistine, and Sartre emphasizes the danger of such social concepts as 'function' or 'duty', which can only be valid to the 'unauthentic' man. The central observation, in this whole tradition, is of great value, but the tendency to equate 'social man' with 'unauthentic man' is highly misleading. For what is being described as a social process is not the experience of the *member*, but of the *subject* or the *servant*. Any society will put pressure on the individuals who are born into it to think and behave in certain ways, but this need not be only the conversion of individuals to social purposes; it is also, in very many cases, an expression of the society's desire to see those individuals survive and grow, according to the best experience the society has.

We must start by recognizing that individuals could not survive and grow except within a social process of some kind. Given this, the real crisis of the 'authentic' and the 'unauthentic' is both an individual and a social process. The valuable element in the existentialist emphasis is the insistence on choice and commitment. It is true that unless an individual, in the process of his growth, achieves a real personal identity, he is incomplete and can be dismissed as 'unauthentic'. He must become deeply conscious of the validity of his ways of thinking and acting, so that he is not merely 'a creature' of the society, but also an individual, a man in his own right. Yet this process, in actual individuals and in different societies, will be exceptionally varied. It is only very rarely limited to conscious appraisal; its ordinary process, while including conscious appraisal in some cases, is a matter of the individual's whole organization: his nervous system, his body, as well as the conscious activities of his brain. In actual growth, the whole complex of feeling and behaviour that constitutes his individuality will stand in a certain relation to the complex of feeling and behaviour that is his society. The stages in his growth which constitute his integration as a particular individual will inevitably be forms of relationship with the whole organization of his society. But these forms of relationship can include what I have called the experience of membership. Particular individuals, in particular societies, can become 'authentic', can deeply commit themselves in terms of their whole organization, to the living organization of the society to which they belong. The 'social' is not necessarily the 'unauthentic'; it is capable of being the 'authentic' and the 'individual'. But it is then necessary to distinguish the kinds of relationship which give existentialist arguments their substance. It is clearly possible for an individual to acquiesce in a way of living which in fact fails to correspond with or satisfy his own personal organization. He will obey authorities he does not personally accept, carry out social functions that have no personal meaning to him, even feel and think in ways so foreign to his actual desires that damage will be done to his own being—often deep emotional disorders, often physical damage to his own organic processes. The marks of this false conformity have been very evident in our social experience, but it is wrong to interpret them in terms of the old 'individual' and 'society' dichotomy. We can best describe them as the roles of *subject* and *servant*, in contrast with *member*.

The *subject*, at whatever violence to himself, has to accept the way of life of his society, and his own indicated place in it, because there is no other way in which he can maintain himself at all; only by this kind of obedience can he eat, sleep, shelter, or escape being destroyed by others. It is not *his* way of life, in any sense that matters, but he must conform to it to survive. In the case of the *servant*, the pressure is less severe, though still, to him, irresistible. The subject has no choice; the servant is given the illusion of choice, and is invited to identify himself with the way of life in which his place is defined. It is an illusion of choice, because again, like the subject, he has no obvious way of maintaining his life if he refuses. Yet the illusion is important, for it allows him to pretend to an identification with the society, as if the choice had been real. The subject will have few illusions about the relationship which is determining him; he will know that the way of life is not his but must be obeyed. The servant, on the other hand, may come to identify himself with the way of life that is determining him; he may even, consciously, think of himself as a member (indeed the old sense of 'member' allows this, for if the individual is an organ of the organism that is society, particular individuals will be higher or lower organs yet still feel themselves as true parts). Yet at many levels of his life, and particularly in certain situations such as solitude and age, the discrepancy between the role the individual is playing and his actual sense of himself will become manifest, either consciously or in terms of some physical or emotional disturbance. Given the right conditions, he can play the role as if it were really his, but alone, or in situations evoking his deepest personal feelings, the identification breaks down. It seems probable, from the experience that has been widely recorded, that this situation of the servant is crucial in our own kind of society. The subject is a more extreme case, theoretically, though in history, and in modern undeveloped countries, it is common experience enough. And in modern Europe and the United States there are still subjects, though the experience of the servant is much more frequently recorded. It is that we are told we are free, and that we are shaping our common destiny; yet, with varying force, many of us break through to the conviction that the pattern of public activity has, in the end, very little to do with our private desires. Indeed the main modern force of the distinction between 'the individual' and 'society' springs from this feeling. It is only from the servant complex that we can both maintain this conviction and yet repeatedly pretend that we believe, wholeheartedly, in the purposes of our society.

The existentialist refuses this complex, and asserts the centrality of personal choice. From this position, with the reality of membership virtually excluded as a possibility, the whole rich repertory of modern individualism proceeds. Yet it is obvious, when we survey this range, that the modes of nonconformity are at least as varied as the modes of conformity. Where we had not only the member but also the subject and the servant, we have now not only the rebel but also the exile and the vagrant. The idea of the *rebel* still carries a strong positive valuation, though in fact rebels are few. The rebel resembles the member in that he has made a strong personal commitment to certain social purposes, a positive identification of his personal existence with a particular pattern of social effort. The ways of his society are not his ways, but in rebelling against one social form he is seeking to establish another. There are obviously important distinctions to be drawn here, between the revolutionary on the one hand, and the reformer or critic on the other. For the reformer and the critic are, in the definition I have given, members. A sincere desire to change this or that aspect of the general way of life is perfectly compatible with adherence to its general values, and with that kind of insistence on the essential continuity and unity of the society to which reformers and critics ordinarily adhere. The revolutionary, by contrast, lacks that sense of membership of a particular society which makes it possible for the reformer and critic to suppose that their own ends can in fact be achieved within the society's existing forms. The revolutionary's relationship with his society is one of declared opposition and struggle, but it is characteristic of him that he opposes the society in terms of the struggle for a different society. This is obvious in the case of political revolutionaries, but the same pattern is evident in rebels of other kinds, in art, morality, religion. The rebel fights the way of life of his society because to him personally it is wrong, but in art, morality and religion, as more obviously in politics, the new reality he proposes is more than personal; he is offering it as a new way of life.

This indeed is his distinction from *exile* and *vagrant*, which are the more truly individual forms. The exile is as absolute as the rebel in rejecting the way of life of his society, but instead of fighting it he goes away. Often he is like the subject in that unless he conforms he will be destroyed or will be unable to maintain his life. But he is unlike the subject in that he has managed to escape, or has been allowed to get away. In some cases, indeed, he will get away to membership of another society, in which he finds his personal reality, his vital system of values and attitudes, confirmed. More usually, perhaps, he will remain an exile, unable to go back to the society that he has rejected or that has rejected him, yet equally unable to form important relationships with the society to which he has gone. This is a tragic and characteristic condition which has been reached again and again in our century. The rebel, while more exposed to real danger in that he is attacking his society at its crucial points, has a degree of positive relationship by the very fact that he is actively living out his personal values. The true exile, on the other hand, is committed to waiting: when his society changes, then he can come home, but the actual process of change is one in which he is not involved.

We have been used to thinking of exiles as men driven from their society, but an equally characteristic modern figure is the self-exile. The self-exile could, if he chose, live at ease in his society, but to do so would be to deny his personal reality. Sometimes he goes away, on principle, but as often he stays, yet still, on principle, feels separate. The Bolsheviks had a useful term for this, in 'internal emigré', and if we realize that this is not confined to politics we can use it to describe a very important modern relationship. This kind of self-exile lives and moves about in the society into which he was born, but rejects its purposes and despises its values, in terms of alternative principles to which his whole personal reality is committed. Unlike the rebel, he does not fight for these principles, but watches and waits. He knows himself to be different, and the pressure of his activity is to preserve this difference, to maintain the individuality which is the term of his separateness. There is great tension in this condition, for theoretically, at least, the self-exile wants the society to change, so that he can start belonging to it, and this involves him, at least notionally, in relationships. But since, unlike the rebel, his personal dissent has remained fixed at an individual stage, it is difficult for him to form adequate relationships, even with other dissenters. He may support the principles of dissenting causes, but he cannot join them; he is too wary of being caught and compromised. What he has principally to defend is his own living pattern, his own mind, and almost any relationship is a potential threat to this. He has become or remained his 'authentic self', but this authenticity cannot be shared with or communicated to others, or, if the effort at communication is made, the commitment involved in it will be characteristically minimal. Whatever he may come to say or do, he continues, essentially, to walk alone in his society, defending a principle in himself.

This condition must be distinguished, finally, from that of the *vagrant*, which in some ways it resembles. The vagrant also stays in his own society, though he finds its purposes meaningless and its values irrelevant. Yet he lacks the exile's pride and his firm attachment to principle. There is nothing in particular that the vagrant wants to happen; his maximum demand is that he should be left alone. Where the exile is usually articulate in distinguishing his personal position, the vagrant often finds as little meaning in himself as in his society. Indeed it is not *his* society to which he objects, but, essentially, the condition of society as such. Whereas to others the society comes through as a particular set of relationships which can be accepted or rejected, to the vagrant society is a meaningless series of accidents and pressures, which as far as possible he evades. He will do anything that is necessary to survive within this, but this activity will have neither personal nor social meaning; it is merely a temporary way of keeping alive, or 'getting by'. For the vagrant has gone so far that he cannot even acknowledge society, even to oppose it. The events that others interpret as 'society' are to him like such natural events as storm or sun; the farthest principle he can see is one of bad luck or good luck, by which he stumbles on money or warmth, endures until he can move away from constraint and cold. These are, moreover, not incidents on a journey, for he is not going anywhere, in the sense of having a particular direction; his life is just happening to be passing this way. When we think of the vagrant we think naturally of such people as tramps and the fringe of society to which many criminals belong, but the condition of the vagrant—the essential negation of relationships which he embodies—is not confined to these obvious examples. In some societies it is possible to live out this condition with considerable material success, and there are signs, in some modern thinking, that the condition of the vagrant is the only available condition of man in society: whatever a man does, this is how he feels, and, given a particular social atmosphere, there is no need even to pretend otherwise. Conformity and rebellion, service and exile, are all alike irrelevant. A man does what he likes, but does not fight for change; serves any master, for immediate convenience, or leaves any service, again as convenience and not principle dictates. The one thing the vagrant is certain of is that all the others who are not vagrants are fools, killing themselves for meaningless meanings, pretending to meanings whereas the only thing that matters is oneself: not even a meaningful self, but simply an organism, as such, keeping going.

We need descriptions such as member, subject and servant, or rebel, exile and vagrant, if we are to get past the impasse of simple conformity or nonconformity. But, like other descriptions, these are not absolutes; they are simply analyses of particular forms of relationship. There is no single 'society' to which these are varying forms of adjustment; indeed 'society' itself takes on the same variations, according to the particular relationship that is embodied. To the member, society is his own community; the members of other communities may be beyond his recognition or sympathy. To the servant, society is an establishment, in which he finds his place. To the subject society is an imposed system, in which his place is determined. To the rebel, a particular society is a tyranny; the alternative for which he fights is a new and better society. To the exile, society is beyond him, but may change. To the vagrant, society is a name for other people, who are in his way or who can be used. Nor are these merely 'subjective' valuations; real societies will necessarily vary according to the kinds of individual organization which compose them. The member and the community, the servant and the establishment, the subject and the imposed system, the rebel and the tyranny, the exile and the lost society, the vagrant and the meaningless society are all forms of active organization, of action and interaction. Further, within actual societies the relationships described are almost always complicated by the existence of different groups and scales. It is possible to be a member of a particular community, yet because of that community's relation to some larger society, to be in the position of a servant or a subject, a rebel or a vagrant, in certain areas of social experience. The rebel or the exile, as we have seen, can in certain conditions find social membership in an alternative group. In fact, because the groups and the alternatives interlock, the total reality of an individual's relations to society is often a compound of the particular kinds of organization described. Moreover, at certain stages of his growth, the individual may move through various kinds of organization; indeed it is commonplace in some societies for adolescents to move through the stages of rebel, exile or vagrant before becoming members or servants. Because it is a form of organization, and not a single substance, the individual's relationship with society will be a complicated embodiment of a wide area of real relationships, although within this certain forms of organization such as those described may be determining.

IV

From the early descriptions of 'the individual' and 'society' to the more refined descriptions of the contemporary debate we can trace a persistent tendency to describe living processes in terms that confer on them the apparent status of fixed and separable objects. The terms we need, to describe the experience adequately, must be essentially active, yet every new description we invent seems to turn, more or less rapidly, into an object, and it is then very difficult both to clarify experience and to remain faithful to it. The crucial fact is that every description, every offered interpretation, is a term of growth. Thus the idea of 'the individual' was not only a reaction to the complex of social, economic and religious changes; it was also a creative interpretation of them, as a way of living. To get rid of restrictive and obsolescent definitions of 'status', to detach human beings from the social function 'to which they were born', to reshape the law, the Church, the economy, the administration, men had to propose the 'bare human being', as the common element by which every kind of restriction and mortmain could be challenged. The individual had even to be detached from his family, if a society based not on birth but on works was to be established. Similarly, the idea of 'society' had to be wrought out, as a creative description, if the problems of human organization were to be considered in terms wider than those set by any particular social system. The later stress on community, and on the social basis of individuality, was again a creative response to practical difficulties which could not be resolved while the idea of the individual as the bare human being remained dominant.

In the long process of actual history, some of these descriptions have come to seem inadequate, but all, in different degrees, have been recharged by experience of an important kind which can apparently be interpreted in only this way. It is very difficult, for example, to live in a modern industrial society and not feel the force of the 'individual and society' distinction. There is a deeply-felt discontinuity, for most of us, between what we as individuals desire to do, and what, by some apparently mysterious process, actually happens 'out there' in society. This feeling is perhaps even stronger now than it was when the sharp distinction was first made. Individuals feel radically insecure when their lives are changed by forces which they cannot easily see or name, and as societies have become larger and more complicated, and as the power to change an environment and real relations within it has greatly multiplied, this insecurity has certainly increased. Such insecurity is a constant source of a particular kind of individualism. As Tocqueville noted:

> Individualism is a novel expression, to which a novel idea has given birth, a mature and calm feeling, which disposes each member of the community to sever himself from the mass of his fellow-creatures and to draw apart with his family and friends.

It may not always be mature and calm, but it is an obvious enough movement, especially now in our own society. I cannot agree with everything that Dostoievski's Zossima says, in *Brothers Karamazov*, but there, quite clearly, is the central paradox:

> They maintain that the world is getting more and more united, more and more bound together in brotherly community, as it overcomes distance and sets thoughts flying through the air. Alas, put no faith in such a bond of union. The idea of the service of humanity, of brotherly love and the solidarity of mankind, is more

and more dying out in the world, and indeed this idea is sometimes treated with derision.

This is not the whole truth, but it is an important part of the truth:

> Everyone strives to keep his individuality as apart as possible, wishes to secure the greatest possible fulness of life for himself; but meantime all his efforts result not in attaining fulness of life but self-destruction, for instead of self-realisation he ends by arriving at complete solitude. Everywhere in these days men have, in their mockery, ceased to understand that the true security is to be found in social solidarity rather than in isolated individual effort.

This is indeed how it often seems, yet the tendency is readily understandable, as a turning towards significance in a manageable area. This is not only a crisis of individuals, but also of a society. The warm house, detached and insulated, where a man can live as he wishes, and find certain satisfaction with his family and friends, makes sense, again and again, in an essentially cold and impersonal society. We can say that the effort will fail, that the insulation will be broken, but still, to very many, it will seem a good risk, against the apparent certainty of a harsh and meaningless society.

Individualism was a term of growth, from the rigidity of a society which, while securing, also restricted and directed men's actual lives. Any growth beyond individualism is necessarily more than a return to old and discredited interpretations. The experience we have now to interpret includes both the gains of individualism and its limits. There is the inescapable fact of mutual dependence, by which alone, as we live, the house can be supplied. Such a meaning has grown, in new ways, with the definitions of democracy and community. But while these direct new energy, the old meanings are continually recharged: the separation between the individual and society is visibly not breaking down. In this continuing tension, the meanings that were terms of growth pass over into meanings that deny growth. Democracy and community have again and again been made over into the old kind of restriction and direction. Individualism has passed into selfishness and indifference by the facts of its own incompleteness. For the turning away is in fact an attitude towards other individuals, and not only to the 'impersonal' society. If we stand on our rights as a bare human being we are forced either to recognize that everybody is in this situation and has these rights, or, in denying or remaining indifferent to them, to diminish the quality of our own claim. We can turn other individuals into 'the masses', from whom we must separate ourselves. We can group other individuals into particular classes, nations or races, as a way of refusing them individual recognition. And some men will be satisfied by this while they are the individuals and others the masses, the excluded group. Yet, inevitably, by this extending process, we are all converted to masses, for nowhere, in a world so composed, can our own individuality be fully recognized by others; they are turning away from us to establish their own. This is the experience we are now trying to face and interpret, at the limit of the meanings we know.

v

The principle we need, to break through to new meanings, is that of the fundamental relation between organism and organization. In interpreting and describing our experience we develop a particular system in terms of which we then live. Every organism both embodies and continues an organization of this kind. Its purpose is the reception and communication of experience in such a form that by adjustment and action the organization itself, and therefore the particular life of the organism, can be continued. Each one of us has within an apparently separate individuality a system of observing, selecting, comparing, adjusting and acting as elaborate and complex as any social system yet described. Yet this particular organization, that we call the individual, exists in terms of a much larger organization with which it is in certain radical ways continuous. The physical evolution of man as a kind is the clearest form of this larger organization. The genetic history of man is the structure of this organization, and is such that it provides ways in which the organization itself can to some extent be changed. The experience of inheritance, of a continuous if changing organization, is still central in human feeling. A man can, in a quite literal sense, feel himself in his parents and in his children, or, in a form of the same experience, feel them in himself. Yet inheritance refers him also to a much wider group, with which again, in certain circumstances, he can feel his continuity. Such organic inheritance produces distinct but related individuals, who live also, however, in terms of another inheritance: an organized society, with particular systems of naming and communicating, acting and reacting, which individuals must learn if they are to survive and grow. Yet further, the human organization itself, and the social organization which develops it in particular ways, lead to the growth of the individual in terms that require a further effort of organization by the individual himself. He is a man and a member of a society, but he only becomes these by becoming himself. It is truly not reproduction, but generation. The human inheritance is in specific terms of variation. The social inheritance will vary widely, and there will be differences in the ways different societies encourage individual growth: some tending towards direct reproduction, others towards a varying range of possibilities. From his actual inheritance the individual will try to complete his own organization. He will separate out, necessarily, but to varying degrees. Yet he cannot separate out altogether, for what he is organizing he will to an important extent share with others, who also remain necessary to his own growth.

In our ordinary thinking, we tend to fix on two states, expressible either as 'the individual' and 'society', or, more actively, as 'person' and 'world'. For certain purposes, these states are efficient, in that they match some parts of our experience; but in other parts, equally, they are continually breaking down. We are accustomed to thinking of the 'generalized other', which we may call the world or society, but which in many kinds of experience breaks down into particulars. We should perhaps think also of the 'generalized self', the individuality of which we are all conscious, yet which again, in experience, breaks down into particular and changing and variously related energies and forms. We have learned to think of certain relationships, notably with our families and immediate friends, as particular. But many other kinds of relationship we come to think of as between the 'generalized self' and the 'generalized other': two fixed states rather than a complex of living processes. Yet in the course of living, to know ourselves and our world, we have continually to break down these fixed states, into the actual processes which are changing us and which we wish to change. We are in practical contact with a vast number of particular organizations, and to know any of these we are forced to recognition of its relationships with other forms. We have to distinguish an organization before we can know it, but the lines we draw, in recognition, are always, potentially, the lines of relationship. If we isolate the individual, we go on to divide him into body, mind and soul; feeling, willing and thinking; conscious and unconscious; ego, superego and id; but to study any of these is to study its relations with the others. If we isolate society, we go on to divide it into groups, classes, associations, but to study any of these is again to study its relations with the others. If we isolate the material world, we go on to divide it into matter and energy, and into particular forms of these, and find again that in studying these we are studying forms of relationship. Yet we sometimes suppose, against this experience, that we can state the substances of individual, society and material world in such a way that there are no relationships between them until, as it were, some signal is given, and having defined the substances as in themselves they are, we can go on now to study the relations between them. But in fact these substances are forms of relationship which we can never finally isolate, since the organization, throughout, is in interlocking terms. We begin to realize, from experience, that the relationships are inherent, and that each organization is, precisely, an embodiment of relationships, the lived and living history of responses to and from other organizations. Organization, that is to say, is enacted in the organism, and to know either fully is to know the other.

In the case of the individual and society we need to learn ways of thinking and feeling which will enable us genuinely to know each in the other's terms, which is as near as we can ordinarily get to saying that we are studying forms of organization in a continuous process: the brain, the nervous system, the body, the family, the group, the society, man. There is no real point at which we can break off this process, to isolate an independent substance. Yet equally we cannot select any one of them and make the others dependent on it. If the old individualism artificially isolated the 'bare human being', there is equal danger in certain trends in the new sociology which isolate the group, the society or the culture as an absolute point of reference. The continuous process of our human organization is itself a continuous action and adjustment in relation to all that is not human, and the central fact of this action and adjustment is a process of learning and communication which has grown through continual variation and the effort to transmit variation. We must not think only of society or the group acting on the unique individual, but also of many unique individuals, through a process of communication, creating and where necessary extending the organization by which they will continue to be shaped. It is right to recognize that we became human individuals in terms of a social process, but still individuals are unique, through a particular heredity expressed in a particular history. And the point about this uniqueness is that it is creative as well as created: new forms can flow from this particular form, and extend in the whole organization, which is in any case being constantly renewed and changed as unique individuals inherit and continue it. This recognition of individual uniqueness, and of the relation of its creativity to general human patterns, is, of course, the permanent basis of the case for democracy as a system of government. It is true that the value and effect of any particular uniqueness will vary considerably, for it will emerge only in a system of real relationships, which will set terms to its degree of communicability and relevance, and beyond this there will be widely varying degrees of success, between individuals, in self-realization and capacity to describe. The fact remains, however, that all human individuals are unique: it was one of the worst results of the old individualism that in asserting the importance of certain individuals it moved, consciously or unconsciously, to denying the importance of others. When we get past this to realize that individuation is in fact the general process of our humanity, and that it is through individuation and communication that we have learned and are learning to live, we must recognize and respect the true scale and complexity of the process, which no one of us, and no group, is in a position to understand, let alone seek to control. If man is essentially a learning, creating and communicating being, the only social organization adequate to his nature is a participating democracy, in which all of us, as unique individuals, learn, communicate and control. Any lesser, restrictive system is simply wasteful of our true resources; in wasting individuals, by shutting them out from effective participation, it is damaging our true common process.

The long conflict between 'the individual' and 'society' resolves itself, as we reach out in these ways, into the difficulty of stating this interlocking process of organism and organization, which are not new terms for individual and society but ways of describing a continuous process within which both are contained. The worst result of abstracting 'the individual' and 'society' is that it limits our thinking to questions of relationship between them. We say this individual is good because he lives in a way that his society values; this society is good because it allows individuals to do these kinds of thing. Yet an individual, in being directed by the norms of his society, may be suppressing a variation which could become generally valuable, or a society, by permitting certain variations, may destroy itself, or other societies, or parts of its environment. These real issues can only be looked at adequately if we recognize the continuity between the many kinds of organization which compose the whole living process. To abstract certain fixed states, and then argue from them, which has been the normal method of approaching this question, is wholly inadequate. Difficult as any new conception may be, it seems absolutely necessary to try to formulate it, and then to learn from it possibly adequate new approaches. In practical terms I think such approaches will be the kind of study of patterns and relationships, in a whole process, which we have defined as the analysis of culture. There, in the practice of creation, communication, and the making of institutions is the common process of personal and social growth.

FOUR

Images of Society

Our thinking about society is a long debate between abstractions and actual relationships. The reality of society is the living organization of men, women and children, in many ways materialized, in many ways constantly changing. At the same time, our abstract ideas about society, or about any particular society, are both persistent and subject to change. We have to see them as interpretations: as ways of describing the organization and of conceiving relationships, necessary to establish the reality of social life but also under continual pressure from experience. In certain periods, the interpretations satisfy experience in such a way that there is hardly any dispute at this level: the descriptions and concepts are deeply built in and accepted. In other periods, there are degrees of discrepancy: a given description is felt to be inadequate, and is disputed; or a description is accurate yet is challenged by an alternative conception of relationships, so that the whole status and future of the society are put into question, usually with deep division and controversy. We have seen how, in such periods of tension and change, the idea of society itself grew and developed. It changed first from the immediate 'society of one's fellows' to the more general 'system of common life', and changed later from reference to a particular system to abstraction of all such systems, the general state of 'society'. There was gain and loss in this process, for on the one hand we need the flexibility and range of the varied conceptual thinking which the abstraction made possible, and on the other hand, if our thinking is to be relevant, we need the continual pressure of actual relationships, an actual common life from which the process of description draws substance. I propose to examine some of the commoner images of society, which have been important in our history, to consider their effects on our present thinking about relationships, and to look at their significance in the actual process of social change.

I

The key to any description is its starting-point: the particular experience that is seized as determining. In general, in thinking about a society, we start from these people in this place, but it is very unusual to retain this simplicity. There is a particular human organization in a particular environment, but we commonly describe and interpret it in terms of some leading element, which we see as its organizing principle. The difficulty is that this element can be very variously identified. For example, a very large amount of ordinary social thinking has started, in effect, from the King. It is not these people in this place, but the King of this place and his subjects. This emphasis, often very rapidly and unconsciously adopted, is of course followed by detailed description: the nature of the place and the people, the system of government and property, the organization of production and trade, the report on institutions and customs. But the emphasis colours the description. We are not merely describing the organization, but assuming its purpose. Again and again, in all kinds of study, we see this practical orientation. It is not merely that this is seen as the effective system, but that the maintenance of this system is seen as the dominant social purpose. You start from the King, or from the existing social order, and then everything that happens is related to that. Thus service at court, in the army or in the fields is the significant social activity, and life outside such functions is conceived and regulated to such ends. Thinking about law and institutions is in terms of the more perfect functioning of this system, and the significant image is that of the single organism, in which each person in the society has 'his part to play'.

Of course many actual societies have been accurately described in these terms. The simplicity of thinking of 'these people in this place' was not abandoned accidentally, but because the facts were that the lives of the people were quite unequally regarded: they were seen, practically, through the needs of the established order. Most feudal and aristocratic social thinking is deeply determined by this fundamental interpretation, and it makes sense that the idea of society as something other than a particular system should have arisen at the time when such societies were being powerfully challenged. What is more surprising is that ways of thinking about society which are reasonable only while the absolute character of the system is maintained should have survived with such power into apparently different societies. Millions of people in Britain are apparently content to describe themselves as 'British subjects', which clearly, in other terms, they are not and ought not to be. Still an important part of law and practical social thinking is concerned with the 'rights and duties of the Queen's subjects', as if there had never been the fundamentally different claim of the 'rights of man'. In part it is the persistence of verbal habit, but to a considerable extent it is a contrived persistence. It has not been the case for many centuries that the meanings and purposes of British society were summed up in the person of the King or Queen, but it has suited many successive kinds of social order to establish the pretence that this is so. The creative interpretation of society as a flexible human organization has been opposed and limited by this different kind of thinking, and a succession of compromises has led to radical confusions: to such a misleading phrase, for example, as the 'liberties of the subject', where 'liberties' means not freedom (though for rhetorical purposes this colouring is added) but simply a permissive area in the margin of an unquestionable duty. Just as persons are practically subordinated to the needs of a defined social order, so the place in which they live undergoes a similar transformation. There is a vital difference between thinking about the place in which we live, and of ourselves in relation to it, and the kind of thinking about 'Britain' or about 'England', which in this use are not real places but particular interpretations which include definitions of duty, function and character. The fact that 'Britain' and 'England' have been, successively, very different places, subject to constant change, is obscured by a mode of description which, like the 'rights and duties of the Queen's subjects', suggests something absolute and permanent rather than something relative and changing. Doing something 'for Britain' or 'for England' may or may not be doing something for ourselves in a particular place, yet the spell of these abstractions is such that it can seem more honourable to do something for 'Britain' than to do something for ourselves.

The nation-state, in subtly different ways, thus powerfully continued a way of thinking about society which started from an existing order and subordinated to this the needs of actual persons. In certain respects, the definition made sense: real needs (as for security) sometimes coincided with the needs that followed from the definition. But they have never necessarily done so, any more than the needs of the serf necessarily included the maintenance of his lord. Any true common interest must include our own interest, but if we start from an abstracted social order we can be persuaded into courses which may actually harm a majority of us. The real question, whether the social order actually serves our needs, cannot be asked when our social thinking is determined by the assumption that it is from the order that we must start.

The most powerful early challenges to this ingrained way of thinking were, first, in terms of the right to pursue certain activities which the defined order either forbade or regulated; second, in terms of the generalized rights of man. The issue of the first challenge has been of vital importance, and from it, slowly, in Britain, emerged a wholly different society. In part this was the growth of democracy, but it is probably true that democracy has never established a really deep social image, of a distinct kind, in Britain. Just because in the main it grew slowly, and by gradual constitutional amendment and compromise, it has always been difficult, here, to separate the principle of democracy from the habitual loyalty to an establishment. The symbols of democracy, in the English mind, are as likely to be institutions of power and antiquity, such as the Palace of Westminster, as the active process of popular decision, such as a committee or jury. A more decisive social image came from the other part of this movement: the rise of economic individualism. Here, instead of thinking of society as an established order, you think of it, essentially, as a market. That it is, of course (in the image) a free market involves radical dissent from any rigid, prescriptive establishment: in this sense it continually overlaps with the kind of democratic spirit which accompanied it. But the most important effect, ultimately, is that a new element in the whole organization is selected as central. You do not now start from the King or the established social order: you start from the activities of production and trading, and increasingly these are seen as the essential purposes of the society, in terms of which other activities must submit to be judged. All forms of human organization, from the family and the community to the educational system, must be reshaped in the light of this dominant economic activity. At the same time, since it was the free economic activity of individuals that was at first emphasized, the whole idea of social purpose underwent radical change. Where the former purpose had been the maintenance of an established order, and thus in these prescribed terms positive, the new purpose was at first largely negative: society existed to create conditions in which the free economic enterprise of individuals was not hampered. Society provided a market, and kept it free. Later, however, the image was more fully developed. With the further development of capitalism, to its corporate stage, society was no longer thought of as merely providing a market: the organization of society itself was essentially a market organization. Whereas, in starting from an established order, the idea of the individual was essentially comprised in 'my station and its duties', the idea of the individual in a market society was, first, the responsible free agent, and, later, the man with something to sell. Obligation and service had been challenged by freedom and responsibility, but then, in the final image, buying and selling became terms in which all human activity could be assessed. In the twentieth century, as perhaps never before in history, people could without loss of respect talk of 'selling' themselves (an operation with archaic connections with the devil), of their 'shop-window', of 'studying the market' and 'being in demand', even when the processes they were engaged in were not commercial in any ordinary sense.

I have isolated these images of society, to try to clarify them, but of course in our actual history they have been both competitive and interacting. The strength of the market image, in modern England, hardly needs stressing: we often speak of the nation as if it were a large firm, with other nations as competitors. We speak of work as the 'labour market' and argue about education primarily in terms of the needs of 'the economy'. At the same time we have already noted the persistence of ways of thinking which 'start from the Queen' or from an abstraction of 'England'. One very powerful model, working in this direction, has of course been the modern army, which, with conscription, extended itself to the sense of a whole society. Here the stress on rank, on corporate spirit, and on single purpose has powerfully taught successive generations a way of thinking about relationships that has perhaps gone much deeper than we know. When we think how many individuals, in our century, have passed through this model, usually in periods of great emotional stress, the effect is hardly surprising. It is remarkable how many social organizations, with quite general and ordinary social purposes (even of a pacifist, reforming or free educational kind) speak of 'recruiting' members, and of their 'rank-and-file'. And it continually surprises me that so many middle-class people speak of their ordinary holidays as 'leave'. The liberal element in the early stages of a market society has to a considerable extent been overridden by a curious fusion of the market and the established order. It is impossible to watch men in actual relationships, in the typical modern industrial or commercial organization, or in an ordinary government or local authority service, without seeing this odd image of a medieval court (as in the graded sitting of officials round a committee table) blended with a modern army unit (particular tones of voice and stiffenings of the body).

And all this, oddly, in a society which would claim, certainly on public occasions, that it is essentially the embodiment of the second main challenge to the idea of an absolute order: not now the free market, but the rights of man. At a certain stage, the market and the absolute order might virtually fuse, by the unexpected process of the organized market becoming the absolute order. But the image based on the rights of man would, we might think, be uncompromising. The difficulty has been, of course, that while 'man' sounds absolute enough, the interpretation of rights has been ordinarily selective; indeed at one level the formula is not far from that of the liberty of the subject. Much of the practical substance of the rights of man was drawn from the conventions of a trading commonwealth: civil society must defend men against certain kinds of absolutism, and assure their liberty to do certain kinds of thing. Thus the idea is often rather limited and negative, and people have been able to use it, on their own behalf, while not admitting its relevance to other kinds of people— the poor, the uneducated, foreigners, men with different skins. It is like the image of democracy, which can be absolute for ourselves and our friends, but relative for others. The basic difficulty, perhaps, has been that the idea is in part conventional, in part abstract: it has sought to unite the necessarily limiting idea of the liberty of the subject, and the necessarily universal idea of the brotherhood of man. Ideas derived from the established order or from the market are continually nourished by practical organizations in their own terms, whereas the revolutionary element, in the idea of the rights of man, is learned as much in despair and aspiration as in convention and practice. Earlier abstract images of a society can be seen to have mirrored, and yet in a sense transcended, their practical counterparts. Thus the 'city of God' drew substance from the actual organization of Church and State, but it did not only rationalize temporal power (the ruler as appointed of God); it also transcended temporal power, by setting a term and a limit to it. At its highest the social purpose, in such an image, was to live in God's ways: through the temporal and spiritual authority of an established order, but with ultimate purposes beyond this, in the 'heavenly kingdom'. An important part of the idea of human brotherhood, underwriting the rights of man, was drawn from this same source, expressed as equality before God. Yet, given this reference, the rights of man are to a considerable extent determined by an assumption of certain absolute relationships which prescribe man's status and define his duties. The idea of the rights of man became universally relevant only when human brotherhood was defined in primarily human terms. It then gained something of the simplicity of 'these people in this place', with no subtly determining prescription of an order to which they are permanently committed. Yet at the same time it could not be local and specific ('this place' became 'this world', or, better, 'these places'): the flexibility and generosity of the conception were practically balanced by its inevitable degree of abstraction.

The most powerful embodiment and clarification of the image of the brotherhood of man has been in the labour movement and in the thinking leading to socialism. Of course brotherhood has often been limited, in the actual history: it has been affirmed and created in such institutions as trade unions and co-operatives, but these, in an actual context, have been as often a brotherhood against something (including other men) as for something. The idea of a new social order, rather than a series of defensive movements, was necessary to transcend this limitation, and socialism has been the main attempt to define such an order. A serious difficulty arises at this stage, for what is proposed is a new established order: intended to be liberating, in that it starts from the needs of all men, on a basis of practical equality, rather than from graded needs according to rank, or the levels established by the free play of the market; in practice, however, in some senses determining, in that it necessarily proposes certain kinds of relationship and duty. Moreover, it is an order which has to be established by overcoming or outgrowing existing real relationships, and it can hardly be denied that while socialism's long-term version of human society is brotherhood, its short-term version is of a very deep conflict. In a hundred ways, the socialist version of human relationship has been shaped by these conditions. Its description of social classes was offered as at once an analysis of existing society and a guide to changing it. But the stage has been reached when the emphasis on class has been seen as the most obvious denial of brotherhood, and when resentments against an existing or remembered class situation have been massively transferred to those who continue to talk about class. At the same time, the history of socialist parties, working for a new order, and of socialist societies, engaged in building it, has provided ample evidence of the practical results of a genuine theoretical difficulty: the commitment to a precise order which is intended to be generally liberating but which in being worked towards has usually included conflict, restriction and even repression. The image of human brotherhood is still there, and only there, but it has been so darkened by the real process of attempting to create it out of societies powerfully organized in other terms that it has been radically confused.

One important consequence of our actual history, with its persistence of thinking in terms of an absolute order, with its subtle transformation of the free market into the laws of the market, and with its confusion of the idea of brotherhood, has been the personal revolt that is modern individualism. Earlier forms of individualism were primarily the assertion of rights to do and say certain things—society was judged and reshaped to guarantee the exercise of this positive freedom. Modern individualism in part continues this tendency, but on the whole puts more emphasis on a negative freedom: the right of the individual to be left alone. There has been a very widespread retreat from social thinking, rationalized by the formula that almost all good things are done by individuals, almost all bad things by societies. The image of society is then of something inherently bad: a restrictive, interfering, indifferent process, whether it claims the virtues of an established order or the creation of human brotherhood. In this personal revolt, nobody is deceived by what societies say they are doing; whatever this may be, the individual is likely to suffer, and the best he can hope for is to minimize its pressures: by detachment, by apathy and scepticism, by seeing that at least he and his family are all right. It is as necessary to acknowledge the great strength and emotional substance of this revolt as to point to its very damaging consequences. Such an idea of society could only gain currency in a context of major social failure, and it is no use trying to beat it down by repetition of the ideas (duty, responsibility, brotherhood) which have habitually accompanied the hated pressures and failures. The experience has been lived, and has to be expressed. But of course the withdrawal from social thinking leaves the bad society as it is. Indeed it is commonly assumed that things will remain much as they are, that fundamental change is inconceivable or would only make things worse, but that individuals, if they turn back on themselves and on 'real' interests, can get by or even be happy.

We must observe the effect of this way of thinking on the creation of the most recent idea of society: that of the mass. This is a very complicated idea, which of course in part simply repeats, in a new way, the idea of the absolute order: the majority of people are the 'masses', and are governed, organized, instructed and entertained by an élite or élites. Such a society may or may not be an *established* order, for the élite will sometimes be largely hereditary or the élites may be continually reselected, by competition or political affiliation. Yet, however the élites are composed, their practical relations with the 'masses' are then defined as directing and directed, as in other kinds of absolute order. But the idea of mass society also repeats, in a new way, the idea of the market. The 'masses' exert their influence on the directions of the society, not by participation, but by expressing a pattern of demands and preferences— the laws of a new kind of market—and this, for the élites, is a starting-point: to be carefully studied (by such techniques as market research and opinion polls), and then worked on. When these two conceptions are joined, they compose a very powerful image, which obviously corresponds with important elements of our experience in very large societies: the concentration of political and economic power, but on a basis of a pattern of demand; the centralized control of highly efficient techniques of popular communication, again on a basis of a pattern of preferences. This combination of wide public reference and a narrow area of actual power is indeed a significant model, but what we must notice about it is its essential impersonality. The élites, necessarily, are not concerned with individuals, but with averaged figures and generalized trends in the mass pattern.

This technique which underwrites and validates their functions becomes, inevitably, an habitual way of thinking about society. Almost one feels, in such a society, that nobody lives here: only classes, consumers and conventions. But if this is the functional way of thinking of the élites, it is also powerfully reinforced by elements of the very reaction against it. The personal revolt asserts individuality, in this world of impersonal abstractions, but the assertion, commonly, is also a withdrawal from social thinking: I and my family and friends are real; the rest is the system. But this, when sufficiently extended, not only confirms the élite's valuation of other people as masses. It also, in its denial or limitation of real relationships, helps people to regard themselves, in their social relationships, as masses. It is no accident, but an element of this structure of thinking, that the terms of the personal revolt so often include contempt for other persons: the crowd, the herd, the benighted masses. A point can be reached when the only reality is 'I and the crowd', and the vacuum this leaves is filled by acceptance of the 'impersonal' system. Romantic individualism and authoritarian and abstract social thinking have again and again, in modern societies, tended eventually to interlock. Power, in such cases, is ultimately rationalized by despair. But in any event, for often individualism will not go so far, a practical division between the 'social' and the 'personal', between 'public' and 'private', will be commonly enforced. The last image of society, and in our own day the most powerful, is that which has separated society from man.

II

The dominant social images that we have inherited—the absolute order, the organized market, the élite and the mass, even brotherhood as expressed in the struggle for power—are alike in this: that they tend to reduce society to two spheres of interest, two kinds of thinking, two versions of social relationship: politics (the system of decision) and economics (the system of maintenance). It is natural for ruling groups to think in this way, and to see the rest of life through these categories that are most closely involved with their power. It is less natural for the rest of us to see society as limited in this way, yet it is significant that even the most powerful reforming groups commit themselves to such a version. For what else is there?, we sometimes ask. When you have said politics and economics you have said society; the rest is personal and incidental.

To limit a society to its systems of decision and maintenance is in fact ridiculous. We must learn to see it as a conditioned reflex to various forms of class society, in which the true nature of society—a human organization for common needs—was in fact filtered through the interests in power and property which were natural to ruling groups. It has been the gravest error of socialism, in revolt against class societies, to limit itself, so often, to the terms of its opponents: to propose a political and economic order, rather than a human order. It is of course necessary to see the facts of power and property as obstacles to this order, but the alternative society that is proposed must be in wider terms, if it is to generate the full energies necessary for its creation. Indeed the political and economic changes might come, and the human order be very little changed, unless these connections are made. A good particular example of this general problem is the question of the definition of work, which has been discussed and then neglected in the socialist tradition. Our common meaning of work has become 'effort rewarded by money': comparable effort, either of a 'private' or 'public' kind, may be as much work, but is described as 'leisure-time activity' or, curiously, 'good works'. The relation between work and effort, which is the central conclusion from experience, has thus become blurred by the forms of a particular kind of society, making a distinction between work undertaken 'in one's own interest' or for some 'voluntary social purpose', and work undertaken for money. It is difficult not to see this as a simple reflection of a society organized on a basis of wage-labour, which a different version of social relationships ought radically to challenge. In capitalist society, the difficulty of the social thinker is to know what to say about activities that are not the production and exchange of things. We tend to fall back, either on the old definition of 'service',

ratified by the persistent influence of thinking of an established order, or on the curious idea of 'leisure', which is a
kind of grace *after* the meal. These meanings may be a true
verdict on present experience: that personal interests and
service to the community have to be set in a separate
category from our ordinary work. But it is hardly something
to be accepted by socialists as a model. The integration of
work and life, and the inclusion of the activities we call
cultural in the ordinary social organization, are the basic
terms of an alternative form of society. In their light, the
system of decision becomes something more than the
traditional version of politics; it necessarily includes, for
example, control over the direction and nature of our
labour. Similarly, just as all men and their work become part
of the process of common social decision (the working community rather than the labour market), so the body of actual
interests, 'private' as well as 'public', 'leisure' as well as
'work', becomes the social purpose. The tradition which I
described in *Culture and Society* is important because it
bases social thinking on our 'general humanity', rather
than on the needs of a received system. But it is an indication of the tenacity of old ways of thinking that this should
have been interpreted as what is called 'a plea for the place
of the arts' (for the arts or education we are expected to
'plead', and some knees seem permanently bent). The real
claim, sustained by the magnificent and necessary relevance
of the arts to our general humanity or to nothing, was that
social thinking must start from the same human assumption,
judging work and politics and property by the general
needs of all the people in the society, rather than underwriting a particular system and working with its definitions.
If socialism accepts the distinction of 'work' from 'life',
which has then to be written off as 'leisure' and 'personal
interests'; if it sees politics as 'government', rather than as
the process of common decision and administration; if it
continues to see education as training for a system, and art as
grace after meals (while perhaps proposing more training
and a rather longer grace); if it is limited in these ways, it is
simply a late form of capitalist politics, or just the more
efficient organization of human beings around a system of

industrial production. The moral decline of socialism is in exact relation to its series of compromises with older images of society and to its failure to sustain and clarify the sense of an alternative human order.

Man in society was traditionally defined as man in social relationships based on a divine order, a received order, or an established order. This was then extended, first by theorists of the market, later by socialists such as Marx, to man in social relationships based on economic activities: as the activities change, so the order must change. This was better, but it still left out too much. It was reasonable to relate the system of decision (politics) to the system of maintenance (economics), but two major kinds of relationship were still excluded. These were, first, the system of learning and communication, which is as central to man as the systems of decision and maintenance; second, the complex of relationships based on the generation and nurture of life, in many ways highly variable and again expressed in particular systems. Since these vital systems were excluded from ordinary social thinking or given merely subordinate places, it was inevitable that separate sciences should be developed to study and account for them. Much of the process of learning and communication could be reasonably explained as social training (a subordinate branch of politics) and vocational training (a subordinate branch of economics). But it is perfectly clear that a vital part of human learning and communication cannot be so reduced: neither art, nor philosophy, nor science has ever served *only* these ends; each has served also the general growth of humanity. In a class society, this problem is evaded by describing such activities as 'liberal', the province of 'free men', which is to say of men disengaged, by their position, from the imperatives of politics and economics. Similarly, education (the system of learning and communication at its most formal) was one thing for 'free men'—a 'liberal education'; another thing for the rest—social and economic training (known respectively as character-building or moral instruction, and vocational training or technical instruction). This division is very far from any useful social thinking about learning and communication: the idealization and the degradation follow as parts of a single error. Thus art is degraded as a mere reflection of the basic economic and political process, on which it is thought to be parasitic; or it is idealized into the separate sphere of aesthetics—if Economic Man, then Aesthetic Man. But the creative element in man is the root both of his personality and his society; it can neither be confined to art nor excluded from the systems of decision and maintenance. To take account of human creativity the whole received basis of social thinking, its conception of what man in society is, must be deeply revised.

The development of a separate psychology, apart from social theory, is to be understood in the same way. A given system of decision and maintenance regards the birth and care of human beings, not as primary but as a process by which it will continue to be supplied. Within such a way of thinking, people have been able to dehumanize themselves to the extent of speaking of children as 'the raw material of the country's future', and when you juxtapose that with the idea of the 'labour market' (a phrase which even educationists now use) the whole status of the family, certainly of other people's families, has been reduced. Yet whatever is said, at this public level, most people are quite clearly not going to be shifted from their ordinary conviction that this is their own real and deepest life. People did not need telling, by the new psychology, that their ordinary experience as parents and children, brothers and sisters, husbands and wives, was of central importance in their own development. If social thinking excluded this experience, by its insistence on man in social relationships based on economic activities, then it was so much the worse for social thinking: we simply separated our family and personal life from the life of society. But of course it is clear that the family, in its changing forms, cannot be separated from society. Either it gets the reduced status of an instrument of supply and training, or it gets the idealized status, that only family relationships are real. The new psychology was able to show that patterns of feeling and behaviour, learned in the primary family relationships, were closely relevant to forms of wider social feeling and behaviour. The idealization began when it was claimed that all social behaviour, including political and economic forms, could be explained in these primary terms: an error very similar to that which, beginning from the evident creativity of art and philosophy, explained social development in terms of the history of forms and ideas. There is just enough truth in both these arguments to encourage the rash extensions which have become commonplace. The abstraction of forms of primary relationship, without reference to their evident historical and geographical variability, was at once the rashest extension and the clue to a more adequate account. The 'permanent' forms failed, but directed attention to the variable forms, and then, with this evidence, it was true that we could never again look at social relationships in the old limited political-economic ways.

We have to try to re-create, from the present complex of interests and disciplines, an adequate sense of a general human organization. It is clear that the reaction against exclusive political and economic social thinking can go too far. The system of decision is clearly crucial: it can quite literally be the life or death of a society. Economic activity is similarly basic, since production and distribution are not only essential for the maintenance of life, but the highly variable ways in which they can be organized quite clearly colour our whole existence, ånd in some cases appear to determine it. The truth about a society, it would seem, is to be found in the actual relations, always exceptionally complicated, between the system of decision, the system of communication and learning, the system of maintenance and the system of generation and nurture. It is not a question of looking for some absolute formula, by which the structure of these relations can be invariably determined. The formula that matters is that which, first, makes the essential connections between what are never really separable systems, and second, shows the historical variability of each of these systems, and therefore of the real organizations within which they operate and are lived. Thus, in certain societies, the family is also a directly economic organization, and its system of decision covers a wide area of activity. Here the relationships between persons will be of a complex yet quite unified kind, in that every person is involved with

every other in more than one kind of activity: the relationships that arise, whether of sympathy, tension, or conflict,
have to be worked out over the whole field. In different
societies, similarly, relationships are in the end worked out
over the whole field, but the ordinary situation, and therefore the ordinary experience, is of an aggregate of apparently
separate relationships: here of work, there of family, there
again of decision or learning. It is the development of
societies of this kind which has led to our conventional
descriptions and separations, although in any actual society,
if we are genuinely open to experience, the descriptions
and separations will be continually breaking down: nobody
can or does actually live as the model of separate orders
would suggest. Our contemporary experience of work,
love, thought, art, learning, decision and play is more
fragmented than in any other recorded kind of society, yet
still, necessarily, we try to make connections, to achieve
integrity, and to gain control, and in part we succeed.

The emphasis falls again, in our analysis of these descriptions of society, on the fact that they are or have been
terms of growth. Politics, economics, aesthetics, psychology
are always, in part, systems of rules learned in a once
living situation, and simply perpetuated unrevised. But
each, similarly, is in part a creative effort, to explore new
situations and to reach for an understanding which is also a
response and a way of control and change. If in studying
human organization we have emphasized not only relatedness but variability, it is to this crucial question of the nature
and origin of change that we are inevitably directed.

III

The systems of decision, maintenance, learning and
generation are necessarily conventional, in that they embody
certain rules which in any real society run very deep.
Further, they are often materialized, and in inheriting
them as institutions we inherit a real environment, which
shapes us but which we also change. We learn this environment in our bodies, and we are taught the conventions.
There is a real tension, always, as the environment and the
conventions are compared, and this comparison takes place

both individually and socially. Individuals arrive at different results, but in communicating and comparing them can work for or establish different conventions, by which we consciously change our environment, while in any event, from the very tension between the lived environment and the received conventions, a process of less conscious change will continue.

Against this theoretical background, we can look at certain kinds of change, as these actually occur. A large part of our history is of change by conquest, when an alien group is powerful enough to take over the system of decision, or a central part of it. The frequent occurrence of change of this kind has led naturally to the isolation of politics as the key to change, and to interpretation of the system of decision as the system of power. It is clear, nevertheless, that the results of conquest have been very varied indeed. The system of decision set up by the conquerors must in practice interact with all the other elements in the conquered society. An economy can be radically changed by alien decision. So can the whole system of learning and communication, even to the extent of a language being suppressed and forgotten and an alien language replacing it. Yet it as often happens that elements of the conquered society will persist, either by tolerance or in spite of intolerance, even when the conquest is prolonged. A structure of real relations, of a whole social kind, will in fact emerge, even if the whole system of decision has been taken over. For the system of decision, however powerful, has to operate in a real material and conventional environment. The conquerors may change with the conquered, and even in extreme cases become indistinguishable from them. More usually, a continually varied balance will result. Of the Norman conquest of England, for example, it is impossible to say that it did not change English society, but equally the eventual result was a very complex change, as can be seen most clearly in the history of the language, which emerged neither as Norman French nor as Old English, but as a new language deeply affected by both. Thus while political change will often be decisive, it will hardly ever be absolutely determining.

Conquest grows out of a structure of real relations that

is often so large in scale that its relevance to relations within the conquered society is extremely indirect. This is the measure of its difference from the otherwise similar capture of the system of decision by a group or class within the society. Whether this is sudden and dramatic, as in civil war and revolution, or a slow process of infiltration and changing control, it will commonly have more meaning in the whole development of the actual society: the political change will express a whole complex of general change. Economic explanations, both of conquest and of internal political change, have incomparably deepened our understanding of history, by taking us beyond that kind of vulgar politics which assumes power as a dominant end in itself, and by showing us that the system of decision is not abstract, but is shaped by the issues it is deciding. But the isolation of economics as the key to change has led, in its turn, to simplification and abstraction. It is indeed impossible to understand the modern world without understanding the growth and nature of capitalism, but it remains true that capitalist societies, in comparable stages of development, are still very different societies, in many respects, and that these differences are not accessible to the most refined kind of political-economic analysis. The danger is, when this has been realized, that we will make a new abstraction of the substance of these differences, as in many theories of culture: it is already a curiosity of language that society commonly indicates a political and economic system, and social life (the ordinary material of sociology) the whole range of activities and relationships which are not directly political or economic. The pattern of meanings and values through which people conduct their whole lives can be seen for a time as autonomous, and as evolving within its own terms, but it is quite unreal, ultimately, to separate this pattern from a precise political and economic system, which can extend its influence into the most unexpected regions of feeling and behaviour. To isolate the system of learning and communication, as the key to change, is unrealistic. The common prescription of education, as the key to change, ignores the fact that the form and content of education are affected, and in some cases determined, by the actual systems of decision and maintenance. Thinkers and artists reveal new meanings and values, as well as expressing conventional meanings and values, but to isolate the most evident creators, as the key to change, is as unrealistic as to overlook them, in some political or economic determinism. Thinkers and artists, and the extension of education, have visibly affected social change, but only within the necessary context of communication. People use art and thought (often deeply distorting actual works) to confirm their own patterns, at least as frequently as they really learn from them. And children, while at school, learn from their whole social environment as well as from the particular curriculum, to say nothing of the fact that when they leave school they have to compare what they have learned with the actual practices of their society. Similarly, we can accept the argument that changes in primary relationships, particularly between parents and children, will have observable social effects, and it is possible to argue that changes of this kind—such as the growth of love and the capacity for loving—are fundamental in the development of a society. It can be immediately agreed that much of our deepest humanity is learned in these relationships, but there is also a very deep crisis at the point of transfer of responses and values learned in this close world to the responses and values conventionalized in a working social system. Once again we are returned to the organization as a whole, but in the active sense that the organization both exists and has continually to be renewed: neither the system dominates nor the learning transforms; people change and are changed.

We can see, looking back, that our ideas of the nature of social change were limited by actual societies and their corresponding conceptions of relationships, so that the emphasis naturally fell on changes in power and property, in their common forms of conquest, revolution, or the rise and fall of classes. The counter-emphasis, on individuals and on learning and communication, was itself a social response, not only to the narrowness of society construed as power and property, but to real changes, which were actually liberating more and more individuals, and which were building ever widening and more powerful means of learning and communication. In the present situation, we are trying to pass beyond both the emphasis and the counter-emphasis, to a new and general conception of change. Our creative power is most evident in our continuing industrial revolution, which is continually confirming our capacity to change our world, and is leading to very much more open feelings, more real willingness to change, than any earlier conception could have foreseen. The democratic revolution, similarly, is insistently creative, in its appeal to all of us to take power to direct our own lives. And we are seeing, increasingly, a new kind of change, by the simple fact of the extension of communications, and by our consequent experience of an expanding culture. The rise of vernacular languages as new channels of general learning; the coming of printing, and then wireless, cinema, and television; the extension of railways, motorways, and air travel; the growth of literacy and systems of universal education: all these have transformed social change itself. Yet whether these means are used for creative growth, or merely as new ways of organizing older human systems, is an open question. Both the industrial revolution and the revolution in communications are only fully grasped in terms of the progress of democracy, which cannot be limited to simple political change, but insists, finally, on conceptions of an open society and of freely co-operating individuals which alone are capable of releasing the creative potentiality of the changes in working skills and communication. The long revolution, which is now at the centre of our history, is not for democracy as a political system alone, nor for the equitable distribution of more products, nor for general access to the means of learning and communication. Such changes, difficult enough in themselves, derive meaning and direction, finally, from new conceptions of man and society which many have worked to describe and interpret. Perhaps these conceptions can only be given in experience. The metaphors of creativity and growth seek to enact them, but the pressure, now, must be towards particulars, for here or nowhere they are confirmed.

We have reasonably adequate and continuing accounts of the rise of industry and the growth of democracy in Britain. But we have no adequate history of our expanding culture:

parts of the process have been documented, but have then too often been fitted into versions of change which seem to me to be based, consciously or unconsciously, on prejudices that are a form of contemporary social action. In my next Part, I shall review some important elements of the cultural expansion: partly to get the record as straight as I can; partly to bring the questions of value involved in the history to the point where commitments can be open. But also I see this cultural history as more than a department, a special area of change. In this creative area the changes and conflicts of the whole way of life are necessarily involved. This at least is my starting-point: where learning and communication are actual, and where through them we see the shapes of a society. What we see in this way we can then try to put to use in a much wider area. We can try to say how, where we live, we see growth and change, perhaps in new ways that are decisively altering our received social thinking.

PART TWO

ONE

Education and British Society

THERE are clear and obvious connections between the quality of a culture and the quality of its system of education. In our own time we have settled to saying that the improvement of our culture is a matter of improving and extending our national education, and in one sense this is obviously true. Yet we speak sometimes as if education were a fixed abstraction, a settled body of teaching and learning, and as if the only problem it presents to us is that of distribution: this amount, for this period of time, to this or that group. The business of organizing education—creating types of institution, deciding lengths of courses, agreeing conditions of entry and duration—is certainly important. Yet to conduct this business as if it were the distribution of a simple product is wholly misleading. It is not only that the way in which education is organized can be seen to express, consciously and unconsciously, the wider organization of a culture and a society, so that what has been thought of as simple distribution is in fact an active shaping to particular social ends. It is also that the content of education, which is subject to great historical variation, again expresses, again both consciously and unconsciously, certain basic elements in the culture, what is thought of as 'an education' being in fact a particular selection, a particular set of emphases and omissions. Further, when this selection of content is examined more closely, it will be seen to be one of the decisive factors affecting its distribution: the cultural choices involved in the selection of content have an organic relation to the social choices involved in the practical organization. If we are to discuss education adequately, we must examine, in historical and analytic terms, this organic relation, for to be conscious of a choice made is to be conscious of further and alternative choices available, and at a time when changes, under a multitude of pressures, will in any case occur, this degree of consciousness is vital.

We cannot begin with the aims of education as abstract definitions. If we look at actual educational systems, we can distinguish three general purposes, but their character is such that we can by no means separate them. We can, for example, distinguish a major general purpose: that of training the members of a group to the 'social character' or 'pattern of culture' which is dominant in the group or by which the group lives. To the extent that this 'social character' is generally accepted, education towards it will not normally be thought of as one possible training among many, but as a natural training which everyone in the society must acquire. Yet when, as often happens, the 'social character' is changing, or when, again, there are alternative 'social characters' within a given society, this 'natural training' can be something very different, and can be seen, by others, as 'indoctrination'. Some writers distinguish this social training from the teaching of particular skills, the former being general atmosphere or background, the latter being specialized instruction. Yet the 'social character' is always and everywhere much more than particular habits of civility and behaviour; it is also the transmission of a particular system of values, in the field of group loyalty, authority, justice, and living purposes. I know of no educational system which fails to contain this kind of training, and the important point is that it is impossible ultimately to separate this training from the specialized training. The teaching of skills prepares a rising generation for its varieties of adult work, but this work, and all the relations governing it, will be found to exist within the given 'social character'; indeed one function of the 'social character' is to make the available kinds of work, and the valuations and relations which arise from them, acceptable. And if we cannot separate general social training from specialized training, since one is given, consciously or unconsciously, in terms of the other, neither can we separate the third distinguishable purpose: what we call a 'general education', or, in Sir Fred Clarke's term, 'education for culture'. Schematically one can say that a child must be taught, first, the accepted behaviour and values of his society; second, the general knowledge and attitudes appropriate to an educated man, and third, a particular skill by which he will earn his living and contribute to the welfare of his society. In fact, just as the particular skill and the accepted behaviour and values are necessarily related, so, we shall find, both are related to, and help to determine, the kind of general knowledge and attitudes appropriate to an educated man. It is never a purely arbitrary selection, nor a simple process of 'indoctrination', for if the governing social character is accepted, even if only by a ruling minority, it is accepted in terms of its value: the general training necessary to a man is bound to be seen in the context of the values which the 'social character' embodies and transmits. If we believe in a particular 'social character', a particular set of attitudes and values, we naturally believe that the general education which follows from these is the best that can be offered to anyone: it does not feel like 'indoctrination', or even 'training'; it feels like offering to this man the best that can be given.

If we turn to historical analysis, the importance of these points becomes clear, for we shall see not only the variations of 'the best that can be given', but the actual and complex relations between the three aims cited: see the training of social character shading into specialized training for particular kinds of work, and the definitions of general education taking their colour from both. I propose to examine the history of English education from this particular point of view: to see the changing complex of actual relations, in social training, subjects taught, definitions of general education, in the context of a developing society. And since we ourselves are not at the end of history, but at a point in this complex development, the historical account will necessarily lead to an analysis of our own educational values and methods.

I

The beginnings of English education show very clearly the close relationships between training for a vocation, training to a social character, and training a particular civilization. The first English schools, from the late sixth century, had a primarily vocational intention, but this was such that it implied a particular social training and a particular definition of a proper general knowledge. The conscious object of these early schools, attached to cathedrals and to monasteries, was to train intending priests and monks to conduct and understand the services of the Church, and to read the Bible and the writings of the Christian Fathers. The break since the withdrawal of Roman power, and the new settlements by peoples of a different language, left a people largely without Latin at a time when the dominant religion, and a large part of all available learning, were in the unknown language. Augustine has been well described as coming to convert England 'with the Latin-service book in one hand, and the Latin grammar in the other' (Leach). Two kinds of school, often in practice connected, were instituted: the grammar school, to teach Latin, and the song school, to teach church singing. Necessarily, in view of their objects, the specialized training of both these schools was part of a general training to Christianity and the particular social character it then carried. Yet the grammar school, especially, could not be confined to this limited aim. Over eight centuries, from before the coming of these schools to England (based, as they were, on Greek and Roman models) until the centuries before the Renaissance, a crucial argument about the content of their education is most interestingly in evidence. Latin must be taught, or the Church could not continue, but ability in it led not only to the Bible and the Fathers, but also to the whole range of Latin literature and 'pagan' philosophy. The problems this raised are well illustrated in a letter from Pope Gregory to Bishop Desiderius in Gaul:

. . . A circumstance came to our notice, which cannot be mentioned without shame, namely that you, our brother, give lessons in grammar. This news caused us such annoyance and disgust that all our joy at the good we had heard earlier was turned to sorrow and distress, since the same lips cannot sing the praises of Jove and the praises of Christ. Consider yourself how serious and shocking it is that a bishop should pursue an activity unsuitable even for a pious layman. We have already in hand the granting of your request, easy in mind and untroubled by doubts, provided that this information which has come to us shall have been proved manifestly untrue, and you will not be shown to spend your time on the follies of secular literature.

Yet 'grammar', the basis of the new schools, was not understood at this time as merely the bones of a language (that is only a late medieval meaning): it was a preparation for reading, especially reading aloud, and was taken to involve comprehension and commentary, so that content was inseparable. On both educational and religious grounds, the 'grammar-book' was the expedient resorted to: first, the anthology, which not only made a variety of texts available but could select them on grounds of suitability of content; later the systematic grammars and the teaching dialogues. The inquiring student could and did read further, especially into Vergil and Ovid, but the nature of the selective tradition was such that a large part of classical thought, particularly in philosophy and science, remained neglected. Several actual curricula have come down to us from this early period. Bede speaks of Theodore and Hadrian, at Canterbury, teaching 'the rules of metric, astronomy and the computus as well as the works of the saints', and Alcuin's account of the teaching at York refers to grammar, rhetoric, law, poetry, astronomy, natural history, arithmetic, geometry, music, and the Scriptures. Yet, when we look at actual textbooks, we see how these subjects were organized by the dominant principles of Latin and the Church. Scripture was the central subject, and rhetoric teaching was mainly a study of verbal forms in the Bible. Grammar was the teaching of Latin, and versification was in the same context, though at times it extended to relate to poetry in the vernacular. Mathematics, including astronomy, was centred on the intricacies of the Church calendar, simple general exercises being an introduction to the all-important 'computus' centred on the controversy about the date of Easter. Music and law were vocational studies for the services and administration of the Church, and the natural history, by contrast with the Aristotelians, was literary and anecdotal. Geography, history, and the natural sciences found little place in such a scheme, though it must be remembered that Bede, with this teaching, wrote a substantial history of England.

It is difficult to be certain how far, if at all, this kind of education was made available to others than intending priests and monks. There was probably an occasional extension, and there are certainly some recorded cases of the education of young members of royal and noble families. In England, in any case, the development of the schools was interrupted by the Danish invasions, to such an extent that the system had to be reconstructed under the influence of Alfred, and we have little positive evidence again until the tenth and eleventh centuries. The new pattern is very similar to the old, even after the Norman invasion when French replaced English as the vernacular medium for teaching Latin. There are grammar schools and song schools, attached to cathedrals, monasteries and collegiate churches, and the vocational curriculum is still evident. Then, in the twelfth century, there is an important expansion, both in institutions and in teaching. The cathedral schools multiplied, and in the following century, in Oxford, the first colleges and the idea of a university appeared. The movement was closely related to extensions of the curriculum, in that rhetoric, at the primary stage, grew to rank equally with grammar, while in the secondary stages, and certainly in the universities, there was a major growth in logic, related to the increasing availability of some of the major writings of Aristotle, and an extension and specialization in the advanced faculties of law, medicine, and theology. Although education remained within a firm Christian framework, the concept of a liberal education, as a preparation for the specialized study of law, medicine, or theology, can be seen shaping itself. The concept of the Seven Liberal Arts (the *trivium* of grammar, rhetoric, and dialectic, the *quadrivium* of music, arithmetic, geometry, and astronomy) goes back to at least the fifth century, but it was only now that it began to be realized with any adequacy, as new material from classical learning, and new attitudes towards it, flowed in. Teachers, instead of being appointed, were now more formally licensed (university degrees were licences to teach). Some extension of studies to practical secular needs is also evident, as for example in the teaching of letter-writing, a growing need as administration became more complex. There is some evidence of writing-schools, as distinct from grammar and song schools, at which letter-writing and practical accounting were taught, for a new class. Some schools again, though needing to be licensed by the Church, were otherwise independent.

A very large part of medieval education remained vocational, but the development of philosophy, medicine, and law had the effect of removing parts of the educational system from the direct supervision of the Church, and the universities' fight for their independence, as corporate learned bodies deciding their own conditions for granting degrees and hence licences to teach, was to an important extent successful. Between the thirteenth and the end of the fifteenth centuries the network of grammar and song schools, attached to cathedrals, monasteries, collegiate churches and chantries, was added to by the creation of virtually independent schools, such as Winchester and Eton, in close relation with new colleges at Oxford and Cambridge. Figures are quite uncertain, but it has been estimated by the best authority, Leach, that for a population, on the eve of the Reformation, of some $2\frac{1}{4}$ millions, there may have been as many as 400 schools, or one school to 5,625 people. (In 1864 there was one grammar school to every 23,750 people.) Yet two other aspects of medieval education must be noted: the apprenticeship system, in the crafts and trades, and the chivalry system, by which young boys of noble family were sent as pages to great houses and lived through a graduated course of training to knighthood. The existence of these two systems, alongside the academic system, reminds us of the determining effect on education of the actual social structure. The labouring poor were largely left out of account, although there are notable cases of individual boys getting a complete education, through school and university, by outstanding promise and merit. For the rest, education was organized in general relation to a firm structure of inherited and destined status and condition: the craft apprentices, the future knights, the future clerisy. The system, while clear, is not perfect, for academic education seems on the whole to have outrun demand. Even with something like one ordained clerk to forty of the population, there was not room for all with an academic education to live by it, and the lower ranks of the clergy were in any case very poor. Further, the clerisy was perhaps recruited from a more varied social background than in the directly class-based apprenticeship and chivalry systems. Provision, in almost all early foundations, for 'poor scholars', can be variously interpreted, but at least the system was reasonably open. In this connection, the nature of the new independent schools, such as Winchester and Eton, is particularly important. At Winchester, apart from founder's kin, there were to be commoners paying their own cost, who would be ruling-class boys, and 'poor and needy scholars, of good character and well-conditioned, of gentlemanly habits, able for school, completely learned in reading, plain-song and old Donatus' (Latin Grammar). Because of their independent status, such schools were not tied to one locality, and admission on a national basis was begun. It has been suggested, perhaps with reason, that such an institution was bound to develop into the public-school as we know it, drawing increasingly on a single class, and combining in its way of life the educational methods of the grammar schools and the social training, by 'boarding-out', of the chivalric system. In view of the close connection between these schools and colleges of the universities, any such development was bound to affect the educational system as a whole.

II

Matthew Arnold once argued that much had been lost in English education because while the schools were reorganized by the Reformation their teaching was not redirected by the Renaissance. In the matter of actual schools, the Reformation of course made many changes, closing or reducing in status a number of old foundations, instituting perhaps an equal number of new. The central institution remained the Grammar School, but there is an important change in sponsorship, of the kind first evident in the fifteenth century. Where the typical medieval grammar school had been a Church foundation, the typical new grammar school was a private foundation, supervised in variable degree by Church and State. Yet the educational tradition of the grammar schools survived, with little change, and we can agree with Milton and Arnold that this was damaging. Greek and sometimes Hebrew were added to the main Latin curriculum, and the main gain was an expansion in the study of literature. But the grammar school's kind of teaching, and even more that of the universities, remained rigid and narrow, and forms such as the theme and the disputation, which had once been creative, were isolated and mechanical. The major achievements of the Renaissance, in the vernacular literatures, in geographical discovery, in new painting and music, in the new spirit in philosophy and physical inquiry, in changing attitudes to the individual, had little effect on the standard forms of general education. Yet, outside these traditional institutions, primary schools in English seem to have increased, in a bewildering variety of forms, ranging from instruction by priests to private adventure schools, often as a sideline to shopkeeping and trade. In many cases, the 'petties' or 'ABCs' were proper schools, sometimes linked to the grammar schools, sometimes, where old endowments had shrunk, virtually taking over grammar schools. In addition, there was some development of 'writing schools', teaching scrivener's English and the casting of accounts—an obvious need in the considerable expansion of trade—and in some cases such teaching became incorporated in grammar schools. It is a complex pattern, yet three trends are clear: the increase in vernacular teaching, the failure of the traditional institutions to adapt either to a changing economy or to an expanding culture, and the passing of most of the leading schools from sponsorship by a national institution to private benefaction.

In the seventeenth century, there were important developments in educational theory, some of which had practical effect. The main educational theories of the Renaissance, in particular the ideal of the scholar-courtier, had had little effect on English institutions, and indeed had the paradoxical effect of reducing the status of schools as such, and setting the alternative pattern, drawing in part on the chivalric tradition, of education at home through a private tutor: a preference, in many families, which lasted well into the nineteenth century. Specific professional institutions, particularly in law, gained in importance, but meanwhile, to serve a different class, new general institutions, the Dissenting Academies, were beginning to appear. Nonconformists, after the Restoration, were seriously discriminated against by the traditional institutions, and replied by setting up their own academies, at a higher secondary or university level of teaching. These varied considerably in quality, but it can fairly be claimed that in the best of them, in the eighteenth century, a new definition of the content of a general education was worked out and put into practice. Here, for the first time, the curriculum begins to take its modern shape, with the addition of mathematics, geography, modern languages, and, crucially, the physical sciences. The older grammar schools, in the same period, changed in differing ways. The nine leading schools, seven of them boarding institutions, kept mainly to the traditional curriculum of the classics, and, while less socially exclusive than they were to become, tended on the whole to serve the aristocracy and the squirearchy, on a national basis. The majority of the endowed grammar schools served their immediate localities, with a reasonably broad social base, but still mainly with the old curriculum. But those older schools situated in the larger cities, greatly influenced by the many merchants and tradesmen whom they served, combined, in the eighteenth century, a quite varied social composition with some broadening of the curriculum, particularly in mathematics and natural sciences. The universities reflected this complex picture, for while there was substantial adherence to the old curriculum, and what seems to have been a decline in teaching standards, there was some serious development in mathematics and the sciences, and the percentage of 'poor' students—sons of farmers, craftsmen, small tradesmen—though falling during the century, was still quite substantial. Of the three old professions, the clergy was still mainly served by the universities, while law and medicine were mainly now outside them. Of the new professions, particularly in science, engineering, and arts, a majority of entrants were trained outside the universities, as were also most of the new merchants and manufacturers. The eighteenth century is remarkable for the growth of a number of new vocational academies, serving commerce, engineering, the arts, and the armed services.

As for primary education, the haphazard system of parish and private adventure schools still survived, and there was some growth in preparatory schools serving the various academies and older foundations. But increasing urbanization was raising new problems, to which solutions were very slow in coming. The Charity School movement, from the end of the seventeenth century, represents the main effort, and its combination of a new kind of intention—the moral rescue as opposed to the moral instruction of the poor—with a more formal definition of elementary education as that appropriate to a particular social class, casts its shadow ahead. By the last quarter of the eighteenth century, with the quickening of pace of the Industrial Revolution, the whole educational system was under new pressures which would eventually transform it.

III

In the seventy years between 1751 and 1821, the population of the British mainland doubled, from seven to fourteen millions, and by 1871, at twenty-six millions, it had nearly doubled again. In addition to this remarkable expansion, the proportion of the population living in towns, including the new industrial towns, and also the proportion of children in the population as a whole, again remarkably increased. These changes would have been enough to disorganize a much better system of education than the eighteenth century actually had, and the first half of the nineteenth century is full of reports showing the utter inadequacy, in part revealed, in part created, by the social and economic transformation. The desire to reorganize education, on a fuller basis than hitherto, was the motive of many of these reports, but at the same time the forces opposed to any general reform were very strong. In 1816, of 12,000 parishes examined, 3,500 had no school, 3,000 had endowed schools of varying quality, and 5,500 had unendowed schools, of a quality even more variable. But to do anything about this the reformers had to get past the representative opinion of a Justice of the Peace in 1807:

> It is doubtless desirable that the poor should be generally instructed in *reading*, if it were only for the best of purposes—that they may read the Scriptures. As to *writing* and *arithmetic*, it may be apprehended that such a degree of knowledge would produce in them a disrelish for the laborious occupations of life.

It is true that at no previous period had the poor, as a whole, been educated, although in exceptional parishes the attempt was made. But there had been provision, again and again, for the exceptional poor boy to get to the university. Under the new dispensation, education was organized on a more rigid class basis.

> To every class we have a school assign'd
> Rules for all ranks and food for every mind.
> (Crabbe.)

Only the last clause was untrue.

But the process of change from a system of social orders, based on localities, to a national system of social classes—a change extending from the fifteenth to the late eighteenth centuries—was now virtually complete, and its result was a new kind of class-determined education. Higher education became a virtual monopoly, excluding the new working class, and the idea of universal education, except within the narrow limits of 'moral rescue', was widely opposed as a matter of principle.

The first new educational institutions of the Industrial Revolution were the industrial schools, providing manual training and elementary instruction, and, much more important, the Sunday schools, available to adults as well as children, and, while varying in methods, mainly organized on the principle noted: that for moral reasons the poor must learn to read the Bible, but that writing and arithmetic, to say nothing of more dangerous subjects, were less necessary or even harmful. In the new kinds of day school, under the rival systems of Lancaster and Bell, teaching was similarly based on the Bible, but by a new method—what Bell called 'the STEAM ENGINE of the MORAL WORLD'—which by the use of monitors and standard repetitive exercises allowed one master to teach many hundreds of children simultaneously in one room. It has been estimated that with the development of Sunday schools and the new day schools, and with the surviving parish and adventure schools, some 875,000 children, out of a possible 1,500,000, attended a school of some kind for some period in 1816, and that in 1835 the figure was 1,450,000 out of 1,750,000. To assess these figures adequately, we must remember that the same inquiries showed an average duration of school attendance, in 1835, of one year. From the eighteenth century some assistance to schools from the rates had been empowered in a few places, and from the 1830s there was a beginning of national assistance in school building. By 1851, the average duration of school attendance had been raised to two years, and by 1861 an estimated 2,500,000 children, out of a possible 2,750,000 may have been in some form of school attendance, though still of very mixed quality and with the majority leaving before they were eleven. The curriculum was broadening a little, usually now including writing and arithmetic, and in some schools other general subjects. The Revised Code of 1862 instituted a system of payment by results in relation to definite standards in reading, writing, and arithmetic (reading a short paragraph in a newspaper; writing similar matter from dictation; working sums in practice and fractions). Increasing public aid to the schools was thus tied to the old criterion of a minimum standard. In 1870, school boards were established, to complete the network of schools and bring them under a clearer kind of supervision, and in 1876 and 1880 this extension was confirmed by making universal elementary schooling compulsory. In 1893, the leaving age was raised to 11, in 1899 to 12, and in 1900 to a permissive 14. Thus by the end of the century a national system of elementary schooling, still largely confined to the provision of a minimum standard, had been set going.

Meanwhile, the old grammar schools had been widely developed, as the institutions of a largely separate class, served mainly, at the primary stage, by an extended network of preparatory schools. Attendances at the old schools, particularly at the leading nine, had begun to revive in the period 1790–1830, and in their different ways Butler at Shrewsbury, from 1798, and Arnold at Rugby, from 1824, had begun to change their character. Arnold's influence was not mainly on the curriculum, but on the re-establishment of social purpose, the education of Christian gentlemen. Butler's influence is perhaps even more significant, for his emphasis on examination-passing marks the beginning of a major trend. By the 1830s, the examination system between these schools and the universities was firmly established, and this, while raising educational standards within the institutions, had the effect of reinforcing the now marked limitation of the universities to entrants from a narrow social class. In the curriculum, classics were 'business' and other subjects were extras, but the establishment of the Civil Service Commission and the Board of Military Education, from mid-century, had the effect of promoting mathematics and modern languages, and of further organizing the schools in terms of examinations. In the 1840s, there were altogether some 700 grammar schools, and more than 2,000 non-classical endowed schools, but an inquiry showed in 1868 that in two-thirds of the towns of England there were no secondary schools of any kind, and in the remaining third there were marked differences of quality. In the late 1860s, through two commissions and the Public Schools Act of 1868, the reorganization of secondary education, still on a narrow class basis, was conceived and in part carried through. The Act of 1868 broke many of the old foundation statutes, and instituted new governing bodies. From this date, the new curriculum (classics, mathematics, one modern language, two natural sciences, history, geography, drawing, and music) and the confirmation of a separate class of 'public schools', were established. The Headmasters' Conference, embracing the many new nineteenth-century schools of this type, and some of the old foundations, was begun in 1869. The Taunton Commission of 1867 envisaged three grades of secondary school: those for the upper and upper-middle classes, keeping their boys till 18 and giving a 'liberal education' in preparation for the universities and the old professions; those for the middle classes, keeping their boys till 16 and preparing them for the Army, the newer professions, and many departments of the Civil Service; and those for the lower middle classes, keeping their boys until 14, and fitting them for living as 'small tenant farmers, small tradesmen, and superior artisans'. Where possible, minorities should be enabled to pass to a higher grade, and in particular there might be a connection between third-grade secondary schools and the elementary schools, enabling some sons of labourers to go on to secondary education. Secondary education, in these three grades, should be made available to 10 children for every 1,000 of the population, and of these 8 would be in the third grade. In practice this would mean a national total of 64,000 children in the first and second grades, and 256,000 in the third grade, out of some 4,000,000 children. 'It is obvious', the Commission commented, in relation to its tripartite grading, 'that these distinctions correspond roughly, but by no means exactly, to the gradations of society.'

In practice, while secondary education was not yet a public responsibility, the effect of this suggested organization was uneven. From the 1850s, a system of University Local Examinations, first called 'Middle-Class Examinations', had enabled endowed and proprietary schools of the first and second grades to aim at some recognized national standard of secondary education, and the extension of the examination system by official and professional bodies had the same rationalizing effect. The campaign for the secondary education of girls was beginning to show results, and then in 1889 Wales took the lead, with an Intermediate Education Act which succeeded in establishing an organized secondary system linking the board and voluntary elementary schools with the universities, and providing for both boys and girls. In 1902 the creation of Local Education Authorities, with responsibility for the full educational needs of their areas, laid the basis for a national system of secondary education. The third-grade school had been overtaken by the raising of the elementary school-leaving age, and it was to the creation of first- and second-grade secondary schools that the new authorities, with varying energy, applied themselves. The Board of Education had come into existence in 1899, and in 1904 it defined a four-year secondary course, leading to a certificate, in English language and literature, geography, history, a language other than English, mathematics, science, drawing, manual work, physical training, and household crafts for girls. If we look back from this to the eighteenth-century curriculum of the Dissenting Academies, we shall see where the main line of the tradition lies.

Meanwhile, in the course of the century, university education had been radically changed. The institution of public examinations, in Cambridge from the eighteenth century, in Oxford from the early years of the nineteenth, had an important effect on teaching, which did not pass without protest that the examination system was making education mechanical. At the same time, the religious exclusiveness of the two ancient universities, and the effective restriction of their curriculum to classics and mathematics, led to the foundation of London University (1828–1836), while the new University of Durham (1832), though governed by the Church, had a notably broader curriculum. Reforming movements at Oxford and Cambridge led to substantial statutory changes in the 1850s, with the dual aim of broadening the range of subjects offered, and ensuring a social representation wider than that of 'prospective parsons, prospective lawyers, (and) young men of rank and fortune'. Further legislative changes in the 1870s and 1880s, and the reorganization and extension of faculties, led to the achievement of modern university status. Meanwhile, university colleges were springing up, and the foundations of Manchester, Nottingham, Reading, Southampton, Leeds, Liverpool, Sheffield, and Birmingham, together with the three Welsh colleges, were being laid.

The nineteenth-century achievement is evidently a major reorganization of elementary, secondary, and university education, along lines which in general we still follow. Both in kinds of institution, and in the matter and manner of education, it shows the reorganization of learning by a radically changed society, in which the growth of industry and of democracy were the leading elements, and in terms of change both in the dominant social character and in types of adult work. At no time in England have the effects of these influences on the very concept of education been clearer, but, precisely because this was so, a fundamental argument about the purposes of education was the century's most interesting contribution. Two strands of this argument can be separated: the idea of education for all, and the definition of a liberal education. The former, as we have seen, was fiercely argued, and the history of the century represents the victory of those who, in the early decades, had been a minority. Two major factors can be distinguished: the rise of an organized working class, which demanded education, and the needs of an expanding and changing economy. In practice, these were closely interwoven, in the long debate, and the victory of the reformers rested on three elements: genuine response to the growth of democracy, as in men like Mill, Carlyle, Ruskin, and Arnold; protective response, the new version of 'moral rescue', very evident in the arguments for the 1870 Education Act in relation to the franchise extensions of 1867—'our future masters . . . should at least learn their letters'; and the practical response, perhaps decisive, which led Forster in 1870 to use as his principal argument: 'upon the speedy provision of elementary education depends our industrial prosperity'. In the growth of secondary education this economic argument was even more central.

The democratic and the industrial arguments are both sound, but the great persuasiveness of the latter led to the definition of education in terms of future adult work, with the parallel clause of teaching the required social character— habits of regularity, 'self-discipline', obedience, and trained effort. Such a definition was challenged from two sides, by those with wider sympathies with the general growth of democracy, and by those with an older conception of liberal education, in relation to man's health as a spiritual being. This interesting alliance is broadly that which I traced as a tradition in *Culture and Society*, and the educational argument was always near the centre of this continuing tradition. On the one hand it was argued, by men with widely differing attitudes to the rise of democracy and of working-class organization, that men had a natural human right to be educated, and that any good society depended on governments accepting this principle as their duty. On the other hand, often by men deeply opposed to democracy, it was argued that man's spiritual health depended on a kind of education which was more than a training for some specialized work, a kind variously described as 'liberal', 'humane', or 'cultural'. The great complexity of the general argument, which is still unfinished, can be seen from the fact that the public educators, as we may call the first group, were frequently in alliance with the powerful group which promoted education in terms of training and disciplining the poor, as workers and citizens, while the defenders of 'liberal education' were commonly against both: against the former because liberal education would be vulgarized by extension to the 'masses'; against the latter because liberal education would be destroyed by being turned into a system of specialized and technical training. Yet the public educators inevitably drew on the arguments of the defenders of the old 'liberal' education, as a way of preventing universal education being narrowed to a system of pre-industrial instruction. These three groups—the public educators, the industrial trainers, and the old humanists—are still to be distinguished in our own time, and we shall see, later, their influence in twentieth-century developments. In general, the curriculum which the nineteenth century evolved can be seen as a compromise between all three groups, but with the industrial trainers predominant. The significant case is the long controversy over science and technical education. If we look at the range of scientific discovery between the seventeenth and the end of the nineteenth centuries, it is clear that its importance lies only in part in its transformation of the techniques of production and communication; indeed lies equally in its transformation of man's view of himself and of his world. Yet the decisive educational interpretation of this new knowledge was not in terms of its essential contribution to liberal studies, but in terms of technical training for a particular class of men. The old humanists muddled the issue by claiming a fundamental distinction between their traditional learning and that of the new disciplines, and it was from this kind of thinking that there developed the absurd defensive reaction that all real learning was undertaken without thought of practical advantage. In fact, as the educational history shows, the classical linguistic disciplines were primarily vocational, but these particular vocations had acquired a separate traditional dignity, which was refused to vocations now of equal human relevance. Thus, instead of the new learning broadening a general curriculum, it was neglected, and in the end reluctantly admitted on the grounds that it was of a purely technical kind. The pressure of the industrial trainers eventually prevailed, though not with any general adequacy until the Technical Instruction Act of 1889, and even here, significantly, it was 'instruction' rather than 'education'. This history was damaging both to general education and to the new kinds of vocational training, and yet it was only an exceptional man, such as Huxley, who could see this at the time and consequently argue in the only adequate way: that science must become a part of general education and of liberal culture, and that, as a further provision, there must be an adequate system of specific professional training, in all kinds of scientific and technical work, on the same principle as the further professional training of doctors, lawyers, teachers, artists, and clergy. We can take only a limited satisfaction in the knowledge that the industrial trainers won, inert and stupid as the old humanists were and have continued to be. Huxley was a public educator, in the full sense, and it was only in this tradition that the problem might have been solved.

The shadow of class thinking lies over this as over so much other nineteenth-century educational thinking. The continued relegation of trade and industry to lower social classes, and the desire of successful industrialists that their sons should move into the now largely irrelevant class of gentry, were alike extremely damaging to English education and English life. As at the Reformation, a period of major reconstruction of institutions was undertaken largely without reference to the best learning of the age, and without any successful redefinition of the purposes of education and of the content of a contemporary liberal culture. The beginnings of technical instruction in the Mechanics' Institutes might have developed into a successful redefinition, but again it was the training of a specific class, whereas in fact the new sciences were radical elements in the society as a whole: a society which had changed its economy, which under pressure was changing its institutions, but which, at the centres of power, was refusing to change its ways of thinking. And then to the new working class, the offered isolation of science and technical instruction was largely unacceptable, for it was precisely in the interaction between techniques and their general living that this class was coming to its new consciousness. Politics, in the wide sense of discussing the quality and direction of their living, was excluded from these Institutes, as it was to remain largely excluded from the whole of nineteenth-century education. It was only very slowly, and then only in the sphere of adult education, that the working class, drawing indeed on very old intellectual traditions and on important dissenting elements in the English educational tradition, made its contribution to the modern educational debate. This contribution—the students' choice of subject, the relation of disciplines to actual contemporary living, and the parity of general discussion with expert instruction—remains important, but made little headway in the general educational organization. Like the individual public educators, their time was not yet.

IV

In the twentieth century, the framework inherited from the nineteenth century has been greatly expanded and improved. Elementary education has been redefined as primary education, ending at eleven, and from this definition, since 1944, it has been possible to provide secondary education for all. A greatly expanded system of combined first-grade and second-grade secondary schools has been brought into being, and arrangements for a substantial minority to pass from primary schools into this system, and for a much smaller minority to pass on to higher education, have been if not completely at least effectively established. A large number of third-grade secondary schools, with limited connections to the minority system, are in process of creation, and vary considerably in quality. In primary education, a notable expansion of the curriculum is perhaps the century's major achievement; it is mainly here that the influence of the public educators has been effective. The universities, if unevenly and at times without clear definition, have expanded their curricula in vitally important ways. It is at the level of secondary education, whether 'grammar' or 'modern', that the essential argument continues, in terms that reveal again the close relationship between curriculum and organization.

In theory, the principles of the public educators have been accepted: that all members of the society have a natural right to be educated, and that any good society depends on governments accepting this principle as a duty. In practice the system is still deeply affected by other principles, as a few examples will show. The continued existence of a network of private education, in the preparatory and public schools, may or may not be socially desirable, but in any case it shows the kind of education, and the necessary level of investment in it, which a particular social group accepts as adequate for itself. The large class, for example, has haunted public education from the beginning: from Lancaster's 1,000 children under one master, through the 60–80 of the urban board schools, to the still common 40–50 of our own day. In the private network, very much smaller classes, and the necessary investment to ensure them, have been accepted as a private duty, in a quite different way from the interpretation of public duty in the national system. Similarly, by the same social group, the necessary minimum level of education of all its members has been set as at least the second-grade school, usually followed by further professional training, whereas the public definition, for the members of other social groups, is at the lower minimum of what is still very much the old third grade. Again, this minimum level, for the limited social group, is set to include subjects which are only available to a minority of the society as a whole. It is not easy to argue that this limited social group has no right to provide the education it thinks fit for its own members, but the contrasts between this and the general provision show very clearly the survival of a familiar kind of class thinking, which has limited the practical execution of a formally accepted public duty. In the analysis of our present educational system, this point is usually neglected in favour of an argument in terms of levels of intelligence, and it is often argued that we face wholly new problems, in the education of the 'masses', because levels of measured intelligence vary so widely. There are problems indeed, but in fact the education of this limited social class has throughout its history had to deal with this same kind of mental variation, and it has been the level of education required by a member of this class, rather than the level thought appropriate to a particular mental measurement, that has in fact governed its organization. If we put the matter in this way, that because a child will be this kind of adult, he must be brought to a given degree of education, we can begin to see the pattern more clearly.

Differences in learning ability obviously exist, but there is great danger in making these into separate and absolute categories. It is right that a child should be taught in a way appropriate to his learning ability, but because this itself depends on his whole development, including not only questions of personal character growth but also questions of his real social environment and the stimulation received from it, too early a division into intellectual grades in part creates the situation which it is offering to meet. The effect of stimulation on intellectual performance has been interestingly described, in our present context, by Professor Vernon:

After 11, in Britain, we do get bigger divergences in environmental stimulation. Children are now at an age when they should be acquiring complex concepts and modes of thought, and the different kinds of schooling provided in grammar, modern and other schools, together with the different intellectual levels of their homes, may well affect their growth. At 15 the majority leave school and enter jobs which do little to exercise their 'brains', and their leisure pursuits are mostly non-stimulating. But a privileged minority continue to receive intellectual stimulation to 17, 18, 21 or later, and are more likely to enter jobs where they use their minds, and to indulge in cultural leisure-time pursuits. Hence we would expect, as has been clearly proved, that education during the teens does affect the ultimate adult intelligence level. The man with full secondary and university education has on the average a 12 IQ point advantage over the man who was equally intelligent at 15 but has had no further education since then.

This is the reality behind the confident use of mental measurement to ratify graded systems of education. To take intelligence as a fixed quantity, from the ordinary thinking of mechanical materialism, is a denial of the realities of growth and of intelligence itself, in the final interest of a particular model of the social system. How else can we explain the very odd principle that has been built into modern English education: that those who are slowest to learn should have the shortest time in which to learn, while those who learn quickly will be able to extend the process for as much as seven years beyond them? This is the reality of 'equality of opportunity', which is a very different thing from real social equality. The truth is that while for children of a particular social class we have a conception, however imperfect, of a required minimum of general education whatever their measured intelligence might be, we have no such conception, or a much lower conception, for the majority of those outside this class. This fact in itself, together with other social processes, magnifies natural inequalities, in a persistent way. For of course there is no absolute correlation between intelligence and membership of a particular occupational group. The mean IQ of children of such groups varies, but the differences within groups are greater than those between the groups. And then, if longer education can be bought by a few, and if more favourable learning environments are perpetuated by the social inequality resulting from previous inequalities of real opportunity, natural inequalities are again magnified and take on a direct social relevance. If one is asked, at any point in this process, to 'stop being utopian and consider the hard facts about educating the masses', it is very difficult to be patient. While we shall always be faced with substantial differences in learning ability among all children, we have to face the really hard fact that we are now meeting this problem in a particular way which serves in the end to magnify the differences and then pass them off as a natural order. We can only change this way if we get rid of conscious or unconscious class thinking, and begin considering educational organization in terms of keeping the learning process going, for as long as possible, in every life. Instead of the sorting and grading process, natural to a class society, we should regard human learning in a genuinely open way, as the most valuable real resource we have and therefore as something which we should have to produce a special argument to limit rather than a special argument to extend. We will perhaps only get to this when we have learned to think of a genuinely open culture.

The conception of graded secondary schools, in nineteenth-century thinking, rested firmly on the assumption that the existing class structure would be reproduced. The educational standards aimed at were, in consequence, class standards—what a gentleman, or a professional man, or a small tradesman would need. We have now added what a technician or an operative will need, but are still far short of the principle I am trying to establish: what a member of an educated and participating democracy needs. Advance to this principle has been confused by one real change and reform. We are now all aware that developments in the professions (including teaching) as a result of expanded social services, in administration as a result of the growth of large-scale organizations, both democratic and commercial, and in industry as a result of highly developed productive techniques, have created a new and expanding class, quite different in character from the old gentry and the old bourgeoisie. In one way, this new class has much more in common with the old working class, in that it lives neither by property nor by trade, but by offering its labour for hire. At the same time, the labour offered is of a skilled kind, requiring specific training, and though this is also increasingly true of the working class itself, it has happened that the preparatory training of the new class has been carried out within the educational system, while the working class is still largely trained 'on the job'. To train this new class, the old education of gentlemen has been largely replaced by the new education of public servants; it was indeed in this connection that the ideology of 'service' was so greatly emphasized, first in the reformed public schools, later in the secondary system modelled on them. In fact, at every stage, and still today, provision for the education of this new class has lagged seriously behind actual need: at first under the influence of traditional educational ideas, later by reluctance to face the effect of this need on the older class system. By the second half of the nineteenth century it was obvious that the existing upper and middle classes could not, by themselves, supply the expanding demand, and the national organization of secondary education was in fact the delayed practical recognition of this transforming situation. The bulk of the recruitment would still come from the established upper and middle classes, but facilities would be provided for lower-middle class and working-class boys to fill the residue of vacancies. This policy had the moral appeal of meeting what was felt to be the most substantial criticism of the existing system: that poor boys of exceptional ability might not get their 'chance', might be wasted. The steady expansion of such facilities has been a persistent if always belated attempt to keep pace with the continuing expansion of this new class, and the guiding principle in secondary education has consequently been the supply of this standard of skilled service: a definition which led naturally to a selective principle based on mental measurement rather than on social origin. It was now not so much the continuing education of a class (though in the private network this emphasis remained) as the grading and treatment of a given quantity of raw material, to supply the expanding professional, administrative, and industrial process.

Such training in itself is essential, but the fact that secondary education, and the selective procedures giving entry to it, have been conceived almost wholly in such narrow terms has been very damaging both in practice and at the level of educational theory. Instead of the effort to reinterpret contemporary culture, and to define a general education for our society as a whole, the emphasis, both in the organization of institutions, and in the thinking of educators, has been on the processes of sorting and grading. Such changes and extensions as there have been in the secondary curriculum have again been largely determined by changes in the character of the work of this new class. The relevant 'social character'—a training in reliability, the willingness to take responsibility within a given framework, and the notion of leadership (in practice a conception appropriate to upper and middle servants, the taking of local control and initiative within a heavily emphasized absolute loyalty to the institution to which the 'leader' belongs)—was again worked out in the reformed public schools, and widely and successfully imitated in the national system.

The alternative tradition of public education, which led to the principle of secondary education for all, has remained relatively weak. One has only to compare the simple class thinking of the Taunton Commission's recommended grades with the Hadow, Spens, and Norwood reports, and the practical effects of the 1944 Education Act, to see the essential continuity, despite changes in the economy, of a pattern of thinking drawn from a rigid class society, with its grading by birth leading to occupation, and then assimilated to a changing society, with a new system of grading. The tradition of public education, on the other hand, rests on a broader interpretation of the lines of social change. It recognizes the occupational changes as vitally important, but it insists that these are only one aspect of our general development. By slow steps, not completed until the late 1920s, Britain has become a democracy based on universal suffrage, and this fact, by which the responsibility of deciding major social policy is transferred to the people as a whole, is obviously of central and inescapable relevance to education. Again, the remarkable growth of cultural communication systems—from the developed national press to cinema, radio, and television—has placed the quality of the whole national culture in the hands of the people as a whole, for it is increasingly obvious that standards set in the wide field affect the standards of the most tenaciously guarded minority culture. Further, the occupational changes are developing on such a scale, and seem certain to continue to do so, probably at an accelerating rate, that the selective education of a new skilled class is no longer a problem of dealing with a minority, but is becoming a problem of the preparation for all kinds of work.

Attention has been concentrated, by critics in the public educator tradition, on the organization of secondary education to the point where a common general education, of a genuinely secondary kind, will be available to all. The detailed proposals for this are interesting and many successful experiments have already been undertaken. Yet it remains true that the crucial question, in any such programme, is that of curriculum and teaching method, and it is difficult to feel that the present grammar-school curriculum, or its partial imitation and local extension by the secondary modern school, is of such a kind that the problem is merely one of distributing it more widely. An educational curriculum, as we have seen again and again in past periods, expresses a compromise between an inherited selection of interests and the emphasis of new interests. At varying points in history, even this compromise may be long delayed, and it will often be muddled. The fact about our present curriculum is that it was essentially created by the nineteenth century, following some eighteenth-century models, and retaining elements of the medieval curriculum near its centre. A case can be made for every item in it, yet its omissions are startling. The social studies, even of an elementary kind, are virtually omitted at the level which every child can be certain of reaching, yet it would be difficult to argue that a detailed description of the workings of parliamentary and local government, of the law and public administration, of the organization of industry, of the evolution and character of modern social groups, of the techniques by which a modern society is studied and influenced, is less relevant than, say, the detailed descriptions of the geography of South America which now have traditional sanction. Where education in the social studies is given at all, except in exceptional schools, it is outside 'business', as modern languages and science were outside 'business' in the nineteenth century, and its teaching varies in quality from simple description to the casual and hortatory process—a true descendant of 'moral rescue'—known as 'civics'. In the arts, similarly, it is a meagre response to our cultural tradition and problems to teach, outside literature, little more than practical drawing and music, with hardly any attempt to begin either the history or criticism of music and visual art forms, or the criticism of those forms of film, televised drama, and jazz to which every child will go home. Even in English, despite the efforts of many fine teachers, most children will leave even grammar schools without ever having practised the critical reading of newspapers, magazines, propaganda, and advertisements, which will form the bulk of their actual adult reading. Meanwhile, in science, the vast and exciting *history* of scientific discovery and its social effects will have been given quite inadequate attention.

But it is not only a question of subjects. Our teaching methods, especially in grammar schools, are still to a considerable extent determined by traditional patterns of thinking, some of which are irrelevant. Modern languages are still widely taught by methods developed for the teaching of a dead language, and it is surely remarkable, in the present state of international communications, that an Englishman should be teaching French paradigms to English children in Dover, while a Frenchman teaches English paradigms to French children in Boulogne. In other subjects, the replacement of the disputation by the examination had important organizing effects, but the ability to use knowledge, and to acquire skill in ordinary public argument, was at least an intention of the older system (and one directly relevant to any effective democratic life), which the newer organization at least diminishes where it does not exclude. A form of instruction for memory tests, which at its worst the modern system has become, has less relevance, to our actual needs, than training in the selection and use of knowledge as a way of making responsible choices between possible courses of action.

The ordinary objection to any criticism of the existing curriculum is that it is already overloaded; this indeed was the nineteenth-century answer to proposals for the teaching of science and even history, and in immediate practical terms it has always some substance. But it is at this point that the grading model, with its terminal ages nicely adjusted to future occupation, can be seen as the main limitation. If, in a working democracy and a popular culture, we are failing, within the existing system, to give adequate education in these fields, while doing our best to maintain education preparatory to various grades of work, that is a choice, a deliberate expression of values, and subject both to challenge and to change. We can see a certain way ahead, on existing lines: making better provision for the training of teachers and for more adequate school buildings; reducing the size of classes; raising the leaving-age to sixteen. These are practical and necessary reforms, but we must ask whether having made them we shall be much better placed to give an adequate general education. In practice we still think of required levels of general culture, according to certain classes of work, and some people would interpret this as classless education because every child is given the opportunity to go as far as he can, to 'choose' the class he will enter. But this choice, this kind of opportunity, depends on the coincidence of a particular child's learning ability with certain defined courses, and, further, we cannot in our kind of society call an educational system adequate if it leaves any large number of people at a level of general knowledge and culture below that required by a participating democracy and arts dependent on popular support. For the majority of our people, education now ends at fifteen: that is to say at an age which, even if the education preceding it had been wholly satisfactory, many of the distinctive adult processes and choices, to whose quality education can clearly contribute, will not have become relevant. If children of moderate learning ability cannot acquire, in the time now given, the essentials of a contemporary general education, the only sensible answer is to give more time, not to dismiss some of the essentials with a resigned regret. We shall have to think (as with difficulty people in the nineteenth century learned to think, reaching levels we now all accept) of an even further expansion, governed by our needs rather than by our inherited models.

What are these essentials? There is no clear consensus, because we have not on the whole been thinking in this way, being preoccupied by organization and otherwise simply repairing a nineteenth-century definition. As a basis for discussion, I would put down the following, as the minimum to aim at for every educationally normal child:

(a) Extensive practice in the fundamental languages of English and mathematics;

(b) General knowledge of ourselves and our environment, taught at the secondary stage not as separate academic disciplines but as general knowledge drawn from the disciplines which clarify at a higher stage, i.e.,

   (i) biology, psychology,

  (ii) social history, law and political institutions, sociology, descriptive economics, geography including actual industry and trade,

  (iii) physics and chemistry;

(c) History and criticism of literature, the visual arts, music, dramatic performance, landscape and architecture;

(d) Extensive practice in democratic procedures, including meetings, negotiations, and the selection and conduct of leaders in democratic organizations. Extensive practice in the use of libraries, newspapers and magazines, radio and television programmes, and other sources of information, opinion and influence;

(e) Introduction to at least one other culture, including its language, history, geography, institutions and arts, to be given in part by visiting and exchange.

In terms of such a definition, we could revise our institutions. We ought perhaps not to keep adolescents at schools of the present kind beyond sixteen, at which age at latest their human growth has entered a new stage. Much of the most interesting work in the curriculum might be done after this age, in a much greater variety of institutions than we now have, and with provision in many cases for the beginning of specific vocational training alongside the continuing general education. Among possible institutions are the county colleges, technical colleges, evening institutes, junior colleges in relation to local universities, 'sandwich' courses, colleges of apprenticeship, day-release organizations, overseas schools, adventure schools. The criterion should be that everyone should have some form of continuing education, and that it is a condition of all offers of employment that this is seriously provided for. As the nature of work changes, there is less hurry than there was to get people out into what was thought of as the 'labour market', and if the institutions are of a kind acceptable to adolescents and young adults, and if the democratic training is given substance by their participation in the immediate government of the institution they attend, we could greatly diminish the already diminishing resistance to an education which for the majority is set in terms of the needs of children, and which, damningly, is seen as of little relevance to the adult living that lies ahead. A variety of institutions, at this period of growth, is more likely to meet the problems of varying capacity and interest than the crude grading of two or three 'types of mind', followed by leaving one large 'type' to its own devices. There is a marked tendency, in our culture, for people between about sixteen and twenty-five to think of themselves as a distinct group, setting their own standards and refusing to be children one day and mature adults the next. Here is the great educational challenge and opportunity, which we can only rise to if we take secondary education as a preparation for this phase. We might then be expressing the shape of our own society, rather than reproducing the patterns of others.

Utopian thinking is that which supposes we shall get an educated and participating democracy, industries and services with adequate human communications, and a common culture of high quality, by proclaiming the virtue of those things and leaving our training institutions as they are. I do not doubt that the proposals suggested above will be called Utopian, but they are in fact the reverse. It is a question of whether we can grasp the real nature of our society, or whether we persist in social and educational patterns based on a limited ruling class, a middle professional class, a large operative class, cemented by forces that cannot be challenged and will not be changed. The privileges and barriers, of an inherited kind, will in any case go down. It is only a question of whether we replace them by the free play of the market, or by a public education designed to express and create the values of an educated democracy and a common culture.

TWO

The Growth of the Reading Public

I T is open to the historian to choose several different dates for the beginning of a reading public in Britain, according to the variable interpretations which such a term carries. It is only in our own century that the regular reading even of newspapers has reached a majority of our people, and only in our own generation that the regular reading of books has reached a bare majority. Yet in the nineteenth century there was a major, and at times spectacular, expansion in reading, while in the eighteenth century there was again an important expansion which both created regular journalism and changed the social basis of literature. Going back beyond these centuries, we find real if uneven growth in the seventeenth century, and then find ourselves tracing the development back to the introduction of printing in the 1470s. In fact, however, if we take a minimum definition, and look for the regular production of multiple copies of books, we must go back, in this country, at least to the eighth century. In Rome it had been the practice to organize multiple production by a system of group copying from dictation, and it has been claimed that in this way an edition of between five hundred and a thousand copies could be completed within a day of the delivery of the work. A similar method of publication was certainly adopted in the *scriptoria* of the monasteries, and we have a record of such production from York in the time of Alcuin. Though very slow by modern standards (the edition in a day depended on thousands of available slaves and if true would be exceptional) it is easy to underestimate the number of books thus made available, and while much of the copying was of course for immediate professional purposes, there is some evidence of books being sold outside the monasteries and, later, outside the universities, which joined the monasteries in production. Certainly, in the fourteenth and fifteenth centuries, before the introduction of printing, manuscript books were being sold by dealers at fairs, by pedlars, and in London by shopkeepers, principally grocers and mercers. It seems fair to conclude that the largely professional reading public, of the clergy, of scholars and students, of doctors and lawyers, grew steadily throughout the Middle Ages, and that they were joined, in the later centuries, by a small but significant number of general readers. It is interesting that when Caxton began printing, some of his most prominent publications were in the field of general literature and in the vernacular, which, while pointing to major trends of the future, can be seen also as a response to a known demand from the later manuscript period. We know very little, unfortunately, of the growth, at this time, of a kind of reading very different not only from the medieval stock of the Scriptures, the Christian Fathers, and Latin and Greek secular authors, but also from the schoolbooks, the vernacular translations, and the poems, histories and romances. Yet the popularity of the chapbook, the jest-book, the ballad and the broadsheet dates at least from the six-teenth century, and this presupposes a reading public, however small and irregular, of a general kind. Estimates of literacy at this time vary from the more than 50% implied by More ('farre more than fowre partes of all the whole divided into tenne coulde never read englishe yet') to Gardiner's 'not the hundredth part of the realme'. In 1518 Copeland wrote, in dramatic reply to an author's request to him to print his book:

> At your instaunce I shall it gladly impresse
> But the utterance, I thynke, will be but small.
> Bokes be not set by: there times is past, I gesse;
> The dyse and cardes, in drynkynge wyne and ale,
> Tables, cayles, and balles, they be now sette a sale.
> Men lete theyr chyldren use all such harlotry,
> That byenge of bokes they utterly deny.

Certainly, if we set book prices then against the income even of priests and schoolmasters, it is easy to understand this complaint, prophetic as it is of so many to come. There has hardly been a generation since in which 'bokes be not set

by: there times is past, I gesse' has not been repeated, by
some of those directly concerned. Yet there were enough
books around, and apparently in demand, to make Colet,
at St Paul's School, 'abbanysh and exclude' such works as
'ratheyr may be called blotterature thenne literature'. The
appearance of this now familiar judgement makes one feel
that at least the beginnings of a true reading public, and of
the problems ever since associated with it, were then in
existence.

The history of the reading public, at anything more than a
technical level, is in fact complicated, throughout, by two
very difficult, and often confused, problems of value, which
in many cases have affected even a plain record. On the
one hand there is the fear that as the circle of readers extends,
standards will decline, and literature be threatened by
'blotterature'. Related to this, but involving other prejudices,
has been an essentially political fear that, if the common
man reads, both quality and order (sometimes the one
standing for the other) will be threatened. Intense feelings
about the threat to quality have led, too often, to quite
unrealistic accounts of the actual history of reading, of the
'then came Defoe' or 'then came *Tit-Bits*' kind of deluge.
At the same time, different authorities have at certain periods
openly exerted their power to prevent or limit the growth of
reading, or to prevent or limit the education from which it
naturally follows. No issue is more central in the history of
our culture, for the argument about quality and the argument about democracy are here so deeply intertwined as to
appear inseparable, and this has led again and again to a
deadlock in the cultural argument which has been profoundly discouraging and confusing. We must try to look at
the record again, setting the formulas aside.

The distinction between desirable and undesirable reading
is, through these early centuries of the formation of a reading
public, basically doctrinal, in relation to religion. For several
centuries, as we have seen in our study of education, the
distinction between improving Christian authors and distracting or debasing 'pagan' authors was repeatedly urged.
In the later Middle Ages there was a significant break from
this distinction, and the Renaissance spirit brought more

and more Greek and Latin authors from the 'pagan' into the 'classical' category. Yet this gain was limited, and in part cancelled, by two forces: first the long period of religious controversy, in reformation and counter-reformation, which led to new definitions of the desirable and the undesirable, in terms of orthodoxy and heresy; second, the renewal by Protestantism of the old distinction between works which improve and works which distract or corrupt the mind. In the former case, a proclamation of 1538 set up a censorship over books in English, whether home-produced or imported, and an Act of 1543, 'for the advancement of true religion and for the abolishment of the contrarie', forbade reading of any English Bible by artificers, journeymen, serving-men under the rank of yeoman, husbandmen, labourers, and all women other than those of noble or gentle rank. Meanwhile in the area of secular literature, there was a continuous campaign against plays and romances, which were not serious reading (a distinction that survives to this day in interpreting public library statistics), as contrasted with books on manners and behaviour, household management, travel, natural history, and public affairs (usually not contemporary). Such interventions and judgements as these of course influenced the development of reading, but they did not, in the end, determine it. A great deal of fiction and romance could be disguised as works of travel, history or manners, and the same elements, together with an otherwise stifled contemporary comment and criticism, were the basis of the popular trade in chapbooks and broadsheets and ballads. As late as the Elizabethan period, respect for the manuscript, and distaste for the publishing market, had important effects on the circulation of literature, and there were many of this courtly persuasion, as well as the Puritan opponents of fiction, to complicate the question of the reading public and its standards. Yet the publication of the plays of Shakespeare, Jonson and others marks a temporary advance: here was high literature, resting on both the classical and popular traditions, and evidently permanent, in spite of the Puritan objection to idle plays, the courtly objection to the vulgarity of the book trade, and the academic objection to the claim that English plays could be regarded as true literary works. This was also the great period of translations, and the quality of books available to the English reading public in fact rose steadily, though in ways that cut across most contemporary definitions of 'standards'. It is ironic to consider how many of the works for which we now honour the period would have been condemned by substantial sections of opinion as evidence of the idleness and vulgarity of the times.

The rise in reading, and in quality, was in fact steady. Prices ranged from Holinshed at 26s. to Shakespeare at 4d. or 6d. (the latter, however, the price of two dinners). The number of printers had risen from two or three at the beginning of the sixteenth century to 13 in 1558, 34 in 1563, 40 in 1577, and as many as 97 between 1590 and 1595. Trade protection, through patents, later limited the number of houses, but there were at least 60 in London in 1649 and again in 1660, and in the 1690s a quite rapid further expansion began, especially into the provinces. It is difficult to estimate the actual output of books as distinguished from ballads and pamphlets, but the trend is evident from figures of 13 titles in 1510, 28 in 1530, 85 in 1550, to perhaps 150 in 1581, a figure generally maintained until the further rapid rise in the period of the Civil War and Commonwealth. The Restoration brought a decline, and the average annual production settled at about 100 titles until the middle of the eighteenth century. At the same time sizes of editions rose from the sixteenth-century limit of some 1,500 (excepting grammars and prayer-books which went to 3,000) to an average of 2,000 which was maintained until well on into the eighteenth century. *Paradise Lost* sold 1,300 copies in two years, and the very popular *Emblems and Hieroglyphikes* of Quarles 5,000 in two years. Meanwhile we can gauge the size of the more general reading public by noting that one of the many popular 'prognosticating Almanacks' sold an average of more than 16,000 copies between 1646 and 1648, and the ballad, broadsheet and chapbook public must have been at least of the order of 20,000. In these early stages of the formation of the reading public, we can see a pattern to be repeated later on a much larger scale: the steady growth of a public interested in literature, philosophy and similar works; the more rapid growth of a public interested primarily in more occasional and ephemeral reading. The distinction of quality is not absolute, however, for a proportion of the occasional reading, especially in pamphlets, tracts, and ballads, marks on the one hand the transfer of popular traditional amusements into print, on the other hand a rise in social and especially political interests, reaching a climax in the Civil War.

After the Restoration, the situation becomes extremely difficult to analyse. The imperfect evidence that we have, in a number of fields, suggests on the one hand a continuation of the general pattern of the expansion—slow growth of the serious public, more rapid growth of the occasional public, but also the apparent confinement of the expansion to the growing middle class. The attitude to popular education was undoubtedly different, in the new period, and it seems probable that general literacy did not increase, and may even have declined, in the period between the Restoration and the end of the eighteenth century. It is from the 1690s that the growth of a new kind of middle-class reading public becomes evident, in direct relation to the growth in size and importance of a middle class defined as merchants, tradesmen, shopkeepers, and administrative and clerical workers. New forms of reading, in the newspaper, the periodical and the magazine, account for the major expansion, and behind them comes the novel, in close relation from its beginnings to this particular public. The 60 London printing houses at the Restoration had become 75 by 1724 and between 150 and 200 by 1757. By the 1740s the *Gentleman's Magazine* was selling 3,000 an issue, and leading newspapers were in the same range. The sales of novels increased, for example *Joseph Andrews* selling 6,500 copies in thirteen months, *Roderick Random* 5,000 in a year, *Sir Charles Grandison* 6,500 in a few months. These developments affected the whole structure of relationships between writers, book-sellers and readers, and Defoe could note in 1725:

Writing . . . is become a very considerable Branch of the English Commerce. The Booksellers are the Master Manufacturers or

Employers. The several Writers, Authors, Copyers, Sub-Writers and all other operators with Pen and Ink are the workmen employed by the said Master-Manufacturers.

This observation was converted by Goldsmith into the familiar qualitative judgement, of

that fatal revolution whereby writing is converted to a mechanic trade.

More sharply than in the earlier period, the spread of print could be seen as a threat to literature and learning, and the condemnation of light periodicals, of newspapers, and of novels was often made. Again, however, the judgement becomes difficult, when seen in historical perspective. The newspapers and periodicals, bad as they often were, seem, as new forms, an absolute cultural gain, while a proportion of the novels must be seen as a major literary contribution, comparable in importance to the high Elizabethan drama, which had itself rested on a large amount of inferior work.

Yet, while this expansion continued, there was surprisingly little change in the general output of books. Until well after mid-century the annual number of titles remained what it had been in the seventeenth century, and a print of 2,000 copies of Johnson's *Dictionary* took more than four years to sell. When we look at prices, this situation becomes clearer. Pope's *Iliad* sold at six guineas the set; a volume of Clarendon's *History* at 30s.; Hickes's *Thesaurus* at £5. Meanwhile novels were sold at 3s. bound, or 2s. 3d. unbound, per volume, so that *Tom Jones* could be bought for 18s. or 13s. 6d., while *Robinson Crusoe*, in a different form, was available at 5s. At these prices, book-buying was obviously socially limited, and it is significant that the eighteenth-century public depended, to a considerable extent, on devices of corporate buying. Proprietary libraries, usually attached to Literary and Philosophical societies, dealt mainly with history, philosophy, poetry, theology and science. Book clubs developed in many towns, buying more generally. For fiction, the circulating libraries, characteristically first prominent in the spas, spread rapidly, though the subscription, at lowest 10s. 6d., was again a limiting factor. Even newspapers and periodicals, their prices reckoned in pence, were widely read through coffee-houses and clubs. These factors determined the rate of expansion of the middle-class public, but if popular education had been better a more general expansion would have been possible, using similar devices. As it was, the demand for almanacs, chapbooks, ballads, broadsheets and pamphlets seems not to have slackened, and may well have increased. Pamphlets sold at 3*d*. to 1*s*., chapbooks and broadsheets at 1*d*. to 6*d*., ballads at ½*d*. to 1*d*., and we know of at least one pamphlet selling 105,000 copies in 1750. A number of novels were serialized in newspapers and chapbooks, and it seems probable that in London and the larger towns the reading public (and the read-to public) was reasonably large.

It is in the last third of the century that new factors enter. Through the Methodists, who vigorously organized popular reading and produced tracts to serve it, and through the wider Sunday-school movement, the beginnings of a more general expansion were visible. The rise in political interest produced a situation roughly comparable with that before the Civil War. In 1776 Price's *Observations on the Nature of Civil Liberty* sold 60,000 copies, and in 1791, Paine's *Rights of Man*, even at 3*s*., sold 50,000 copies within a few weeks, and in its cheaper edition sold very widely indeed, though the estimated figure of 1,500,000 is difficult to believe. It seems clear that the extension of political interest considerably broadened the reading public by collecting a new class of readers, from groups hardly touched by the earlier expansion. The annual output of books was now also rising sharply, and averaged 372 in the years 1792–1802, as compared with the 100 at which it was still stuck in the 1750s. In the matter of price, a curious situation emerged in this period, in that the ordinary price rose very sharply, after 1780, and small editions at high prices became more popular with publishers than larger editions at mid-century prices. On the other hand, the first regular cheap reprints date from the same period: Bell's *Poets*, *British Theatre*, and *Shakespeare*, at as low as 6*d*., followed by other standard reprint series including fiction. The development of serialization, which had been popular throughout the century, was a notable advance, and while the orthodox publishers went on raising prices, many newcomers, using everything from respectable reprint series to pirating and undercutting, permanently enlarged the book-reading public to a point where it came into proportion with the expanded public for newspapers and periodicals.

Once again, the basic trends of the growth of a reading public are evident, but the period now being entered brought so marked an increase in the pace of the general expansion that the problem of proportion became acute. The real break to a very rapid expansion did not come until the 1830s. The generation of the French Revolution, and that of Peterloo, was deeply affected, in its reading, by the political crisis, in a number of ways. The eighteenth-century expansion continued along familiar lines, with a marked increase in the annual issue of books, from 372 in the years 1792–1802 to an average of 580 between 1802 and 1827. A large part of this increase was in fiction, and directly related to the success of the circulating libraries. The annual issue of novels rose sharply in the 1780s, and went on increasing at a rapid rate. Yet book prices also continued to rise and the reading public did not increase proportionately with the increase in titles. The ordinary size of editions varied from an average of 750 for more serious works to about 1,250 for a circulating-library novel. The most popular author, Scott, sold 11,000 copies of *Marmion* in a year, at 31s. 6d., and 10,000 of *Rob Roy*, at the same price, in a fortnight. These figures represent only a modest advance over the popular novels of the mid-eighteenth century, whereas the annual sale of newspapers, over the same sixty years, had risen from 7,000,000 to over 24,000,000. In the field between books and newspapers, the success of serialization, or number-publication, continued, and cheap reprint series continued to appear, though still on a very limited scale. Radical writers continued to expand the public, John Wade's *Black Book* selling 10,000 an issue, and Cobbett's *Address to the Journeymen and Labourers* selling 200,000 in two months. But it was here, precisely, that active measures were taken against the expansion, on the grounds of the political dangers of too widespread reading. The heavy taxation of newspapers was supplemented by a series of prosecutions aimed at killing the whole radical press. A different response to the same danger was the development of cheap tracts, of an 'improving' kind, designed to counter the success of Cobbett and others, and these were heavily subsidized in this first stage. Meanwhile, at the really popular level, the sale of almanacs, ballads and broadsheets continued to increase, and the most remarkable publishing figures of the whole period are those for the products of James Catnach, whose accounts of murders and executions reached a climax with 1,166,000 copies of the 'Last Dying Speech and Confession' of the murderer of Maria Marten. If we look at the whole situation as the 1830s are entered, we find a range in reading matter basically similar to that of the first period of printing, but with two critical changes: a growing disparity between the actual circulation of literature on the one hand and the broadsheet on the other; a new middle range of novels, magazines and newspapers, serving the still expanding middle-class public. It was in this new range, in the 1830s, that the next major phase of the expansion occurred.

Newspapers led the way, with the first application of steam-printing, and in the 1830s Sunday papers of the police-gazette kind and very similar to the old broadsheets took a lead which they have never lost over the mainly political newspapers established in the eighteenth century. Cheap magazines followed, although the radicals were replaced by the popular educators, and both, in the 1840s, by a range of 'improving' family publications. Serial fiction expanded its public, and an edition of 400 for the first number of *Pickwick* grew to 40,000 for the fifteenth, about the same circulation as the *Penny Magazine*. Figures of 100,000 for serial fiction were later reached both by Dickens and by Reynolds. An expansion in cheap reprints of both fiction and non-fiction followed the spread of steam-printing to books in the 1830s and 1840s, and there was a marked reduction in price following the development of new methods of binding, with boards and cloth replacing leather. The annual issue of titles rose from 580 in the 1820s to more than 2,600 by mid-century, and the average price of new books fell from 16s. to just over 8s. A large proportion of the increase in titles was in fiction, and a large part of the reduction in average price was due to the cheap series, many other prices actually rising.

The population was rapidly increasing, through this same period. A mainland population of some seven million in 1750 had become eleven million in 1801, nearly twenty-one million in 1851, and thirty-seven million in 1901. It is probable that until the end of the eighteenth century the literate proportion of this population increased only slowly, and the rise was still gradual with the slow and uneven development of nineteenth-century elementary education. Yet a rise it certainly was, and we can gain some indication of the trend from one narrow field in which, from 1837, national statistics were kept. Ability to sign the marriage register is obviously a meagre indication of capacity to read a book, but it was a period in which reading was much more commonly taught than writing, and the rate of change may be of some importance. A sample shows:

Able to sign	Men	Women	Total
1839	66·3%	50·5%	58·4%
1873	81·2%	74·6%	77·9%
1893	95·0%	94·3%	94·65%

We already know from the history of elementary education that there was no sudden opening of the floodgates of literacy as a result of the 1870 Education Act. The basic history of literacy in the century seems to be a steady expansion, led by the towns (though unevenly between new and old) and by men, and this simple expansion was also a steady development of real reading capacity, as the length of schooling increased. While this expansion affected the reading public (giving some basis, for example, for the radical and Sunday press), it is misleading to think of the general expansion of the reading public, at this time, in simple relation to the question of literacy. Not only in books, but also in magazines and newspapers, the expanded reading public at mid-century was still well below the lowest possible estimate for general literacy. The true history is much more the bringing of cheaper reading matter to the already literate part of the population. If we make a rough calculation of the situation in 1830 and then in 1860, translating sales into readership and expressing this as a percentage of the adult population, we find the following results. In 1820, the public reading daily newspapers is about 1%, that for Sunday newspapers just over 1%, that for magazines about 3%, and that for occasional broadsheets about 10%. In 1860, the daily newspaper public has risen to 3%, the Sunday newspaper public to 12%, the magazine public to nearly 20%. All these figures are well below the actually literate proportion of the population, at either period. If we turn to books, we find a similar rate of growth in actual editions, though the number of titles had greatly increased. Where *The Lady of the Lake* had sold 20,000 in a year, *In Memoriam* sold 25,000 in its first eighteen months, and the *Lays of Ancient Rome* 46,000 in a cheap edition. In fiction, *Uncle Tom's Cabin*, in 1852, sold 150,000 in the first six months, but this was exceptional. While Dickens and Reynolds might reach 100,000 in serial form, Thackeray's estimate of his readership, in 1857, was 15,000, and a marked success like George Eliot's *Adam Bede* sold, in its first year, 3,350 in its original edition, and 11,000 in a cheaper edition. It would seem that the book-reading public, at mid-century, was still a tiny minority, though it was certainly increasing, both as a proportion of the population, and in real figures. However, with the general expansion under way, the relationship between what can be called the literary public and the more general reading public was significantly changing. The difference had always been there; the 'prognosticating Almanack' had sold ten times more widely than *Paradise Lost*, just as the *News of the World* now sold ten times more widely than *Adam Bede*. But the disparity in actual figures was now becoming startling, and the familiar arguments about quality, with the development of a 'mass' reading public, acquired a new urgency.

In fact, as we have seen, there was no 'mass' public at this stage. In the most popular form of reading, the newspaper, there was not even a majority public until our own century, Sunday papers reaching this stage before the 1914–1918 war, and daily papers just after it. Yet at the end of the first period of major expansion, in the 1850s, the outline of the new publishing situation was sufficiently clear. Since the 1830s, but now at an increasing rate, the reading public was becoming large enough to attract a new kind of speculator. Defoe's description of writing as a 'very considerable Branch of the English Commerce', and of its organization in the typical forms of capitalist industry, had been an accurate foresight of a situation which only fully revealed itself when the market became really large. Bell in newspapers, Catnach in broadsheets, Lloyd in penny fiction, were the forerunners of a new kind of organization. The problem of distribution was crucial, and in books, by the middle of the nineteenth century, the success of the circulating libraries had reached the point where the tastes and demands of their proprietors had an important effect on what was published. At the same time, serving that part of the public which could afford an annual subscription of a guinea (at a time when the average lower-middle-class income was £90, and the middle-class range was £150–£400), the circulating libraries tended to keep prices high, and to limit expansion. Several factors combined to break through this situation, and to revolutionize the distribution not only of magazines and newspapers, but of books. The railway system is the most evident, for it was in the bookstalls at the new stations, notably those of W. H. Smith, that the public could be reached in a new way. The cheap Parlour Library, and then the Railway Library, poured through this new outlet: the yellow-backs, with glossy covers, illustrated in colour, and carrying advertising on their backs. The last taxes were withdrawn from newspapers, advertisements, and paper. Printing machinery was being rapidly improved, and new paper-making processes (esparto from 1860, wood pulp from the 1880s) were successfully developed. The general income level was rising, and the middle and lower middle classes in particular were rapidly expanding, in a changing society and economy. This was the period of opportunity, but while the speculators seized it, the pub-

lishers of traditional books, largely tied to the old circulating-library public, were very slow to react. As late as 1880,
Matthew Arnold observed:

> As our nation grows more civilized, as a real love of reading comes
> to prevail more widely, the system which keeps up the present
> exorbitant price of new books in England, the system of lending-
> libraries from which books are hired, will be seen to be, as it is,
> eccentric, artificial and unsatisfactory in the highest degree. It is a
> machinery for the multiplication and protection of bad literature,
> and for keeping good books dear.

Instead of new writing of quality being immediately available at the low prices now possible, the market was being
dominated by

> a cheap literature, hideous and ignoble of aspect, like the tawdry
> novels which flare in the bookshelves of our railway stations, and
> which seem designed, as so much else that is produced for the use of
> our middle-class seems designed, for people with a low standard of
> life.

It will certainly help us to understand the problems of the
expansion if we remember in this now familiar kind of judgement Arnold's ascription of a low standard to the 'middle
class'. For the essential argument *must* be detached from its
ordinary confusion with vicarious contempt for a 'lower'
social group. The whole argument about 'cheap literature' has been compromised by its use as a form of class-
distinction, whereas the real problem is always the relation
between inexperience and the way this is met. Certainly, in a
limited way, it would do middle-class people good to remember that these problems did not arrive with working-class
literacy; that new middle-class groups made all the same mis-
takes and were as evidently exploited. We shall never see this
problem straight if we convert it to the truly endless snigger-
ing of the arrived (the most corrupt culture now existing in
Britain is that broad range of laughing at the comic working
classes, from *Mrs Dale's Diary* to *Take it from Here*, from the
Daily Telegraph to the *Daily Mirror*, and from the average
West End revue to the party-pieces in which young educated
people speak in amusing 'common' accents). To be against

the people who face these new problems is a trivial evasion of the real issues which Arnold (though himself at times guilty of just this error) both defined and worked to resolve.

In the second half of the nineteenth century, the size of the publishing industry—this 'Branch of the English Commerce'—was growing very rapidly. It was an important new period in the expansion of magazines, and in books, eventually, cheap reprint series of standard literature took their place alongside the yellow-backs. The high-price circulating libraries slowly declined, and by the end of the century cheaper libraries—notably Boots' from 1900—were taking their place, with a larger public. The public libraries, growing slowly from mid-century, added an increasingly important sector.

By 1900, the characteristic modern forms of organization of the reading public had been discovered and set, and both their advantages and their limitations were evident. The history now becomes one of expansion within these forms. The great expansion in newspapers and magazines will be studied separately. In book publication, the annual issue rose from 2,600 in the 1850s to 6,044 in 1901, and to 12,379 in 1913. Falling during and just after the First War, it was back to 12,690 (including 3,190 reprints) in 1924, and by 1937 had risen to 17,137 (including 6,347 reprints). The annual average fell again during the Second War, but was back to 17,072 (including 5,334 reprints) by 1950 and in 1958 was 22,143 (with 5,971 reprints). Costs have risen again, and the most notable change of recent years has been the increasing number of paper-backs, mainly reprints but including, interestingly, a proportion of new works. This is a development of great importance to the expansion as a whole.

The commercial circulating libraries have continued to grow, at different levels, and it has been estimated (for there are no complete figures) that they now issue nearly 200 million volumes a year. Serious booksellers are still insecure, but for paper-backs many new selling points have been found, from tobacconists' shops to garages, to add to the railway book-stalls and the chain store. The public library service was available to 62·5% of the population by 1911, and to 96·3% by

1926. It is now almost universally available, though with many inequalities between different kinds of community. The figures for public library book issues have steadily risen, and had reached 312 million in 1948–1949 and 431 million in 1957–1958. Taking all kinds of book distribution into account, a figure of about 15 books read annually per head of population is about the present stage, or 20 per head of the adult population. The average, of course, conceals very unequal individual uses, but it is probable that in the 1950s, for the first time, we had a majority book-reading public (as compared with a majority Sunday-newspaper public by 1910 and a majority daily-newspaper public by the 1914–1918 war).

With this expansion, the argument about quality—the old distinction between literature and 'blotterature'—has inevitably sharpened. But this can only be negotiated in terms of historical analysis and by reference to the development of all parts of the society. The worst error is to suppose that our ancestors—the date may vary, but they are always ancestors—had no such problems. On the evidence this is plainly untrue; it has been a problem of the whole expansion. The more relevant inquiry is into the changing character of both literature and 'blotterature'—in different societies and ways of life. On the one hand we must remember that two forms condemned in their day as low and idle—the Elizabethan popular drama and the eighteenth- and nineteenth-century novel—are now heavily represented in our standard literature. The preservation of quality is by no means wholly the preservation of traditionally sanctioned forms. The newspaper and the periodical are also substantial gains, in themselves, in spite of very many bad examples. On the other hand there is that body of work best described by Coleridge as

> characterized by the power of reconciling the two contrary yet coexisting propensities of human nature, namely, indulgence of sloth and hatred of vacancy.

Reading as this kind of easy drug is the permanent condition of a great bulk of ephemeral writing. But the question still is one of the circumstances in which the drug becomes necessary. I think there are certain circumstances—times of ill-ness, tension, disturbing growth as in adolescence, and simple fatigue after work—which are much too easily over-looked in sweeping condemnations of 'reading as addiction'. I doubt if any educated person has not used books—any books—in this way. The kind of attention required by serious literature is both personally and socially only variously possible. The conditions of social variation ought to command our main attention: the association of railway travel with an increase in this kind of reading is obviously significant. More difficult to analyse is the evident distinc-tion between ways of living which stimulate attention and allow rest, and ways which produce neither attention nor rest, but only an unfocussed restlessness that has somehow to be appeased. These are radical questions about the society as a whole, and my own view is that there are deep reasons in our social organization for the especial prevalence of this mood: in particular the difficulty of living a restlessness through to some of its sources, as we find so many channels blocked. These problems cannot be solved in the field of publications alone, but within this limited field we can all see the difference between relatively harmless and harmful drugging, and such evidence as that adduced by Q. D. Leavis and more recently by Richard Hoggart is of great importance, if its full social context is always taken into account. It is the business of education to discover, teach and discuss this difference, as well as the larger difference between literature and the ephemeral. It is the business of the society (neglected except in the much less important field of 'ob-scenity', which has been thoroughly muddled) to create and maintain the conditions in which this necessarily difficult growth can go on, in particular by the creation and strength-ening of institutions based on some more adequate principle than that of quick profit, with the speculators setting the pace. The changes we have traced, and the consequent realization that forms of production and distribution are not permanent, may at least clear the way to our consideration of the next stage.

THREE

The Growth of the Popular Press

THE development of the press in England, in particular the growth of the popular press, is of major importance in any account of our general cultural expansion. The vital period of development is significant in itself, from the establishment of a middle-class reading public in the late seventeenth and early eighteenth centuries, through the widening of this public to the virtually universal readership of our own time. And the newspaper, as a continuing element in this period of growth, is an obviously significant element for analysis, both because of this continuity, and because of its status as the most widely distributed printed product.

Some of the facts of the development are very difficult to establish—a few indeed are impossible, due to records lost or not kept. But there are quite enough facts to establish a general pattern, and the histories of newspapers reproduce these faithfully enough. When it comes to analysis, however, there are two general defects. There is still a quite widespread failure to co-ordinate the history of the press with the economic and social history within which it must necessarily be interpreted. Even more, there is a surprising tendency to accept certain formulas about the development, which seem less to arise from the facts of press development than to be brought to them. The general cultural expansion has been interpreted in a particular way, and the history of the press has been fitted, often against the facts, to this general interpretation.

The most common of these formulas is that before the coming of *Tit-Bits* and *Answers* in the 1880s, and of Northcliffe's halfpenny *Daily Mail* in 1896, there was no cheap popular press in England. The basis of the new press, it is said, was the Education Act of 1870, by means of which the ordinary people of England learned to read. At this point, the formula has alternative endings. Either, as a result of this process, a popular press, the keystone of a lively democracy, could be established. Or, with the entry of the masses on to the cultural scene, the press became, in large part, trivial and degraded, where before, serving an educated minority, it had been responsible and serious.

Now these alternative endings hardly matter, and the debate between them is really irrelevant, for the fact is that to anyone who knows the history of the press, or the history of education, such an account is nonsense. It can be traced, interestingly enough, to Northcliffe, who said to Max Pemberton in 1883:

> The Board Schools are turning out hundreds of thousands of boys and girls annually who are anxious to read. They do not care for the ordinary newspaper. They have no interest in society, but they will read anything which is simple and is sufficiently interesting. The man who has produced this *Tit-Bits* has got hold of a bigger thing than he imagines. He is only at the beginning of a development which is going to change the whole face of journalism. I shall try to get in with him.

This is the frank thinking of a speculator (and was noted as such by Gissing in *New Grub Street*). As an indication of attitude it is important. But it became something more. R. C. K. Ensor, in the Oxford History *England 1870–1914* referred to 1870 as a watershed, and spoke of a 'dignified phase of English journalism' which

> reigned unchallenged till 1886 and indeed beyond. Yet the seed of its destruction was already germinating. In 1880, ten years after Forster's Education Act . . . Newnes became aware that the new schooling was creating a new class of potential readers—people who had been taught to decipher print without learning much else. He started *Tit-Bits*.

After this, the formula was firm in most educated minds, and has found its casual way into print an uncountable number of times. We find even the 1947 Royal Commission on the press saying:

> The 1890s saw the introduction of newspapers sold at a halfpenny and addressed, not to the highly-educated and politically-minded

minority, but to the millions whom the Education Act of 1870 had equipped with the ability to read.

But if, as commonly, we start an inquiry with an assumption like this, offered as fact when it is not fact, it is unlikely that we shall go on to ask the really relevant contemporary questions, or reach the point at which our present urgencies can be illuminated by the actual lessons of history.

The facts, it is hoped, will become clear in the account that follows. But it seems worth setting down first, in summary, the cardinal points of the history, and the questions they indicate. The newspaper was the creation of the commercial middle class, mainly in the eighteenth century. It served this class with news relevant to the conduct of business, and as such established itself as a financially independent institution. At the same time, in periodicals and magazines, the wider interests of the middle class as a whole were being served: the formation of opinion, the training of manners, the dissemination of ideas. From the middle of the eighteenth century, these functions, in part, were additionally taken up by the newspapers. In relation to the formation of opinion, successive Governments tried to control and bribe the newspapers, but eventually failed because of their essentially sound commercial basis. When one of these newspapers, *The Times* in the early nineteenth century, claimed its full independence, it found that it was there for the taking, and with the new mechanical (steam) press as its agent, a powerful position, and wide middle-class distribution, could be achieved. The daily press, led by *The Times*, became a political estate, on this solid middle-class basis.

Before this had been achieved, however, other points of growth were evident. Between the 1770s and the 1830s, but particularly in the last twenty years of this period, repeated attempts, against severe Government repression, were made to establish a press with a different social basis, among the newly organizing working class. These attempts, in their direct form, were beaten down, but a press with a popular public was in fact established, in another way. This was through the institution of the Sunday paper, which, particularly from the 1820s, took on a wholly different character and function from the daily press. Politically, these papers were radical, but their main emphasis was not political, but a miscellany of material basically similar in type to the older forms of popular literature: ballads, chapbooks, almanacs, stories of murders and executions. From 1840 on, the most widely selling English newspaper was not *The Times*, but one or other of these cheap (penny) Sunday papers.

In 1855, with the removal of the last of the taxes on newspapers, the daily press was transformed. A cheap (penny) metropolitan daily press, led by the *Telegraph*, quickly took over leadership from papers of the older type, led by *The Times*, and gained rapidly in an expanding lower-middle class. At the same time, a provincial daily press was firmly established. With improvements in printing, with falling prices for newsprint, and with railway distribution, circulations grew rapidly, and were around 700,000 in 1880. Still, however, the Sunday press was in the lead, and by 1890 had reached 1,725,000, with a leading paper selling nearly a million. In the 1870s and 1880s, meanwhile, a new kind of evening paper, taking much of its journalistic method from the Sunday press, was successfully launched.

In the 1890s, after a period of renewed expansion in popular periodicals, the spread of the daily paper through the rapidly-growing lower-middle class, especially in the large towns, was notably forwarded by a cheaper daily paper, the halfpenny *Daily Mail*—a conscious imitation of *The Times* for a different public. The basis of the change was economic, in the substitution, for the old kind of commercial class support, of a new revenue, based on the new 'mass' advertising. By 1900, the daily public had climbed (in a still quite gradual curve) to 1,500,000, and by 1910 to 2,000,000. The Sunday press was still well in the lead, with its older and somewhat different public.

In 1920, after the demand for news in the war, the daily public was above 5,000,000, and the Sunday public above 13,000,000. It was now, in the period between the wars, that expansion of the daily press to the working class really began, although by 1937 the daily public was still smaller than the Sunday public had been in 1920. It was now, also, that the transformation of content of the daily papers radically occurred, in the course of a race for circulation and thus for the 'mass'-advertising revenue without which the papers would be running at a great loss. The *Mail* was overtaken by a new type of paper, the *Express*, which carried the mixture of political paper and magazine miscellany much further than hitherto—a mixture clearly visible in changing appearance. The full expansion, to something like the full reading public, took place in the daily press during the second war, reaching over 15,000,000 in 1947. The Sunday press, meanwhile, had increased to over 29,000,000. The really steep curves, and the real establishment of a popular press, occur, in the Sunday press between 1910 and 1947, in the daily press between 1920 and 1947. It was an establishment, moreover, first on the basis, for the press as a whole, of the traditional content and methods of the Sunday papers since the 1820s, and, second, in terms of the new economic basis of newspapers—running at a loss and making up with the revenue from 'mass' advertising. In this same period, however, a new type of Sunday paper (*Observer*, *Sunday Times*), consciously imitating the methods of the older daily press, won a growing public, while the surviving older-style papers also markedly gained.

During the last decade of the major expansion, a new type of paper, the *Daily Mirror*, took over leadership from the *Express*, and is now clearly ahead. This is an even further application of the technique of combining a news sheet with a miscellany, and involved a further change of appearance. In method and content, the *Mirror* draws partly on the traditional Sunday newspaper, partly on the techniques of the new advertising which was now the daily paper's commercial basis. In the 1950s, the general expansion has slowed, with the whole reading public effectively covered, and there appears to be taking place within the achieved situation a kind of polarization, with success going, on the one hand to the most extreme form of paper-miscellany, on the other hand to the most clearly surviving newspapers of the older style. Papers representing earlier stages of the mixture between newspaper and miscellany are losing readers.

Now the questions one asks from these cardinal points

(which need to be amplified from the fuller account that follows) are these. First, what is the real social basis of the popular press as now established? It grew, in content and style, from an old popular literature, with three vital transforming factors: first, the vast improvement in productive and distributive methods caused by industrialization; second, the social chaos and the widening franchise, again caused by industrialization and the struggle for democracy; third, the institution, as a basis for financing newspapers, of a kind of advertising made necessary by a new kind of economic organization, and a differently organized public. Literacy was not a transforming factor, in itself, even supposing that the 1870 Act was the basis of popular literacy, which it was not. There were enough literate adults in Britain in 1850 to buy more than the total copies of the *Daily Mirror* now sold each day. Literacy was only a factor in terms of the other changes. In seeking improvement in the popular press, therefore, while it is wise to work for a higher literacy, we shall only arrive at the centre of the matter by asking questions about the social organization of an industrial society, about its economic organization, and about the ways in which its services, such as newspapers, are paid for.

Second, what is the communication-basis of the popular press? The eighteenth-century *Advertisers*, and the nineteenth-century *Times*, had, as their basis, the image of a particular kind of reader, in an identifiable class to which the owners and journalists themselves belonged. The twentieth-century popular press has, as its image, a particular formula, which, beginning perhaps in the 1840s, has been rapidly developed since the institution of the new advertising in the 1890s. This formula is that of the 'mass', or 'masses', a particular kind of impersonal grouping, corresponding to aspects of the social and industrial organization of our kind of capitalist and industrialized society. The essential novelty of the twentieth-century popular press is its discovery and successful exploitation of this formula, and the important question to ask about it, while it is wise to attend to the detailed devices of the formula, is a question about the relation of the 'masses' formula to the actual nature of our society, to the expansion of our culture, and to the struggle for social democracy.

These questions are at once the means of understanding our press in some depth, and the means of understanding the nature and conditions of our expanding culture, to which it is so important an index. To ask them, and to look for answers in the field which they open, is the real consequence of our actual press history. While we hold to existing formulas we shall ask wrong questions, or be left to the sterile debate between those who say that at any rate the press is free, and those who say that at any price it is trivial and degraded. We need to get beyond this deadlock, and the history of the press is the means.

I turn now to the actual history, in seven periods: 1665–1760, the early middle-class press; 1760–1836, the struggle for press freedom, and the new popular press; 1836–1855, the popular press expanding; 1855–1896, the second phase of expansion; 1896–1920, the third phase; 1920–1947, the expansion completed; the 1950s, and the new tendencies within an achieved expansion.

(i): 1665–1760

The story of the foundation of the English Press is, in its first stages, the story of the growth of a middle-class reading public. The first half of the eighteenth century is a critical period in the expansion of English culture, and the newspaper and periodical are among its most important products, together with the popular novel and the domestic drama. The expansion is significant, in that it took place over a wide range and at many different levels. The development of the press fully reflects the range and the levels, and sets a pattern in this kind of expansion which is vitally important in all its subsequent history.

The cultural needs of a new and powerful class can never merely be set aside, but the ways in which they are met may be determined by various legal, technical and political factors. The factors which most clearly affected the press, in the late seventeenth and early eighteenth centuries, were, first, the state of communications, in particular the postal services, and, second, the passage from State-licensed printing to conditions of commercial printing for the market. State control over printing was, in its turn, an obvious political control over the powerful new means of disseminating news and opinions.

There had been many efforts, in the sixteenth and early seventeenth centuries, to use printing for this obvious social purpose, but all had been hampered by direct political censorship. In one form or another, the *Corantos*, *Diurnalls*, *Passages* and *Intelligencers* did their best to break through, yet all these were still, essentially, books or pamphlets. The establishment of the weekly public post in 1637 made possible a new technique, that of the news-letter, which was circulated by subscription to booksellers, and which, being handwritten by scriveners in the booksellers' employ, escaped the restrictions on printing. This advance in freedom was, however, obviously technically regressive, and when the same freedom found a progressive technique the news-letters were left far behind. This was not to happen, however, until nearly the end of the century.

The important technical advance, the development of a news *paper* instead of a book or pamphlet, in fact took place under official direction. This was in 1665, when an official *Oxford Gazette* was 'published by Authority', in the new single-sheet form. This later became the *London Gazette*, now only an official publication, but then a true newspaper. In the same period, however, State control of printing was being put on a new basis. The Licensing Act of 1662, to prevent 'abuses in printing, seditious, treasonable and unlicensed books and pamphlets', limited the number of master printers to twenty; and in 1663 a Surveyor of the Press (L'Estrange) was appointed, with a virtual monopoly in printed news. Thus, while the right technical form was being found, the conditions for its exploitation were firmly refused.

Yet the balance of political power was now evidently changing, and as 1688 is a significant political date, so 1695 is significant in the history of the press. For in that year Parliament declined to renew the 1662 Licensing Act, and the stage for expansion was now fully set. In addition to the new freedom, there was also an improved postal service, with country mails on Tuesday, Thursday and Saturday, and a daily post to Kent. The expansion was not slow in coming, for in the years between 1695 and 1730 a public press of three kinds became firmly established: daily newspapers, provincial weekly newspapers, and periodicals. Between them, these new organs covered the whole range of the cultural expansion.

The first daily newspaper, the *Courant*, appeared in 1702, and was followed by the *Post* (1719), the *Journal* (1720), and the *Advertiser* (1730). Many thrice-weekly morning and evening papers began publication in the same period, on the days of the country mails. At the same time, provincial weekly papers were being established: two in 1695–1700; eight in 1701–1710; nine in 1711–1720; five in 1721–1730. In periodicals, Defoe's *Weekly Review* began in 1704, and Steele's *Tatler* in 1709. Almost immediately, however, a new form of State control was attempted, with the imposition of a Stamp Duty ($\frac{1}{2}d$. or $1d$. according to size) and an Advertisement Tax ($1s$. on each insertion), not to raise revenue, but as the most 'effectual way of suppressing libels'. The new form of control is characteristic of the new conditions: the replacement of State licensing by a market tax.

The pressures of the expansion in fact fairly easily absorbed these impositions. The daily press, in particular, was serving so obvious a need of the new class that hardly anything could have stopped it. A glance at its contents makes this clear, for the commercial interest could hardly have been better served. The news at first is mainly foreign, including news of markets and shipping. Of home news, a principal item is 'the Prices of Stocks, Course of Exchange, and Names and Descriptions of Persons becoming Bankrupt'. Lists of exports and imports are given, and after these come a few miscellaneous items of such other news as marriages, deaths, and inquests. Finally comes the material which was in fact to sustain the eighteenth-century newspaper: the body of small commercial advertisements. With the growth of trade, this last item became for a time the principal feature, and the *Advertiser*, 1730, conveniently marks this emphasis. It began as a strictly commercial sheet, and then broadened itself, when advertisements were short, to include 'the best and freshest accounts of all Occurrences Foreign and

Domestick'. It became the leading mid-eighteenth century newspaper, and the priority it gave to advertisements, in putting them rather than news on its front page, initiated a format of obvious subsequent importance.

At the same time, however, the broader interests of the rising class were being served, at many levels, by the periodical press. The daily newspapers ordinarily abstained from political comment, not because comment was thought unnecessary but because this could obviously be more conveniently done in periodical publications. Defoe's *Weekly Review* is the first of these political periodicals, and it had many successors and imitators. There was also, however, the need for social commentary, on manners and polite literature and the theatre. This was met by the *Tatler*, which again was widely imitated. After the first phase of establishment of these classes of periodical, a wide expansion took place between 1730 and 1760. The word 'magazine' conveniently marks the expansion, beginning with the *Gentleman's Magazine* in 1730 and going on, in rising scale, to the *London Magazine*, the *Universal Magazine*, the *Town and Country Magazine*, the *Oxford Magazine*, the *Magazine of Magazines*, and the *Grand Magazine of Magazines*. These publications illustrate very clearly the broadening cultural ambitions of the class of readers they served. Their contents vary in quality and intention: from original work that can properly be classed as literature, through polite journalism, to an obvious 'digest' function. It is what one has learned to recognize as characteristic of such a stage of expansion in a culture: a range of publications serving everyone from those who want a first-hand acquaintance with facts, literature, and opinion, to those who want these in summary and convenient form as a means of rapid cultural acquisition. In the whole field it is an impressive record of work, though it must not be idealized. There is much good writing, but also much self-conscious 'pre-digested' instruction in taste and behaviour, and some exploitation of such accompanying interests as gossip and scandal about prominent persons. There is not only Steele's *Tatler*, but Mrs de la Riviere Manley's *Female Tatler* (Mrs Manley was the author of *Secret Memoirs and Manners of Several*

Persons of Quality, of both Sexes); not only Johnson's essays in the *Universal Chronicle*, but also the *Grand Magazine of Magazines, or Universal Register*, 'comprising all that is curious, useful or entertaining in the magazines, reviews, chronicles . . . at home or abroad'. The fact is that when a culture expands it does so at all its levels of interest and seriousness, and often with some of these levels exploited rather than served.

Meanwhile, the daily newspaper was changing, alike in contents, organization, and ambition. Increasingly, features that had been left to the periodical press were being absorbed into the daily papers: comment, general news, and 'magazine interest' such as theatrical notices, light literature, and reviews. This expansion took place on the basis of a solid and growing commercial function. Since the 1740s, advertising had grown in volume, and a successful newspaper was an increasingly profitable business enterprise. One mark of this development is the beginning of a new type of ownership. Ordinarily, the first papers had been the property of printers, who had welcomed their regular printing as a way of keeping presses fully occupied. From a sideline, papers were becoming in some instances a main activity—a development which as a whole is not complete until the early nineteenth century. In this situation, the floating of joint stock companies to run newspapers, the printers being hired agents rather than proprietors, was a natural commercial development of the times. The first such company was formed in 1748, to run the *London Gazetteer*, and the change was later to be of considerable importance.

Circulations continued to rise. A total annual sale of 2,250,000 in 1711 had become 7,000,000 in 1753. Readership was much larger than sales, for more papers were taken in by coffee-houses and similar institutions than by private individuals. The raising of the Stamp Duty in 1757 did no more to check the expansion than had the original imposition. The time was coming, in fact, when with increased prosperity the papers would aspire to a higher political status. Their political importance was already sufficiently recognized to make them the objects of persistent Government bribery: Walpole, for example, paid out more than £50,000 to news-

papers and pamphleteers in the last ten years of his administration. But the time was coming when the freedom of the
press, as a political institution in its own right, would be
seriously claimed. The key issue in this was the freedom to
report Parliamentary proceedings, and here the periodicals
had been in the van. Cave began to report Parliamentary
debates in 1736, in the *Gentleman's Magazine*. When in
1738 this was declared a breach of privilege, Cave continued
to publish reports, as of the 'Senate of Lilliput', and in 1752
resumed direct reports, with only the first and last letters of
speakers' names. The battle was not yet won, but the claim
had been staked. For the next three-quarters of a century,
the freedom and political status of the press were to be
dominating issues in its development. For the newspaper
had broken out into the open market, and had prospered:
it now sought, with all those whose history had been similar,
to take a greater share in the government of the country.

(ii): 1760–1836

The first number of Wilkes's *North Briton*, in 1762, is a convenient introduction to the coming battle for independence.
Wilkes wrote:

> The liberty of the Press is the birthright of a Briton, and is justly
> esteemed the firmest bulwark of the liberties of this country.

By the end of the decade, the liberty had been taken, in the
remarkable series of Letters of Junius in a daily newspaper
of the old commercial kind, *The Public Advertiser*. Then, in
1771, at Wilkes's instigation, several papers began printing
full Parliamentary reports, and privilege, though not formally set aside, was successfully defied. This victory, however, was to some extent offset by Lord Mansfield's judicial
interpretation of the law of libel, in a case arising from a
Junius letter. This had the effect of making the Crown, rather
than a jury, decide whether a given publication was libellous,
and there were several prosecutions and sentences on printers,
in these terms, until the Libel Act of 1792 restored the
decision of substance to juries.

Yet while individual printers suffered, the press as a
whole was buoyant in these years. Two very important

newspapers, the *Morning Chronicle* and the *Morning Post*, were founded in 1769 and 1772 respectively. With these, the London daily press had reached the beginnings of its political establishment. *The Times* followed, in 1785. Although the Stamp Duty had been again raised, in 1776, circulation continued to grow. The 7,000,000 total annual sale of 1753 had become 12,230,000 in 1776, and by 1811 was to reach 24,422,000. In 1784 there were eight London morning papers, in 1790 fourteen. Distribution had been improved, first by the coming of the Mail Coach, in 1784, and then, in 1785, by the separation of newspaper distribution from the ordinary mails. The first regular evening paper appeared, as a result of these improvements, in 1788: the *Star*, which gained a circulation of 2,000. The *Courier* followed, in 1789, and reached a circulation of 7,000. The leading morning newspapers at this time had circulations varying between two and three thousand, and a profit could be shown on this. When the *Morning Post* temporarily declined, in the 1790s, circulation fell to 350 before closure was threatened. Meanwhile, in 1779, the first Sunday paper, the *Sunday Monitor*, had appeared, and was followed by many short-lived imitators and by others destined for success, *The Observer* (1791), *Bell's Weekly Messenger* (1796), and *The Weekly Dispatch* (1801). In every direction, the press was expanding, but at just this time taxes on it were sharply increased. In 1789 Stamp Duty was raised to 2*d.*, and the Advertisement Tax to 3*s.* In 1797, Stamp Duty went up to 3½*d.* In 1789 the practice of hiring out papers was forbidden, though not stopped. These measures produced a temporary decline in circulation, though demand continued to grow. In the excited political atmosphere following the French Revolution, the influence of the press was deeply feared by the Government. The Tory *Anti-Jacobin Review* puts the issue, and its context, most clearly, in 1801:

> We have long considered the establishment of newspapers in this country as a misfortune to be regretted; but, since their influence has become predominant by the universality of their circulation, we regard it as a calamity most deeply to be deplored.

The matter was not left at deploring alone. The subsidy system had been continued, and surviving accounts show substantial expenditure in 1782–1783, 1788, and 1789–1793. The latter years show nine papers in receipt of subsidies, from £600 p.a. to the *Morning Herald* and the *World*, through £300 to *The Times* to £100 to the *Public Ledger*. Production costs for the *Oracle* in 1794 show an annual expenditure of about £6,864, and for *The Times* in 1797 £8,112. Thus the subsidies quoted formed a notable but not necessarily decisive element in a paper's finances: the subsidy would clearly be welcome, but at the same time the *Oracle* could make a profit given a daily circulation of 1,700, and *The Times* in fact did make a profit on a circulation around 2,000. These figures exclude overheads on the debit side, and advertisement revenue to credit, but clearly, taken overall, the commercial position of the successful papers allowed independence if it was desired. At the same time, there were other means of Government influence. Direct payments were made to journalists, at least £1,637 in the year ending June 1793. Later, and rising to a peak in the 1820s, the Government tended to confine its advertisements to favourable newspapers. When the situation is seen as a whole, it seems that while influence could obviously be bought, it was bought because of the strength and effect of the press, and that this strength and effect—small circulations being multiplied by multiple readership, and made financially possible by the advertisement revenue which had throughout been the key to development—would make possible the achievement of real independence whenever a determined bid was made. There were, however, new counter-measures to come. In 1815, Stamp Duty was raised to 4*d*, and the Advertisement Tax to 3/6. As a direct result of these new impositions, an important new factor was introduced into press development. Cobbett, by dropping news and concentrating on opinion, sold his *Political Register* unstamped, and at 2*d*. weekly achieved the extraordinary sale of 44,000 (nearly half a million in actual readership). Wooler began his *Black Dwarf* in 1817, and achieved a sale of 12,000. Here, in these critical years, a popular press of a new kind was emerging, wholly independent in spirit, and reaching new classes of readers. The marked rise in the political temperature was creating a fully independent political press, and behind Cobbett and Wooler in this new spirit, if not in opinion, were the outspoken new quarterlies (The *Edinburgh Review*, 1802, and the rival *Quarterly Review*, 1809, each sold 14,000 in 1818), the Radical weeklies (*News*, 1805, and *Examiner*, 1819), and the growing independent spirit of *The Times* (Barnes was made editor in 1817). The spirit of independence came from all these sources, but Cobbett and Wooler were extending it to a new public. The Government was not long in counter-attack: the Circular Letter of 1816, and then two of the Six Acts of 1819, were directly aimed at suppressing press opinion ('blasphemous and seditious libels'), and the power of the new popular press was, if not crushed, at least gravely weakened. Lord Ellenborough explained the Government's attitude clearly:

> It was not against the respectable Press that this Bill (Newspaper Stamp Duties Act, 1819) was directed, but against a pauper press...

Ever since this period, there has been an important factual split between the 'pauper press', expressing new kinds of political and social opinion, and the 'respectable press', advancing to financial independence and editorial independence within the terms of 'respectable opinion'. It is easy to write the history of the press in terms of the latter alone, but the history of the independent radical press is fundamentally important. Against open repression, Cobbett, Wooler, Carlile, Hetherington and many others fought hard and well, and the Chartist press was an important temporary success. But the economic basis of such papers was and has remained profoundly difficult. As the line is followed down through Blatchford and Lansbury to the *Daily Worker* and *Tribune* of our own day, it is a story of continual financial pressure met by persistent voluntary or ill-paid effort, not only from journalists but from collectors and sellers serving a cause rather than a commercial enterprise. The resources of the 'respectable press', in advertising revenue and organized distribution, have hardly ever been available to this kind of paper, yet the new ventures have kept coming, in direct relation to phases of political change. Without this dissenting press, the history not only of journalism but of politics and opinion would be very different.

The fact is that the economic organization of the press in Britain has been predominantly in terms of the commercial middle class which the newspapers first served. When papers organized in this way reached out to a wider public, they brought in the new readers on a market basis and not in terms of participation or genuine community relationships. As the new public appeared, in the time of Cobbett, the beginning of this long history was evident. The community as a whole was not providing its newspapers, but having them provided for it by particular interests. The radical press diverged, on a political basis, while the 'respectable' press went on to commercial independence, not only from the Government, but eventually from the society.

The years between 1820 and 1850, in which the independent radical press made its first sustained effort, saw *The Times* move to a new position. Opposing the Government on Peterloo, taking the popular side in the Queen Caroline controversy, it steadily emerged as the principal organ of 'respectable' Reform, with a cohering and growing middle-class public. Its sales had reached 7,000 by 1820, and in the Caroline controversy rose temporarily to more than 15,000. With its more radical rivals openly suppressed, it moved ahead on the basis of its solid commercial organization, with growing advertising support from the class which it politically represented. That *The Times* took the lead, rather than some other paper of the same general kind, is due to the combination of this economic basis for independence with the decisive desire for it, in the adoption of a Reform policy in the critical years between 1815 and 1832. There is another, technical, reason. From its foundation, *The Times* had been closely connected with improvements in printing (it was in fact founded to advertise the new 'Logographic' press). Now, in this decisive period, it was always technically ahead. The first steam printing machine in the world printed *The Times* in 1814 (after experiments since 1807). From 250 sheets, the hourly rate was raised to 1,100 and then 1,800 (900 on both sides), and further improvements, in

The Times office, raised this by 1827 to 4,000 on both sides. Expansion of circulation had been limited, previously, by just this printing-rate factor. Thus, its commercial status, its policy of middle-class reform, and its technical superiority, gave *The Times* its decisive lead. The factors are interrelated, for alike in its commercial, political and technical elements, *The Times* was the perfect organ of the middle-class reading public which had created the newspaper press, and was now carrying it with it to a share in the government of the country.

Certain other aspects of press development in this period must be briefly noted. The most important is the growth of the Sunday papers, whose beginnings have been noted. By 1810, these had circulations well above those of the daily papers, with a leading circulation of 10,000, which was not to be reached by *The Times* until the 1820s. Most of the leading papers were for Reform, and had an important political influence. At the same time, however, led by the *Dispatch*, they were beginning to give a good deal of space to detailed accounts of murders, rapes, seductions, and similar material, and also to sport (racing, wrestling and prize-fighting). From 1815 on this tendency is clearly marked, and a typical front page of the 1820s, from *Bell's Life in London*, describes its contents as 'combining, with the News of the Week, a rich Repository of Fashion, Wit, and Humour, and the interesting Incidents of Real Life', which in practice means a column of foreign news, a column report of a lively election meeting, half a column of general domestic news, an account of some 'amusing cases' of corpulency, and a miscellany including reports of two murders, a prison-break attempt, and a robbery. The style of reporting is direct, and there are only small headlines. Since the increase in Stamp Duty, all papers had used small and close print, and avoided any waste of space. All are consequently very difficult to read compared even with eighteenth-century papers. It should be noted, incidentally, that repeated attempts were made to declare Sunday newspapers illegal, but in spite of great strength of feeling in the matter, all the attempts failed. While allowing for the terms of polemic in this context, it seems probable that the Sunday papers reached poorer people than did the 'respectable' daily press.

The other main development in this period was in magazines. The successful quarterlies were joined by such monthlies as *Blackwood's* (1817) and the *London Magazine* (1820), and by a new type of weekly, widely regarded as 'scandalous', in *John Bull* (1820), which quickly achieved a 10,000 circulation. There were successful new literary weeklies, and then, in the early 1830s, the extraordinarily successful cheap magazines, *Chambers'*, *Penny*, and *Saturday*, all founded in 1832, which achieved circulations varying between 50,000 and 200,000—a decisive expansion into a new reading class. Though intended for the working class, however, these magazines seem largely to have been bought by middle class and lower-middle-class people, who were still starved of print. It was said in 1830 that a middle-class household with an income of £200–£300 p.a. could not afford a taxed daily paper at 7d. per issue, and it was evidently to such people that the penny magazines mainly appealed. The expansion of daily newspapers into this public had to await the next important legislation affecting the press, which initiated a new period.

(iii): 1836–1855

In 1836, Stamp Duty was reduced from 4d. to 1d., and in 1833 the Advertisement Tax had been reduced from 3/6 to 1/6 per insertion. These changes led to a considerable expansion, both in the daily press, dominated now by *The Times*, and, more remarkably, in the Sunday press.

Though at exceptional times in the twenties the circulation of *The Times* had risen to above 15,000, its average circulation in 1830 was about 10,000. This rose a little in 1831, but by 1835 was distinctly lower than it had been in 1830. The political importance of the paper was already established, but its next phase of expansion did not begin until after the 1836 reduction, and then most notably in the 1840s. From 11,000 in 1837 it climbed to 30,000 in 1847, and continued to climb until it had reached nearly 60,000 in 1855. The surprising thing, at first sight, about these figures, is that the rise in circulation was not even greater, for *The Times* now had no real competitor—the other dailies were all still below 10,000. The key is price, for at 4*d*. or 5*d*. a paper of one's own was limited to a still narrow income range. The *Daily News* (1846) reached a circulation of 22,000 at 2½*d*., but was insufficiently capitalized and fell back.

Meanwhile, however, masked from normal interest by the rise of *The Times*, the expansion that one looks for was taking place in the Sunday press. Already by 1837 two Sunday papers, the *Dispatch* and *Chronicle*, were selling about 50,000 an issue, and in the 1840s there is a remarkable general rise, in a fiercely competitive sphere. The two typical papers are *Lloyd's Weekly* (1842) and the *News of the World* (1843). By 1855, both had circulations in the region of 100,000. The estimated total Sunday circulation in 1850 was 275,000, as against 60,000 for total daily circulation. Here, it is clear, is the first phase of expansion of the modern commercial press.

The contents of Sunday papers in the 1820s have been noted, and the new papers of the 1840s were their true successors, alike in their predominantly Radical tone and in their selection of news. At first, however, to avoid even the 1*d*. stamp, *Lloyd's Weekly* published no actual news, but serial stories and fictitious news, with ample illustrations. By 1843, however, it had conformed to the older style, and a distinctive 'Sunday paper look' had been established. A few examples can be given. From February 27, 1842, there is *Bell's Penny Dispatch*, subtitled *Sporting and Police Gazette, and Newspaper of Romance*. The main headline is 'Daring Conspiracy and Attempted Violation', and this is illustrated by a large woodcut and backed by a detailed story. This was an ordinary format, though it should be noted that the first number of the *News of the World* gives its (unconnected) 'Extraordinary Charge of Drugging and Violation' a very small headline and no illustration.

The provenance of this class of journalism is in fact not far to seek. There is a long history of chapbooks and ballads carrying this kind of material, especially in relation to murders, executions, and elopements. These had been exceptionally popular in the eighteenth century, and the woodcut illustration, with title headline, had been typical of their format. These continued into the nineteenth century, and the circulation of comparable fiction similarly expanded, but the time came when the newspaper, with its advertisement revenues, its political news and opinion, and its superior techniques, was clearly the most effective means of buying and selling the same material. Just as the eighteenth-century newspaper had absorbed a proportion of 'magazine interest', so these nineteenth-century papers absorbed the chapbook, ballad, and almanac interest, and at a much cheaper price. This is the recurring tendency in the history of journalism: the absorption of material formerly communicated in widely varying ways into one cheaply-produced and easily-distributed general-purpose sheet. The economics of the newspaper business had, from the beginning, set this course, and it is clear how appropriate these factors of concentration and cheapness were, in a continually expanding culture. A wide range of interests was being brought into a literate form, and the pioneer of each expansion was the cheapest and most extensive print.

(iv): 1855–1896

In 1855 the last penny of the Stamp Tax was removed, and in 1853 the Advertisement Tax had also finally disappeared. These changes came at a time when the press was already expanding, and also when new techniques in news-collection and in distribution were beginning to be widely exploited. The combined effect of these factors was a new and remarkable phase of general expansion. Before we turn to examine this, however, we should try to make some estimate, in social terms, of how far the expansion had already gone, and of other social factors, such as literacy, which were obviously to affect it.

A distinction must be clearly drawn between the daily and the Sunday press, if we are to understand this process of expansion with any accuracy. The impression one gains, from the beginning of Sunday newspapers, is that a class different from readers of the daily press was being catered for. From the very day of their publication, they were never part of the 'respectable press', and, in the first decades of the nineteenth century, their readers were commonly identified as the 'lower classes'. Yet a typical Sunday paper of the 1820s sold at 7*d*, on a par with the daily papers, and at this price few even among middle-class people would normally have bought them. The key here, as in the earlier history of the daily press, is buying by institutions. New coffee-houses were started, at which nearly a hundred papers and magazines were available, and a typical price for reading at one of these, through the extended hours made possible by gas-light, was 1*d*. Papers were also collectively bought, and even read aloud, in workshops, but the public-house and the barber's shop were, increasingly, the main reading places. In both these places, Sunday morning was the most popular time, and this undoubtedly is the explanation of the lead in expansion that was taken by the Sunday press in the first half of the nineteenth century; a lead, it should be noted, that has been maintained to our own day. Even as the price of papers came down, and more people could buy private copies, the Sunday papers retained their advantage, since they appeared on the only day on which the majority of people had any real leisure. The figures already quoted for 1850—275,000 total Sunday circulation, 60,000 total daily—show clearly enough the two publics, and the disparity in readership was probably even greater than this, since it seems likely that a higher proportion of Sunday papers were collectively bought and read at this time. When it is further remembered that distribution was to a large degree still concentrated in London, it would seem that by mid-century a Sunday press that can be genuinely called popular was firmly established in the capital, and that the history of the expansion as a whole must be rewritten in these terms. The daily press expanded, through the rest of the century, largely into an expanding middle class. The history of the popular press, in the nineteenth century, is the history of the expanding Sunday press, aimed at a largely different public.

Between 1816 and 1836, the period of the 4*d*. Stamp Tax, there was a 33% rise in newspaper sales. Between 1836 and 1856 the rise was 70%. In the quarter-century following 1856 the rise was at least 600%, and the major expansion had begun. As a direct result of the 1855 tax abolition, two new elements appeared: a cheap metropolitan daily press, and a widespread provincial daily press. While these rose and flourished, the Sunday papers and the more expensive daily papers also reached out to large new circulations.

Conditions for expansion were exceptionally favourable at this period, quite apart from the effect of the tax abolitions. There was still regular improvement in printing techniques: the hourly rate of 4,000 in 1827 had been raised to 20,000 in 1857. The price of paper was falling again: a ream which had cost 21s. in 1794 cost 55s. in 1845, but by 1855 was down to 40s. Paper duty was abolished in 1860, and there was considerable subsequent improvement in manufacturing techniques: the price of this main raw material continued to fall. General improvement in commerce led to a rising demand for advertising space, although most newspapers were slow to increase their rates and take full advantage of this. In the collection of news, the electric telegraph had been available since 1837, and had been regularly used since 1847, though its full exploitation was not to come until the 1870s. Distribution by railway was becoming widely available, and by 1871 sale-or-return distribution to railway bookstalls had become established. All these factors operated within the general mood of the whole economy, which was confident and expansive.

The repeal of the Stamp Tax became law on June 20, 1855, and on the same day the newspaper appeared which for forty years was to lead the expansion of the daily press: the *Daily Telegraph*. Within three months it was selling at 1d., and by 1860 it had a circulation of 141,000. The *Morning Star*, at 1d., appeared in 1856, and the *Standard* reduced to 1d. in 1858. With the *News* and *Standard* as principal competitors, the *Telegraph* had reached nearly 200,000 in 1870, 250,000 in 1880, and 300,000 in 1890. From the 1870s, new machines were printing at 168,000 an hour.

The *Daily Telegraph*, which set the pace in this rise of the cheap daily press, was conceived as serving 'an entirely new public who never saw the weeklies and monthlies': it was 'the paper of the man on the knifeboard of the omnibus'. In style it had certain obvious differences from the early Victorian *Times*, but it was not, of course, even in the daily press, the first newspaper to adopt a light style of journalism. The pioneers in this had been the *Morning Post* and the *World*, back in the 1780s, and we must remember that the Victorian *Times* was itself much heavier in manner than at any earlier stage in its career. Labouchere observed of the *Telegraph* that

> when persons entirely unconnected with literature themselves are the owners of newspapers, they naturally sacrifice all decorum to the desire to make the journal a remunerative speculation.

The owners of the *Telegraph* were the printing family of Levy, but Labouchere's implication that the separation of literature and journalism was new is impossible to accept. The separation between writers and journalists is clear, in spite of occasional overlaps, before the end of the eighteenth century, and printer-ownership had always been common. What is certain is that Levy had a new kind of paper in mind: 'what we want is a human note', he instructed new entrants to the *Telegraph*, and politics must not be assumed to be the sole interest of its readers. Matthew Arnold, observing the result, called it the 'new journalism'.

In terms of contents, it is not really new. But undoubtedly, in this period, an attention to crime, sexual violence, and human oddities made its way from the Sunday into these daily papers, and also into older papers like the *Morning Post*. As early as 1788, the *Morning Post* had written:

> Newspapers have long enough estranged themselves in a manner totally from the elegancies of literature, and dealt only in malice, or at least in the prattle of the day. On this head, however, newspapers are not much more to blame than their patrons, the public.

The Victorian *Morning Post* had become respectable, but under Borthwick (1852–1908) it certainly published very full reports of crimes. The 'new journalism' is complex, because the expansion was producing something new: distinct levels of seriousness within the daily press. The period from 1855 is in one sense the development of a new and better journalism, with a much greater emphasis on news than in the faction-ridden first half of the century. In a period which saw the consolidation of sentiment from the middle class upwards—a unity of sentiment quite strong enough to contain constitutional party conflicts—most newspapers were able to drop their frantic pamphleteering, and to serve this public with news and a regulated diversity of opinion. On the other hand, this change in political atmosphere had to a large extent removed politics from the primary place which it had in the cheap press of the first half of the century, and allowed the new emphasis on a more general news miscellany. *The Times* and a few of the older papers served the established classes with a new and more objective journalism; the *Telegraph* and the new papers served a new lower and rising middle class, with a new journalism in which liveliness was applied, not only to politics, but to other kinds of news. The ordinary reaction of readers of *The Times* was the same as the later reaction to the halfpenny *Daily Mail*: 'lively, but crude and vulgar'. It must again be emphasized that no lion of the new journalism would have had anything to teach eighteenth-century journalists in the matter of crudeness and vulgarity, but, given the rate of the expansion, the emphasis was now very evident. 'Extraordinary Discovery of a Man-Woman at Birmingham', announced the *Telegraph* in 1856; 'Furious Assault on a Female', in 1857; and so on and so on. Burnham (a descendant of the Levy family, who remained associated with the *Telegraph*) writes in his history of the paper:

> Reviewing the files, the honest biographer cannot dispute that the *Daily Telegraph* thrived on crime.

Such items as a three-column description of the hanging of a woman remind us that a popular old item in cheap literature was now establishing itself in the daily press.

There is also, at this time, an evident change in the style of reporting, due to the now regular use of the telegram. The older style was, at its best, that of books; at its worst, what the language textbooks still call 'journalese' (which has survived longest, significantly, in local newspapers, which use telegrams so very much less). The desire for compression, to save money on the wire, led to shorter sentences and a greater emphasis of key-words. There is often a gain in simplicity and lack of padding; often a loss in the simplification of complicated issues, and in the distorting tendency of the emphatic key-word. The balance in these issues has ever since been crucial in newspaper style.

In one other way, the *Daily Telegraph* was a pioneer. It shared with *The Times* and others the organization of public funds, but it was a leader in organizing public functions (such as bringing 30,000 children to Hyde Park for the 1887 Jubilee), and in self-advertising stunts, such as the campaign to keep the elephant Jumbo, in 1882. On the other hand it was still, typographically, conservative: that is to say, it adhered to the dense 'daily paper' look, which had been established in the expensive days of stamped paper and which had already been abandoned by the Sunday press. The clearer layout and rather larger headlines of the American press of the period (itself roughly comparable to the mid-twentieth-century news pages of *The Times*) were frequently condemned and certainly neglected. To be classed with the Sunday papers was really what the cheap daily press feared.

Meanwhile, from 1855, a flourishing daily provincial press was being established. Seventeen new papers of this kind were established in 1855 alone, and the development of news agencies increasingly freed them from dependence on the London press. The most successful reached circulations of up to 40,000: though this is small for the period, the spread of so many of these papers represents a considerable further expansion of the newspaper public. Because of their provincial position, they escaped the competition for different levels of the public which was appearing in the London daily press. Seeking to serve all the readers in their area, they followed a general rather than any angled policy. It is no accident that several of them have developed into some of the best newspapers of our own time.

The forces making for cheap newspapers gathered strength as the press moved into the 1870s and 1880s. An unsuccessful halfpenny newspaper (the *London Halfpenny Newspaper*) had appeared in 1861, but there were successful halfpenny papers in the provinces from 1855. In London, the evening *Echo* came out at a halfpenny in 1868, and it was in evening papers, in the seventies and eighties, that this new stage of the cheap press began. With the rise of interest in sport, particularly football, the evening paper had a new function, and the new London evenings of the eighties (*Evening News*, 1881; *Star*, 1888) were eventually to found themselves on this as a main interest. The *Evening News* was at first unsuccessful, as a political paper financed by the Conservatives, but was made successful by Northcliffe in the nineties. By then there was a successful model, the *Star*, which in method is a landmark. Techniques such as the interview, the cross-heading, and American-style headlines had been introduced by Stead's *Pall Mall Gazette* (founded 1865; edited by Stead from 1883), and these and other features of the new journalism were taken further by O'Connor's *Star*. O'Connor promised:

> We shall have daily but one article of any length, and it will usually be confined within half a column. The other items of the day will be dealt with in notes terse, pointed and plain-spoken. We believe that the reader of the daily journal longs for other reading than mere politics, and we shall present him with plenty of entirely unpolitical literature—sometimes humorous, sometimes pathetic; anecdotal, statistical, the craze of fashions and the arts of house-keeping—now and then, a short dramatic and picturesque tale. In our reporting columns we shall do away with the hackneyed style of obsolete journalism; and the men and women that figure in the forum or the pulpit or the law court shall be presented as they are—living, breathing, in blushes or in tears—and not merely by the dead words they utter.

The description is apt, but O'Connor's policy is a landmark, not a revolution. The tendencies that have been noted in the cheap morning papers were now being extended in the new product, the cheap evening paper. The essential novelty of the *Star* is that the new distribution of interest which the second half of the nineteenth century had brought about was now *typographically* confirmed. From now on, the new journalism began to look like what it was.

The first issue of the *Star* sold 142,600 copies; the *Daily Telegraph* was still at around 300,000. But the really big circulations were still in the Sunday press. In 1855 the total circulation of the Sunday papers had risen to about 450,000, with the leading paper at 107,000. By the end of this period, total circulation was about 1,725,000, and the leading paper, *Lloyd's Weekly News*, was at 900,000 in 1890, and 1,000,000 in 1896. As previously emphasized, the growth of a large-circulation press was, from the 1820s, led by the Sunday press, and the existence of circulations like these, before Northcliffe, is a radical factor in assessing the nature of the 'Northcliffe Revolution'. The contents of these successful Sunday papers are what one would expect from their tradition. The Jack-the-Ripper murders, for example, did much to push *Lloyd's Weekly News* towards the heights. Also, the Sunday papers gave the news of the whole week, and were thus welcome to a public which still, after the expansion noted, did not buy a daily paper.

(v): 1896–1920

When the expansion of the period 1855–96 is reviewed more closely, it becomes evident that the most rapid advance came in the period 1855–70, and that there was then a slowing-down. Circulation of daily papers trebled between 1855 and 1860, and doubled again between 1860 and 1870. Between 1870 and 1880 the expansion is just under 30%; between 1880 and 1890 about 12%. On the other hand, the main expansion of circulation in the provincial daily press came between 1870 and 1890, and the evening press was growing markedly from 1880 on.

There are certain probable factors within the press industry itself, in particular the growing importance of a new kind of advertising. The commercial prosperity of the old newspapers had depended on a large number of small advertisements, of the kind we now call 'classified'. In other media, notably billposting, the style of advertising had been changing since the 1830s, but the attitude of the press remained cautious. In particular, editors were extremely resistant to any break-up in the regular column layout of their pages, and hence to any increase in display type. Advertisers tried in many ways to get round this, but with little success, and the pressure on newspapers to adapt themselves to techniques drawn from the poster (which was eventually really to change the face of journalism) began to be successful only in the 1880s. The change had come first in the illustrated magazines, with a crop of purity nudes and similar figures advertising pills, soaps and the other pioneers of new advertising methods. Eventually, with Northcliffe in the lead, the newspapers dropped their column rule, and allowed large type and illustrations. It was noted in 1897 that 'The Times itself' was permitting

> advertisements in type which three years ago would have been considered fit only for the street hoardings,

while the front page of the *Daily Mail* already held rows of drawings, from the new department stores, of rather bashful women in combinations. Courtesy, Service and Integrity acquired the dignity of large-type abstractions.

Behind these changes were important changes in the economy. The great bulk of products of the early stages of the factory system had been sold without extensive advertising, which had grown up mainly in relation to novelties and fringe products. Such advertising as there was, of basic articles, was mainly by shopkeepers: the classified advertisements which the newspapers had always carried. In this comparatively simple phase, large-scale advertising and the brand-naming of goods were necessary only at the margin, or in genuinely new things. In the second half of the century, the range widened (branding is especially notable in the new patent foods) but it was not until the 1890s that the emphasis deeply changed. The Great Depression which in general dominated the period from 1873 to the middle 1890s (though broken by occasional recoveries and local strengths) marks the turning point between two moods, two kinds of industrial organization, and two basically different approaches to distribution. After the Depression, and its big falls in prices, there was a more general and growing fear of productive capacity, a marked tendency to reorganize industrial ownership into larger units and combines, and a growing desire to organize and where possible control the market. Advertising then took on a new importance, and was applied to an increasing range of products, as part of the system of market control which, at full development, included tariffs and preference areas, cartel quotas, trade campaigns, price fixing by manufacturers, and economic imperialism. There was a concerted expansion of export advertising, and at home the biggest advertising campaign yet seen accompanied the merger of several tobacco firms into the Imperial Tobacco Company, to resist American competition. In 1901, a 'fabulous sum' was offered for the entire eight pages of the *Star*, and when this was refused four pages were taken, to print

> the most costly, colossal and convincing advertisement in an evening newspaper the wide world o'er.

The system of selling space changed, from the old eighteenth-century shops which 'took in' newspaper announcements, through systems of agents and brokers, to the establishment of full-scale independent advertising agencies, and, in the newspapers, full-time advertising managers who advanced very rapidly from junior to senior status. Pressure was brought on the newspapers, by advertising agents, to publish their sales figures. Northcliffe, after initial hesitations about advertising (he wanted to run *Answers* without it) was the first to realize its possibilities as a new basis for newspaper finance. He published his own sales figures, challenged his rivals to do the same, and in effect created the modern structure of the press as an industry and an expression of market relationships with the 'mass reading public'.

The production costs of newspapers were in any case increasing, if a large circulation was to be won. By tying the policy of newspapers to large circulation, Northcliffe found the formula and the revenue from the new advertising situation. He was then able to make quite rapid technical advances in journalism itself. He started the halfpenny *Daily Mail* in 1896 with new and expensive machinery (new rotary presses had raised the hourly printing rate to 200,000, and the Linotype type-setter, which came into use in the 1890s, had achieved a rate ten times as fast as that of a hand compositor), and also with new arrangements for rapid sale (by 1900 he had set up separate printing of the same paper in Manchester). The improvements meant a considerable cut in the price of a single copy, if a large circulation could be achieved, and the new scale of advertising revenue was a capital factor in the necessary investment. The true 'Northcliffe Revolution' is less an innovation in actual journalism than a radical change in the economic basis of newspapers, tied to the new kind of advertising.

Northcliffe had begun, like Pearson who was to found the *Daily Express* in 1900, in the periodical business. There had been two phases of growth in this field since the penny magazines of the 1830s: first, the rise of illustrated magazines, from the 1840s, reaching circulations of 200,000 and above; second, the development of consciously light weeklies, in the sixties and seventies (*Vanity Fair* (1868), *World* (1874)). In 1881, a new phase started, with Newnes's penny *Tit-Bits*, and its subsequent imitators *Pearson's Weekly* and Northcliffe's *Answers*. Essentially these represent an emphasis of the 'miscellany' trend in the daily papers since 1855, and in the Sunday papers from the 1820s, but now separated altogether from news in the ordinary sense. The 'bittiness' of these weeklies has often been adversely noticed, and the reaction of this method on the reporting of serious news is certainly deplorable, but the right emphasis, finally, is on the similarity of their function to that of earlier periodicals, at particular stages of cultural expansion: the mid-eighteenth century magazines, the penny magazines of the thirties. There is a marked 'popular educator' emphasis, particularly in Northcliffe, and the lowering in quality, despite this, is a significant sympton of general cultural history: in particular of the increased distance of their promoters from real education and literature. The existence of marked cultural 'levels', of real cultural class-distinctions, is much more evident in the 1880s than in either of the earlier periods. Moreover, many of the people who were serving real popular education in late Victorian England would, at an earlier stage, have been serving it through the press. Pearson, Newnes, and Northcliffe were speculators, in the strict sense. The circulation of their periodicals was deliberately built up by advertising stunts: some an exploitation of the uneven development of services (such as the free insurance with readership which Newnes started, and which was to be a major selling-point in the popular press until the 1930s); others in the form of gambling (sovereign treasure-hunts, £1 a week for life for winning a guessing competition, and so on). At least two of the latter were soon declared illegal, but by then the trick had been done: not only in getting readers, but in getting money for further investment in this kind of press. For example, Northcliffe's *Answers* sold 12,000 of its first issue, and at the end of a year sold 48,000. Then came the £1-a-week-for-life competition, later judged illegal, and with it sales climbed in the second year to 352,000. Again it is not so much the journalistic novelty, in the strict sense, that marks the advance but the appearance of a new kind of sales and advertising policy. The tenfold increase in Northcliffe's profits enabled him to expand: first to other periodicals, *Comic Cuts*, *Forget-menot* and *Home Chat*, then to buying the *Evening News*, and finally, on the success of these new enterprises, to the *Daily Mail*.

In 1896 the leading daily paper, the *Telegraph*, was selling around 300,000 copies: after its initial rapid expansion it had reached a relatively static period. Northcliffe, with his halfpenny paper based on a different economic conception, took the expansion into its next stage. At first the *Mail's* average sale was about 200,000, and in 1898 over 400,000. By 1900 it had reached 989,000, and a new period had decisively come. It must be emphasized at this point that, by comparison with the Sunday papers, the *Mail* was relatively traditional in method: there were advertisements on its front page, and the main news-page was similar to the new evening papers in layout, with single-column headlines, cross-heads, and a general lightening of the page. It looked, and was meant to look, not unlike the existing morning papers; its changes were matters of degree. Its success, and its dominance of the press in its immediate period, are remarkably similar, in analytic terms, to the rise of *The Times* earlier in the century. For, first, it was based on a clear conception of the economic basis of a newspaper— a large volume of advertising interacting with circulation; second, it was technically in the lead, both in production and distribution methods; third, it pursued a popular politi-

cal policy—the Imperial sentiment in the *Mail* corresponding to the Reform sentiment in *The Times*. Just as *The Times*
reached its first peak with the Reform Bill controversy, the
Mail reached its first peak with the South African War.
The Times's public had been the commercial middle class;
the *Mail's*, primarily, was the lower-middle class of small
businessmen, clerks, and artisans. The effect of the success
of the *Mail* was to double the daily-newspaper-buying
public in the period 1896–1906, and then, with its competitors, to double it again by the outbreak of war in 1914. The
expansion is striking, but it must be remembered that even
after the further increase during the war years, which for
obvious reasons brought a considerably increased demand,
the daily-newspaper public was still, in 1920, only 5,430,000
as compared with over 15,000,000 in 1947. Large-scale
expansion of the daily newspaper into the working-class
public did not take place until the years between the wars,
and the war of 1939–45. The Sunday press was considerably ahead, throughout. Indeed, in this period 1896–1920,
which appears to be dominated by the rise of the *Daily
Mail*, the biggest expansion is again in the Sunday papers.
By 1920, these sold 13,000,000—nearly two and a half
times the total daily-newspaper public, and a figure not to
be reached by the daily press until the war years of 1939–45.
The history of the popular daily, evening, and weekly press
is, throughout, an expansion of these types of paper into a
public already served by the Sunday press. Yet in nearly all
discussions of the history of the press this fact is ignored, in
favour of the idea of a new public which had read nothing
until the 1870 Education Act had taken effect.

The real novelty of this period, it must again be emphasized, is a change in the economics of newspaper publishing.
The effect of the *Daily Mail*, embodying the new conception,
on the existing papers, conceived in older ways, is very striking. *The Times*, of course, had already been outdistanced by
the *Telegraph*, and this, in social terms, seems to record the
increasing emphasis on the division of the middle class into
upper and lower sections, with the *Telegraph* serving the
numerically larger latter. From 1870 the circulation of *The
Times* had been declining; by 1908 it was down to less than

it had been in 1855, and it was bought by Northcliffe, after a struggle with Pearson. The *Telegraph*, itself outdistanced by the *Mail*, lost readers slowly—it was down to 180,000 by 1920. Of the other popular penny papers, the *Standard* declined heavily, and ceased publication in 1917, while the *News* also declined until it lowered its price to $\frac{1}{2}d$. These facts are significant in showing that the *Mail* did not serve only a new daily public, but a substantial part of the older public.

Following Northcliffe, Pearson started a daily paper of the new type (*Morning Herald*, later *Daily Express*) in 1900. The other member of the trio of penny-weekly publishers, Newnes, had tried and failed with a penny paper, the *Daily Courier*, in 1896. In terms of journalistic method, the *Express* was more novel than the *Mail*: it had news on its front page from the beginning (following the fashion of the successful cheap evening papers), and was the first to introduce streamer headlines. Then Northcliffe introduced another new paper, the *Daily Mirror* (1903), which failed in its original design as a paper for women, but succeeded when it was reduced to a halfpenny and turned into the first picture-newspaper. From 1911 on, the *Mirror* had an even larger circulation than the *Mail*—it reached its million (the first daily paper to do so) in 1911–12.

Thus the change in the economics of newspaper publishing led to changes in methods of ownership, of far-reaching importance. Occasionally, in earlier periods, the same printer or proprietor had owned two or three small-circulation papers but the rule, throughout, had been the ownership of a single paper, either by a printer, a printing family, or a joint-stock company. Now, around the new kind of speculative owner, whole groups of papers and periodicals were being collected or begun. Capital was built up with a first successful enterprise in the penny-weekly field, then invested in new periodicals, which in their turn were the basis for starting new papers or acquiring old ones. Thus *Answers* was capitalized to start the *Daily Mail* and then the *Daily Mail* was capitalized, the first time a daily newspaper had gone to the investing public. By the end of 1908, Northcliffe had not only his group of periodicals, but the *Daily Mail* and *Daily Mirror* as new enterprises, and *The Times*, two Sunday papers (*Observer* and *Dispatch*) and an evening paper (*News*) acquired. Pearson, at the same time, had his group of periodicals, and then the *Daily Express*, new, and the *Standard* and *Evening Standard* (including the *St James's Gazette*) acquired. Other similar organizers were waiting in the wings, and among new papers founded in this general way were the *Sunday Pictorial* (Rothermere, 1915), *Sunday Graphic* (then *Illustrated Sunday Herald*; Hulton, 1915—Hulton already owned the *Sporting Chronicle*, *Sunday Chronicle*, *Daily Dispatch*, and *Daily Sketch*), *Sunday Express* (Beaverbrook, 1918). Thus, in the general expansion, and conditioned by the new kind of 'mass' advertising, the real 'Northcliffe Revolution' in the press occurred, taking the newspaper from its status as an independent private enterprise to its membership of a new kind of capitalist combine. The real basis of the twentieth-century popular press was thus effectively laid.

(vi): 1920–1947

Between 1896 and 1920 there had been an expansion of readership and a concentration of ownership. After 1920, the expansion of readership continued, the concentration of ownership appeared in new areas of the press while relaxing a little in others, and, for the first time in the whole history of the press, a decline began in the actual number of newspapers. These positive and negative aspects of expansion are the basic factors within the period to be examined.

Expansion of readership took place in two phases: 1920–37, and 1937–47. In the first phase, the main expansion is in the national daily press, and this was promoted, as is well known, by extraordinary non-journalistic measures, of the kind begun by the *Daily Telegraph* and rapidly developed by Newnes, Pearson and Northcliffe: the organization of functions and campaigns, the offering of insurance, and (now particularly developed by Southwood for the *Daily Herald*) the offering of many kinds of goods with readership. Since all the popular papers vied with each other in these characteristic forms of commercial advertising, the effect was a general expansion in readership rather than the emergence of a single leading newspaper, as had been normal in earlier periods of growth. From a daily total of 5,430,000 in 1920, the national morning papers had reached 8,567,567 in 1930, and 9,903,427 in 1937. In 1920 there had been two papers with a million-plus circulation; in 1930 there were five; in 1937, two above two-million and three above a million. The *Mail* had continued to lead until 1932, but was then passed by the *Express* and *Herald*. By the mid-thirties, the expansion had reached into all social classes, though not evenly. There is at this time heavy buying in the income groups above £500 a year, and quite heavy buying in the group between £250 and £500, but in the group between £125 and £250 buying is distinctly less heavy, and in the group below £125 comparatively light. The comparison with Sunday papers is still significant: in 1930 a Sunday total of 14,600,000 against a daily total of 8,567,567; in 1937, 15,700,000 against 9,903,427. It will be noted, however, that the rate of Sunday expansion between 1920 and 1937 is much slower than that of daily expansion: a 20% as against an 80% increase in total sales. Meanwhile in the provincial press, there is no expansion at all, but even a slight decline.

The period had begun with considerable difficulties for the press. Newsprint, which had been £10 a ton in 1914, was at £43 in 1920, and £22 in 1922; by 1935 it was to drop again to £10. In the early years of high costs, several newspapers ceased publication, and the mounting cost of the competition for circulation reinforced this tendency. Between 1921 and 1937, the number of national morning papers declined from 12 to 9, and national Sundays from 14 to 10. Provincial morning papers declined from 41 to 28 in the same period, and provincial evening papers from 89 to 79. Associated with this decline in the provincial field, though not its primary cause, was the extension of combine control into large areas of the provincial press. Chain ownership of provincial morning papers increased from 12.2% in 1921 to 46.35% in 1937, and of provincial evening papers from 7.86% to 43.01%. There was also an increase in combine ownership of the Sunday press, 28.64% to 47.11%; but in the daily national press control by the leading combines became less during this period, falling from 50% to 22%.

In the matter of style, the popular press was led, between 1920 and 1937, by the *Daily Express*. There is a marked influence from American newspaper practice, in terms of headline styles and page-composition, but there is also assimilation of two existing English newspaper styles: that of illustrated papers like the *Mirror*, and of the magazine-style Sunday papers. The *Express* of August 5, 1914, has a streamer headline in quite small type, and then a front page with ordinary straight-column setting, and small headlines which are little more than cross-heads except that two or three of them may appear above each item. By 1937 (the radical change having come in the late 1920s) the headlines are much larger, there is much more illustration, and the page is made up in the now familiar staggered jigsaw. The 1914 *Express* has 5⅜ columns of ordinary printed news out of 7 columns; the 1937 *Express* 3½ columns. By 1937, the other papers of this type are a virtual imitation of the developed *Express*, except that the *Mail* still has advertisements on its front page. Meanwhile, by the same date, the illustrated papers, *Mirror* and *Sketch*, give only about a third of their front pages to ordinary printed news.

In the period between 1937 and 1947, in spite of news-print shortage during the war itself, there was a remarkable further expansion in the press as a whole. Total daily sales rose from 9,903,427 in 1937 to 15,449,410 in 1947, and Sunday sales rose even more strikingly from 15,700,000 to 29,300,000. There was also an expansion in London evening papers, from 1,806,910 to 3,501,599. The pattern of this expansion is somewhat changed, for among daily papers two now took a decisive lead, the *Express* and *Mirror* both nearing 4,000,000, while their competitors advanced much more slowly. In the Sunday press there is a comparable pattern, with the *News of the World* rising from under 4,000,000 to nearly 8,000,000, and two other papers (*People* and *Pictorial*) rising above 4,000,000. It is of course impossible to say when an expansion of this kind is complete, but it would seem that it is in the period 1937–47 that the daily paper becomes fully popular, being widely and regularly bought by people in all classes, even though the aggregate sales are still only a little over half those of the Sunday press. At the same time, having reached this peak of expansion, papers of all types were encountering new kinds of difficulty. In the war years and after, the greatly increased price of newsprint had been offset by very much smaller papers. Now, with the limits on size about to be removed, a new kind of competition was to begin: no longer to expand the buying-public as a whole, but for increasing shares of the existing public. The expansion between 1920 and 1937 had been marked by some decline in the number of papers; between 1937 and 1947 by relatively stable conditions. The phase that lay ahead was to see renewed pressure towards concentration.

It must be noted, finally, as a significant fact about this period, that newspapers of the older kind (*Times*, *Telegraph*) made an aggregate gain in their percentage of the total daily public, and that there were also important gains by the new kind of Sunday paper (*Observer*, *Times*). In particular, in the 1937–47 expansion, these 'quality' papers made substantial gains in circulation: not being driven down or out as in earlier expansions, but slowly expanding their share of the expansion as a whole. This is only one sign of the new stage which the expansion had reached.

(vii): The Present

In Britain, there are 609 copies of daily newspapers for every 1,000 people—the highest figure in the world—and an average 88% of the adult population read a daily paper, 65% an evening paper, and 93% a Sunday paper. Putting it another way, if we translate sales into readership, using the average figure of 3 readers a copy (which will be an underestimate in earlier periods and a slight overestimate in later) and then expressing readership as a percentage of the varying adult population, we can see how the expansion has gone, to its present stage. The daily press rose from 1% in 1800 to 1.2% in 1850, to $11\frac{1}{2}$% in 1875, to 18% in 1900, to 19% in 1910, to 54% in 1920, to 75% in 1930, and to 120% in 1947. The Sunday press rose from 1.3% in 1800 to 5% in 1850, to 19% in 1875, to 33% in 1900, to 60%

in 1910, to 125% in 1920, and to 233% in 1947. Thus the daily press became a majority press during the First War and immediately after, and a fully distributed press during the Second War. The Sunday press was a majority press by 1910, a fully distributed press by 1920, and by 1947 had achieved more than twice total coverage.

Sales from 1937 into the 1950s are as follows:

	1937	1947	1957
Total dailies:	9,903,427	15,449,410	17,000,000
Total Sundays:	15,700,000	29,300,000	26,888,000

In purely numerical terms, it would seem that the expansion at this level is in its final stages.

At the same time, the actual number of newspapers has been steadily falling:

	1921	1937	1947	1959
National morning	12	9	9	9
London evening	4	3	3	3
Provincial morning	41	28	25	23
Sunday	21	17	16	15
Provincial evening	89	79	75	75
Weekly papers	1485	1303	1162	686

This contracting field has further emphasized the concentration of ownership. In the national daily press, four groups control 77% of total circulation, and the same four control 57% of Sunday circulation. Two other large Sunday groups control a further 14% and 24%, putting 95% of Sunday ownership into six groups. Two of these same six groups control 66.7% of London evening circulation, and one of these two and one other of the six control more than 30% of provincial evening circulation. Chain ownership is widespread in the shrinking local weekly press, while in magazines recent amalgamations have produced two almost wholly dominant groups, which are also two of the leading six newspaper groups. The contrast between a majority press and minority ownership, within a diminishing area of real choices, is already striking, and seems likely to go much further yet. The same groups, it should be noted, already have important holdings in commercial television.

What is happening, within the general expansion, to different types of newspaper? If we take the usual rough classification, into 'quality', 'popular' and 'tabloid', we find the following trends:

	1937	1947	1957
	% shares of actual sales		
'Quality' dailies	8	9·5	9·5
'Popular' dailies	71·7	62·4	55·5
'Tabloid' dailies	20·3	28·9	35
'Quality' Sundays	3·5	3·5	5·5
'Popular' Sundays	82	76·5	71
'Tabloid' Sundays	14·5	19·5	23·5

These figures do not support the idea of a steady if slow development, in relation to improving education, of a better press. The rise of the 'quality' papers is continuing, quite steadily, but the significant development is the rise of the tabloid press, and this is even more important when it is noted that there has been a steady development, in magazines, towards the same kind of journalism. There the market is being steadily specialized, in direct relation to advertising income, and the popular magazine for all kinds of reader is being steadily driven out. This does not even begin to look like the developing press of an educated democracy. Instead it looks like an increasingly organized market in communications, with the 'masses' formula as the dominant social principle, and with the varied functions of the press increasingly limited to finding a 'selling point'.

What, finally, is the social distribution of different kinds of newspaper? Here are some recent figures, by the advertising agents' definitions of social class (almost all readership figures are now collected in relation to advertising, which shows the dominant principle clearly enough), and by age-groups:

	AB	C1	C2	DE
By 'Social Class'	5,580,000	6,570,000	11,692,000	13,783,000
	%	%	%	%
Mirror	16	28	44	39
Express	36	36	32	28
Mail	25	20	13	12

By 'Social Class'	AB 5,580,000	C1 6,570,000	C2 11,692,000	DE 13,783,000
	%	%	%	%
Herald	4	9	18	17
Sketch	9	12	13	11
Chronicle	11	12	12	11
Telegraph	25	11	3	2
Times	10	2	1	1
Guardian	7	3	1	1
Observer	19	8	2	2
Sunday Express	47	33	21	17
News of World	24	36	55	58
Pictorial	20	34	49	41

By Age Group	16–24	25–34	35–44	45–64	65+
	%	%	%	%	%
Mirror	42	43	41	32	20
Express	32	32	35	33	26
Mail	14	15	15	17	16
Herald	14	12	14	16	13
Sketch	13	13	13	11	7
Chronicle	8	9	11	13	14
Telegraph	5	7	8	7	8
Times	3	3	2	3	2
Guardian	3	3	2	2	1
Observer	6	7	6	5	4
Sunday Times	6	6	6	6	5
Sunday Express	24	27	28	25	23
News of World	54	47	46	30	42
Pictorial	48	53	44	33	21

Here again, we find no simple process of desirable evolution, nor quite the simple class affiliations used in popular discussion. If the age-group tendencies are projected, the trends noted can be expected to continue. In terms of class, it is worth noting that the leading daily paper of the rich and well-to-do is not *The Times* (which is in fact exceeded by the *Daily Mirror*) nor the *Telegraph* (which is roughly equalled by the *Mail*); it is the *Express*, which of all the 'popular' papers is nearest the tabloid style. Similarly in Sunday papers, the *Observer* is just beaten in this class by the *Pictorial*, and both *Observer* and *Sunday Times* are beaten by the *News of the World* and, very thoroughly, by the *Sunday Express*. If the rich and well-to-do are in fact (as is sometimes claimed) defending traditional culture, and the interests of the 'highly-educated and politically-minded minority', against the vulgarity of the intruding masses, they seem, in their buying of newspapers, to be doing it in a very odd way.

Is it all to come to this, in the end, that the long history of the press in Britain should reach its consummation in a declining number of newspapers, in ownership by a few very large groups, and in the acceptance (varied between social groups but evident in all) of the worst kinds of journalism? The process is evidently something other than the incursion of the 1870 masses, or the 1820 masses if the process is merely backdated. It is something that is happening to the whole society, and all the elements—not only the bad journalism but also the questions of ownership and the relation to advertising—have to be considered if the process is to be understood. We do not solve the critical questions by understanding the history, but still an adequate sense of the history, as opposed to the ordinary functional myths, is the basis of any useful approach. I shall return to these questions in my third part.

FOUR

The Growth of 'Standard English'

THE importance of speech as an indicator of social class is not likely to be underestimated by anyone who has lived in England. Our reactions to speech are in any case fundamentally important, for certain sounds, certain words, certain rhythms carry for most of us a very deep charge of feeling and memory. The feeling that we should speak as other members of our group speak is also very strong. Indeed it is in just this imitative desire and capacity that the possibility of language, with its vital communication of our humanity, is centred. At the same time, this imitative process is dynamic, for no living language is ever fixed. There are variations of speech habit within the simplest group, and the complication of experience and of contacts with other groups is constantly modifying the very thing that we are imitating. Since it is both a confirmation and a discovery of our changing experience of reality, language must change if it is to live. Yet within any human lifetime, and within any society, our attachment to known ways will remain significant, and our important sense of belonging, to a family, to a group, to a people, will be vitally interwoven with the making and hearing of certain sounds—the making and hearing being a very large part of our social sense.

There is then a necessary tension in language, between powerful impulses to imitation and to change. This tension is part of our basic processes of growth and learning. In the general history of language, we can see two quite opposite tendencies: an extraordinary evolution of separate languages, and a remarkable growth, in certain conditions, of common languages. Almost all modern European languages, from Welsh and English to Italian and Russian, together with such Asian languages as Hindustani and Persian, have developed and separated, through history, from a common root. And still, in simple societies, there is an almost incredible variation, within tiny regions, so that villages six or eight miles apart can often hardly understand one another, or on an island of 100,000 people there can be as many as forty dialects, often mutually incomprehensible. As a group develops its own way of life, which may extend over a few miles or over half a continent, it will, as part of this development, create its own forms of language. The very factor which gives the group its social cohesion can become the factor cutting it off, to an important extent, from similar groups elsewhere. But, on the other hand, and especially now as communities become larger and develop greatly improved communication systems, certain languages (of which English is notably one) expand and flourish, serving as a common basis for many different groups. Even within these common languages, however, and alongside the powerful tendencies to expanded community of speech, the processes of growth and variation will continue, in different ways in different groups speaking the common tongue. The variations may be of a regional or of a class kind, and the case of class speech is particularly important, for here the tension between community and variation may be seen at its most sensitive.

A class is a group within a geographical community, and not a community in its own right. In certain extreme cases, a class will so emphasize its distinction from the community of which it is a part that it will in fact use a separate language: either one of the various hieratic languages, such as Sanskrit, or, as in nineteenth-century Russia, a foreign language, French, which is thought of as a mark of cultural superiority. More usually, however, class speech will be a form of the ordinary speech of the region, and the relations between this class dialect and the ordinary speech of the region (which will usually itself be further sub-regionally varied) form a complex of great importance in the development of a language. In the case of English, the sensitivity of this complex is very high: a very large number of Englishmen have become tense and anxious about the way in which they speak their own language. This problem has a deep bearing on the development of English society, but it is still not very clearly understood. There is commonly a lack of historical perspective, and there are also many prejudices, both theoretic and practical. Yet English has been served by many fine scholars and historians, and, with certain notable gaps, the material for a better understanding is available. I propose to review the historical material, as a way of gaining perspective, and to suggest, from this review, certain necessary clarifications. The period in which we are now living is of exceptional importance in English, and behind the history and the theory we can surely all feel the pressures of a complex social experience.

II

In England, after the Norman Conquest, two different languages were spoken—French and English—and a third, Latin, was not only the international language of learning, but by scholars was spoken and developing. The division between French and English was on class lines; it is best described by the chronicler known as Robert of Gloucester, writing in about 1300, and here translated:

> Thus England came into Normandy's hand, and the Normans at that time could speak only their own language, and spoke French just as they did at home, and had their children taught in the same manner, so that people of rank in this country who came of their blood all stick to the same language that they received of them, for if a man knows no French people will think little of him. But the lower classes still stick to English and their own language.

But in 1204, Normandy was lost to the English crown, and the French of the Normans began to develop along separate lines, and with influence from English. Old English itself had changed by this time, affected by the Normans' French. Gradually, a new language developed, the product of both these changing tongues, and after the legal recognition of English in 1362, the growth of the common language was paramount, reaching a recognizably modern form in about 1500, and relative stability by about 1700.

The social processes involved in this history are of great interest. We can trace the minor relics of class prejudice in the lasting equation of moral qualities with class names:

base, *villain*, *boor*, and *churl* for the poor; *kind, free, gentle, noble*, but also *proud* and *dangerous*, for the rich. But a more important legacy was that affecting the whole language of learning. English passed, during the separation, into the mouths of the uneducated and the powerless. Thus the greater part of the vocabulary of learning and power, together with the bulk of the vocabulary of a richer way of living, came from Norman sources. The only substantial alternative source, in these matters, was Latin, and down to the fourteenth century this was taught in the grammar schools through the medium of French. Of course, once the common language emerged, the whole vocabulary was theoretically available to all. But the long continuation of education restricted to a minority, which learned Latin and French as well as speaking its own language, gave this limited class an access to the resources of their own language which, for the majority, remained much more difficult. Though wider education can resolve this, extending the area of the truly common language, it is probably still important, in English, that so much of the language of learning should have this special kind of class stamp.

A further consequence of this particular history was the splitting of English into many more dialects than hitherto. Old English had had three or four important regional dialects, but within these there were important centralizing tendencies. In any language, it is the development of major central institutions—government, law, learning, religion, and literature—which leads to the emergence of a reasonably common language among men drawn from various parts of the region to take part in these central activities. But, under Norman rule, this central language was alien, and the removal of these centralizing tendencies in English led to a greater variation in ordinary dialects. When modern English emerged, as the language of these central institutions, the relation of the centre to the outlying areas was more complex than hitherto. However, the centralizing tendencies continued to operate, and slowly the speech of the centre became accepted as the basis of the new common language. The old East Midland dialect, with some influences from other regions, became the basis of the common language of the centre. Yet it is less the rise of one regional dialect than the emergence of a class dialect. The regional dialect had the advantage of being spoken in an area reaching to the capital, London, and the two universities of Oxford and Cambridge. But the new common language, from the beginning, showed marked differences from the speech of the ordinary inhabitants of these cities. If we say the best speech was that of London, Oxford and Cambridge, we mean the evolved common speech of all those who had come to these centres, to take part in government and learning, rather than of the majorities who had been born there. In the written language, particularly, this divergence was quite evident, and it was largely from the forms of this written language, spoken by men who had been trained in these centres and gone back to their regions, that the new common language spread over England. The existence of a common written language, which when spoken still showed the results of regional influence, is the first key to the subsequent history of class dialect in England.

Through the emergence of a common written language, marked regional speech variations still continued, even at the centre. Between the sixteenth and the end of the eighteenth centuries, Englishmen in touch with the central institutions wrote a common language, but still, in diminishing degree, spoke it differently. In Elizabethan London, the divergences of educated speakers were still quite marked, but the signs of unease and self-consciousness about this were already beginning to show. Palsgrave, in 1530, makes the first recorded mention of a 'true kynde of pronuntiacon', and Puttenham wrote:

> Our maker therfore at these dayes shall not follow *Piers plowman* nor *Gower* nor *Lydgate* nor yet *Chaucer*, for their language is now out of use with us; neither shall he take the termes of Northenmen, such as they use in dayly talke, whether they be noble men or gentlemen or of their best clarkes, all is a matter; nor in effect any speach used beyond the river of Trent, though no man can deny but that theirs is the purer English Saxon at this day, yet it is not so Courtly nor so currant as our Southerne English is; no more is the far Westerne mans speach. Ye shall therefore take the usuall

speach of the Court, and that of London and the shires lying about London within LX myles, and not much above. I say not this but that in every shyre of England there be gentlemen and others that speake, but specially write, as good Southerne as we of Middlesex or Surrey do, but not the common people of every shire, to whom the gentlemen, and also their learned clarkes, do for the most part condescend; but herein we are already ruled by th'English Dictionaries and other bookes written by learned men, and therefore it needeth none other direction in that behalfe.

This, indeed, is the shape of things to come, but meanwhile the written language was itself still changing. There was a very important accession of Latin vocabulary and sentence-forms, particularly in the sixteenth and early seventeenth centuries, although parts of this influence were later decisively rejected. And there was also the vitalizing influence of the still varied speech on the written forms: an influence at its greatest at the time of the Elizabethan dramatists. The extraordinary invigoration of English at this period can be seen as the flow of the living and varied speech into the narrower common written language. Only when this extension had been made could the tendency towards uniformity prevail over the varied strengths of the speech.

Puttenham speaks, significantly, of dictionaries, but the real influence of such instruments lay nearly two centuries ahead. The language was still changing, though more slowly than in previous centuries, and changes in the social structure of England were now to exert a decisive effect. The process of standardizing the written language continued, with growing confidence, yet the source of the standard was now a matter of dispute. When Puttenham wrote, the standard was evidently the Court and the Metropolis, with an afterthought of acknowledgment to 'learned men'. But the Court, after the Restoration, with a French-influenced manner that held fashion for a period, was no longer in fact a centre, and Swift, acknowledging its former pre-eminence, could now speak of it as the 'worst school in England for that accomplishment'. Similarly, deprived of the real Court, Thomas Sprat, in his *History of the Royal Society*, looked for an 'impartial Court of Eloquence according to whose censure all books or authors should either stand or fall', yet recommended

> a close, naked, natural way of speaking; positive expressions; clear senses; a native easiness; bringing all things as near the mathematical plainness as they can; and preferring the language of artisans, countrymen and merchants, before that of wits or scholars.

The class-structure of England was now decisively changing, at the beginning of a period which can be summed up as the effort of the rising middle-class to establish its own common speech. By the nineteenth century, after many important changes, this had been achieved, and it is then that we first hear of 'Standard English', by which is meant speech: a very different thing from the written 'standard' established so much earlier. Indeed, its naming as 'standard', with the implication no longer of a common but of a model language, represents the full coming to consciousness of a new concept of class speech: now no longer merely the functional convenience of a metropolitan class, but the means and emphasis of social distinction. It is to the history of this process that we must now turn.

III

The late seventeenth and eighteenth centuries saw a strenuous effort to rationalize English, by a number of differently motivated groups. The Royal Society's Committee 'for improving the English tongue' (1664) represents the effort of a new scientific philosophy to clarify the language for the purposes of its own kind of discourse. A different group, running from Addison and Swift to Pope and Johnson, were concerned with the absence of a 'polite standard' in the new society. Yet behind these intellectual groups there was the practical pressure of a newly powerful and self-conscious middle class which, like most groups which find themselves suddenly possessed of social standing but deficient in social tradition, thought 'correctness' a systematic thing which had simply to be acquired. Eighteenth-century London abounded in spelling-masters and pronunciation-coaches: many of them, as it happened, ignorant men. Yet if they had all been scholars, within the concepts of their period, the result might not have been greatly different. The scholarly teaching of grammar was locked in the illusion that Latin grammatical rules were the best possible guide to correctness in English. And Johnson himself emphatically expounded a doctrine equally false: that the spelling of a word is the best guide to its pronunciation, 'the most elegant speakers . . . (those) who deviate least from the written words'. The new 'standard', therefore, was not, as the earlier common language had been, the result mainly of growth through contact and actual relationships, but to a considerable extent an artificial creation based on false premises. The habits of a language are too strong to be wholly altered by determined yet relatively ignorant teachers, but the mark of their effort is still on us, and the tension they created is still high.

Common pronunciation (as distinct from regional variations) changed considerably during this period: partly through ordinary change, partly through the teaching of 'correctness'. English spelling, as is now well known, is in fact extremely unreliable as a guide to pronunciation, for not only, at best, does it frequently record sounds that have become obsolete, but in fact many of these were obsolete when the spellings were fixed, and moreover certain plain blunders have become embedded by time. *Iland, sissors, sithe, coud*, and *ancor* were altered, by men ignorant of their origins, confident of false origins, to *island, scissors, scythe, could*, and *anchor*, but in these cases, fortunately, pronunciation has not been affected. Similar false alterations, however, such as *fault, vault, assault* (which need no l's), or *advantage* and *advance* (which need no d's) have perpetuated their errors not only into spelling but into sound. The principle of following the spelling changed the sound *offen* into *often, forrid* into *forehead, summat* into *somewhat, lanskip* into *landscape, yumer* into *humour, at ome* into *at home, weskit* into *waistcoat*, and so on, in a list that could be tediously prolonged. Words like these are among the pressure points of distinction between 'educated' and 'uneducated' speech, yet the case is simply that the uneducated, less exposed to the doctrines of 'correctness', have preserved the traditional pronunciation.

An amusing sidelight on this process is the development,

in literature and journalism, of an 'orthography of the uneducated'. It has been one of the principal amusements of the English middle class to record the hideousness of people who say *orf*, or *wot*, even though these can spell the standard pronunciations. The error consists in supposing that the ordinary spelling indicates how proper people speak. We may look at one case among thousands, from a current detective novel (written by an Oxford don's wife), in which there is an awful north-country don:

> Field stood blinking and rubbing his chilblains. Then he smiled woodenly. 'Well, Mr Link, you may have a chance of showing your principles at once' (he pronounced them *channse* and *wonnce*).

The difficulty here is how a nice person (without chilblains) would have pronounced them. If he had followed the plain spelling, his 'chance' would have been as likely to be North-country as anything else, and his 'once' would not have been English at all. Submerged in the demonstration, in fact, are the understood values of *chahnce* (to make it quite certain) and *wunce* (but that belongs to children and the ignorant). It is difficult to estimate when people will know enough about their own language to stop this, so that naked prejudice no longer goes bowing graciously down the street. Meanwhile we can try to see when it started. It is used in Elizabethan plays to indicate such foreign elements as Welsh soldiers or Somerset peasants, and in Restoration plays there are the beginnings of finer distinctions, socially based, whether in the affected pronunciation of fops, or the 'errors' of those from outside the fashionable world. But it is in the eighteenth century, in novels and plays, that the real development is noticeable, and of course by the nineteenth century it is in full spate. I find it interesting to set beside this development the actual letters of eighteenth-century aristocratic women, which contain such phrases and spellings-by-ear as these:

> between you and I, Sis Peg and me, most people thinks, sarve, sartinly, larne (learn), schollards, Frydy, Mundy, byled, gine (join), went down of his knees, jest agoing to be married, the weather has been wonderfull stormie, he is reasonable well agane, I don't see no likelyhood of her dying.

These letters show also a tone which the anxiously correct middle class sought to reform:

> I believe I shall Jumble my Guts out between this and russell street. (Anne Countess of Strafford)

> I was at her Grace of Shrewsbery's who I think is more rediculouse in her talk than ever. She told all the Company as they came in that she was very much out of humour for she had things growing upon her toes like thumbs. (Anne Countess of Strafford)

> I danced with Ld Petre, and he is a nasty toad, for I long'd to spit in his face. (Lady Sarah Lenox)

> She is femenine to the greatest degree, laughs most heartily at a dirty joke, but never makes one. (Lady Sarah Lenox)

We can of course see the standard changing within this class itself, as Mrs Behn found to her cost. Meanwhile, as a last gesture to the 'orthography of the uneducated', we might set down, in its orthodox manner, the speech of an educated late eighteenth-century gentleman, according to known pro-nunciations of that class at that period:

> Aye, he's an ojus feller, if he is a Dook. Her leddyship's more obleegin, I've offen taken a coop of tay in her gyarden, and admired her lalocs, which she thinks more of than goold. A umorous ooman, and her gyearls the prettiest in Lunnon. But to be in the Dook's neighbrood's summat dauntin. He talks only of his fortin and his futer, as if he was some marchant of cowcumbers or reddishes. And he wears a cyap and weskit like a sarvant's, and sits in his cheer like some chaney Injun. You know that kyind.

It is interesting to see how much of this would now slip into the fashionable middle-class exercise in vulgarity.

Between about 1775 and 1850, what was later called 'Received Standard' pronunciation changed markedly. One of the crucial changes was the lengthening of the vowel in such words as *past* and *path*: now a mode of class speech, but until this period a regional and rustic habit. *Boiled* lost its *biled* pronunciation, as did almost all the 'oi' words, and the 'ar' pronunciation (dating from about 1500, in 'correct' London speech) in words like *servant* and *learn* also went out, except in one or two words, such as *clerk* and *Derby*, which, amusingly, are now highly valued, for their anomaly, in class speech. *Had* and *man* verged towards *head* and *men*, as one can still hear. The 'r' in most words was further weakened, *more* moving towards *maw*, and the endings of such words as *orator* diminishing to a mere glide of the voice. Dropping the 'r' in such words as *bird* produced a new and valued vowel sound in what remained. These and similar changes were spread by improved communications, but the main agency, undoubtedly, in fixing them as class speech, was the new cult of uniformity in the public schools. It was a mixture of 'correctness', natural development, and affectation, but it became as it were embalmed. It was no longer one kind of English, or even a useful common dialect, but 'correct English', 'good English', 'pure English', 'standard English'. In its name, thousands of people have been capable of the vulgar insolence of telling other Englishmen that they do not know how to speak their own language. And as education was extended, under mainly middle-class direction, this attitude spread from being simply a class distinction to a point where it was possible to identify the making of these sounds with being educated, and thousands of teachers and learners, from poor homes, became ashamed of the speech of their fathers.

But this takes us on into the continuing social changes of the present century, and we must look at the effect of this history on present theory and practice.

IV

It is now customary, in language theory, to mark three kinds of English speech: Received Standard, whose history we have been tracing; Regional Dialects, the varied survivors of many localities; and Modified Standard, which has gained currency in varying kinds in different areas, representing a development from regional dialects but falling short of Received Standard.

Most people who use this classification are, of course, attached by their own speech habits to 'Received Standard', and this has had important effects, even at a scholarly level. Thus a fine historian of language like H. C. Wyld can slip into special pleading, as when he argues that the long 'a' in

Received Standard *path* and *last* is more 'beautiful and sonorous' than its alternatives (this is a natural affection but quite arbitrary), or that to 'insert' the 'r'-sound in *bird* would lose the quality and length of the vowel (but to me, with different speech habits, the sounding of 'r' is 'beautiful and sonorous'). Or R. W. Chapman can write:

> In phonetics England does not yet groan under a democratic tyranny; we are free, within wide limits, to speak as well as we can.

But to anyone who has thought about language the class-prejudice of this will be especially clear. Chapman goes on to define Received Standard as the speech of

> a class which though not arrogantly exclusive is necessarily limited in numbers. Its traditions are maintained not primarily by the universities, but by the public schools.

Wyld argues that the class among which 'the "best" English' is 'most consistently heard at its best' is that of 'officers of the British Regular Army'. But of course it is just at this point that one sees why 'Received Standard' will not do.

With the growth of towns, and especially the new industrial towns drawing on wide rural areas for their populations; with the increase in literacy, and the vast increase in the dissemination of print; with increased travel and with social mobility affecting wider numbers of people, the evolution of a common English speech was clearly hastened. The difficulty lies in estimating the point we have so far reached in this evolution; it is this question that 'Received Standard' begs. If we look at the situation as a whole, we can see a marked decrease in pure Regional Dialects; it does not often happen now, as it certainly used to do, that men from different parts of the country find plain difficulties of meaning in each other's speech. Moreover, although there are still very many people who speak a clear regional form, though commonly purged of certain extreme habits in vocabulary and construction, there are very many also who, while using regional sounds, in all other respects speak a common tongue. We can say with some confidence that dialects, in the true sense, are rapidly ceasing to exist, and that in their place are a large number of regional ways of speaking a common language. Some of these are, in pronunciation, purely Regional; others seem to represent the growth, over certain extending areas, of forms which are certainly not 'Received Standard' but as certainly not the old local dialects in their earlier forms. Within these two kinds, which in individual cases will be seen to be a continuous shading and not a sharp distinction on either side of a line, the majority of English speakers in this country are contained. But the terms offered to describe them, Regional Dialects and Modified Standard, are both misleading. More accurately they are Regional and Modified Regional forms. 'Modified Regional' is, however, very different in sense from 'Modified Standard', which assumes that everybody in this category is aiming at the class dialect but failing to achieve it.

The next stage in development is, of course, Inter-Regional, and here the real problems of a common language arise. We have seen that 'Received Standard' had as one of its leading elements the habit of where possible pronouncing by the spelling. However misleading this might be, as a principle, it was obviously a general and permanent development. In so far as 'Received Standard' included changes made on this principle, its changes have been widely accepted, even in many recognizably regional forms. But, in other respects, 'Received Standard' was simply the development of a particular Southern form, and it came to include certain purely class elements. Thus, while in certain respects 'Received Standard' was in the general line of evolution, in other respects it moved away from this, by the fact of its becoming identified with a particular class. Of course it became entrenched in education, and then in broadcasting, and so had wide effects on the national development, but at the same time the ordinary linguistic process was operating, through the other kinds of social change. Indeed, in becoming identifiable as 'Public School English', which is in fact its more accurate description, certain barriers were raised against its general adoption, and these have to be set against the effects in education and broadcasting. In the latter, interestingly, there is already considerable variation, because the class dialect is not universally acceptable. The standard accent of the popular entertainer or commentator is as often pseudo-American as Public School or its derivatives. The class and region complex is avoided by an imported or synthetic alternative.

It looked, indeed, for a time, as if Public School English would be the effective Inter-Regional Speech, but it now seems quite certain that it will not be, in the forms then envisaged. Every use of the form for class distinction (and this, of course, has been widespread) reduced its chance of becoming a true common speech. Its identification with power, learning and material success (factors naturally making for its imitation) was countered by strong feelings against it, in the explosive human area of snobbery and resentment. The way things would go was first shown by an interesting adaptation of the 'orthography of the uneducated' to an orthography of Public School English (particularly applied to Wyld's 'best class'—officers of the British Regular Army), e.g.:

> We head a chahnce of pahchasing that fohm, but a bahd in the hend seemed maw vehluable, evenchalleh.

Here the class form encountered the powerful current of pronunciation by spelling, and of course once the so-called 'Received Standard' could be used not only for comic representation but also as a distinction from the 'correctness' of pronunciation by spelling, its chances of common adoption, in spite of all the powerful factors in its favour, were small. What in fact has happened is that Public School English, too hastily called Received Standard, has itself begun to shed certain sounds found wrong on the 'correctness' principle, and the actual inter-regional speech that is developing is a combination of old 'Received Standard' and some of the more important Modified Regional forms. The breathed sound which acknowledges the 'h' in 'what' and similar words, counted as not Received Standard in the nineteen-twenties, is becoming normal, even in 'Received Standard' speakers, because of the spelling. The 'r'-sound, also, is making its way back, though as yet not emphatically, and the vowel-sound in words like 'more' and 'bird' is noticeably changing, again under the influence of the spelling. The crucial 'a' sounds are also changing, so that while 'chance' is still 'chahnce' the length of this stress is reduced, while in words like 'had' the tendency towards an 'e'-sound has been reversed, The crucial factor in all this, more important than the dropping or softening of sounds which had been identified as ridiculous, is the speaking-by-spelling of a more widely educated society. 'Received Standard', as defined thirty years ago, is becoming a local form, for there are now many thousands of people who do not make these distinctive sounds yet who speak an English that has lost any obvious regional identification. The change is more marked among men than women, but already it is fair to say that the sounds crucially identified as 'Received Standard' are passing into local and historical use. And we cannot say that 'Received Standard', as the best form, is evolving. The fact is that we are at still too early a stage, in the development of a common pronunciation, for anything like a standard to have been introduced.

There are now not only inter-regional but international problems in this. To American ears 'Received Standard' was always unacceptable, and there has in fact been a considerable interaction between American and English forms, with American predominating. Not only have hundreds of American words, speech forms and pronunciations been taken, often unnoticed, into English, but American speech has had an influence on almost all kinds of traditional English speaking, and it is worth noticing that it works against every single sound that was identified as peculiarly 'Received Standard'. Moreover, by giving other accents to power and material success, it has deprived Public School English of its former monopoly in this respect. The process is still going on, but it is not simply the Americanization of English; it is, rather, the addition of another factor to the long and complicated history of spoken English.

It is by no means certain that any one form will emerge as universal, but in any case what matters is that we should reduce the area of mystification and prejudice. The U and non-U controversy, at its popular level, was pathetic rather than dangerous, for it showed, in the end, how shifting the class boundaries, in this case of vocabulary, are. There will doubtless always be people and groups who are anxious to show that they are not as other men, but the deep processes of the growth of a great international language will not be much affected by them, though they may for a time be blurred. We want to speak as ourselves, and so elements of the past of the language, that we received from our parents, are always alive. At the same time, in an extending community, we want to speak with each other, reserving our actual differences but reducing those that we find irrelevant. We are almost past the stage of difficulties of meaning, in ordinary discourse, though with a limited educational system there are still serious and unnecessary difficulties wherever the world of organized learning is touched. For the rest, the problems are of emotional tension, and these, while certain to continue, can be much reduced if we learn to look at them openly and rationally, with the rich and continuing history of English as our basis of understanding. 'Vor bote a man conne frense me telth of him lute', wrote Robert of Gloucester, noting the social superiority of the Norman French of the masters of the time, but the language he noted as superior is even farther from us, in the same country, than the language in which he noted it. Nor did history end around 1800, or in the nineteen-twenties. The living language offers its deciding witnesses.

FIVE

The Social History of English Writers

WE argue a good deal about the effects on literature of the social origins of writers, their kind of education, their ways of getting a living, and the kinds of audience they expect and get. Theoretical questions, often very difficult, are of course involved in this argument, but the most obvious difficulty is the lack of any outline of facts by which some of the theoretical principles could be tested. There are occasional agitated debates in which people quote lists at each other, to prove their own version of the origins and affiliations of valued writers. Yet the principle of selection, in these lists, is usually quite obviously related to the particular thesis. We seem to need an outline of such facts based on a standard list, and then to restart the argument from there. I have attempted such an outline, based on the index of the Oxford *Introduction to English Literature*, and with the *Dictionary of National Biography* as main authority. Ideally, of course, we need a much more extensive piece of research, but this examination of nearly 350 writers, born between 1470 and 1920, may perhaps serve as a preliminary sketch. The questions asked are in three categories: social origin; kind of education; method of living. For social origin, eight reasonably continuous kinds of family, based on the economic and social standing of the father, have been listed: nobility, gentry, professional men, merchants, tradesmen, farmers, craftsmen and labourers. For education, four kinds of schooling have been listed: national grammar (since the 1860s called 'public schools'), local grammar, dissenting academy, and home or private. For universities, the traditional division between Oxford and Cambridge, and others, has been used. For method of living, three general categories have been used, to indicate main source of income: independent (inherited or propertied); employed (in work other than that for which the writer is known); and vocational (main income from work in the field in which the writer is known). A good deal of overlapping has been found, especially in the last category, and this has been allowed for. It is obvious also, of course, that kinds of family, and their relative importance in the society, have varied historically, and that this must be remembered as the significance of origin is assessed. In spite of these difficulties, I think the general outline that emerges may be useful.

The historical periods used have been half-centuries. For several reasons, including the terminal date, the actual periods used are 1480–1530; 1530–1580; 1580–1630; 1630–1680; 1680–1730; 1730–1780; 1780–1830; 1830–1880; 1880–1930. As it has turned out, I think these periods are more relevant to the actual history of literature than any other regular division. The assignment to periods has been on the basis of the tenth year after the particular writer's birth, since this is obviously a crucial age in one of the decisive factors—education. This also means that no writers born later than 1920 have been included, and for such writers there is of course as yet no reasonably standard list.

In the first period studied, from 1480 to 1530, we are looking at the men who created Tudor literature. Of the twenty-one writers listed, the origins of three are uncertain. Of the remaining eighteen, eleven came from the nobility and gentry (three and eight respectively) and four from professional families closely related to the gentry. Only three are known to come from outside these classes: two from farming and one from a craftsman's family. The homogeneity of this predominantly gentry culture was greatly advanced by the universities of Oxford and Cambridge, to which seventeen are known to have gone. Of the four exceptions, one is a nobleman, two as Scots went to Scottish universities, and one is not recorded. Schooling is less unified, in terms of institutions: of the fourteen for whom there are records, four went away to national grammar schools, five went to local grammar schools, and five were educated at home. In content, the literature of the period has a high proportion of theological and educational writing, and it is only in relation to this emphasis that we find as many as ten living by the vocation for which they are known, mainly in church and university. Three vary, in different periods of their lives, between vocation and employment and six are mainly employed. The close interconnection of institutions and families is shown in kinds of employment: service at court or as tutor in a royal or noble family. Only two seem to have been wholly independent, though in many cases there was supplementary family income from property.

In the next period, from 1530 to 1580, we are looking at the men who created Elizabethan literature. Of thirty-eight writers, the origins of two are uncertain. Of the remaining thirty-six, fifteen are from the nobility and gentry (three and twelve respectively), and nine are from professional families, now less regularly connected with the gentry. The appearance of twelve from the families of merchants, tradesmen and craftsmen (four, three and five respectively) marks an important change. Yet the importance of Oxford and Cambridge, as linking institutions, is still great. Of the thirty-six for whom there are records, twenty-seven went to Oxford and Cambridge. Two attended universities abroad, and seven (including one noblemen and one page at court) attended no university, three of these being the sons of tradesmen or craftsmen. Of the nineteen for whom schooling is recorded, eight went away to national grammar schools, nine went to local grammar schools, and two were educated at home and court. In method of living, seven were wholly independent, two combined substantial independence with service at court, and eleven were employed, away from their vocation as writers, in court, church, law, university and as secretary or tutor in a noble family. Some of the earlier vocational basis remains, in the church, but this period saw the emergence of a class of professional writers: the first generation of Elizabethan dramatists, centred on the London theatres. The ordinary earlier ties between drama and church or academic institution had been largely replaced by the new theatres. It is significant that almost all these dramatists came from the newly represented classes: either professional families not related to the gentry, or tradesmen and craftsmen. This is the radically new element, while in the rest of the national literature the distribution of content and origins is very much that of the earlier Tudor period.

In the next period, 1580–1630, we are looking at the Jacobean dramatists, the metaphysical poets, and the Cavalier and Puritan poets, together with political theorists up to Hobbes. Of the thirty-three writers listed, the origins of three are uncertain. Of the remaining thirty, there are nine from the gentry, thirteen from professional families, one from a merchant family, four from trade, two from farming, and one from the family of a craftsman. The continued importance of Oxford and Cambridge as linking institutions is marked: twenty-eight of the thirty for whom there is information went to these universities. Twelve went away to national grammar schools, nine to local grammar schools, and three were educated at home or at court. It is notable, in many individual careers, that meeting at university was a critical factor in the lives of many of the poorer men. There was some evidence of this in the previous half-century also. The result is a good deal of social mobility once Oxford or Cambridge has been reached. In method of life, the dramatists can still follow their vocation in the theatres (it is perhaps interesting that their social origins are rather different from the Elizabethan generation, with a shift back towards the gentry and professional families related to the gentry, and a marked decline in those coming from the merchant-tradesman-craftsman group). More writers are now employed, away from their vocation as writers, both in the older institutions and, with a significant increase, as secretary or tutor in a noble family of whom a member has been met at university. Seven of the thirty-three are wholly independent, and there is a decline in the number of those based on the church.

In the next period, 1630–1680, we are looking mainly at Restoration writers, and at some of the early Augustans. Of the twenty-two writers listed, the origins of twenty-one are known. In the smaller total, there is a proportionate swing back towards the nobility and gentry, who provide nine representatives (two and seven respectively). Seven are from professional families, three (one of whom did not publish until the eighteenth century) from trade, and two (one of them Bunyan) from craftsmen. It is both a more limited and a more clearly class-based culture than that which preceded it. The importance of Oxford and Cambridge is still evident, with these universities taking thirteen of the twenty-one for whom there is information. Three others went to Irish and one to a French university, while two of the four remaining are noblemen, and two poor. Of the eighteen for whom there is information on schooling, six went away to national grammar schools, seven went to local grammar schools, one went to a dissenting academy, and four were educated at home. In method of living, the smaller number of dramatists were still largely based on the fewer theatres, and these account for most of the ten who lived by their vocation. Eight were employed, significantly often now in government service, while four were wholly independent.

In the next period, 1680–1730, we are looking at the Augustans and the mid-eighteenth-century novelists, poets, dramatists and philosophers. On the whole, between about 1640 and the 1730s there had been a slowing-down in the general expansion of the national literature, and proportionately less writers are recorded. The period 1680–1730 shows a marked change in social origins, with thirteen out of nineteen writers listed coming from professional families of a mainly middle-class kind, only two from the nobility and gentry, and four (one, two, one) from the merchants, tradesmen and craftsmen. The relative importance of Scots and Irish is much higher, and for the first time less than half those listed (eight out of nineteen) went to Oxford or Cambridge. Of those for whom there is information on schooling, six went away to national grammar schools, nine went to local grammar schools, and two were educated at home. In method of living, only two of these writers were wholly independent. It was becoming possible for some writers to live wholly, if often inadequately, by their profession, and the emergence of a class of professional writers, many of them hacks, was noted in the period. Most of the writers we now read combined authorship with some form of employment, normally in the professions (including the church but less often than in earlier periods) and in some cases in the old form of service as secretary or tutor. More government posts were also becoming available. Money through marriage is notable in a number of cases. This was a period of patronage, and of the emergence alongside it of a more organized bookselling market. The ordinary career of a good writer was exceptionally uneven, with irregular income from a variety of sources, and with a good deal of hand-to-mouth living until some favourable opportunity, either in patronage or from the market, turned up. There is also a distinct sense of emerging classes of writers, with a division between those following traditional forms usually with some patronage, and those adapting to the new market. But in several careers this division was blurred, for the whole period is one of overlapping of different systems and forms.

In the next period, 1730–1780, we are looking at late-eighteenth-century writers and some of the first generation of Romantic writers. The predominance of writers from professional families continues, with eleven out of twenty-five listed. Only two are from the nobility, and none from the gentry. The new element is the greater representation from tradesmen, farmers and craftsmen, who between them supply eleven (four, four, three), an equal number with the professions. One is from a merchant's family. The relative importance of Scots and Irish continues. Again, as in the earlier period, the significance of Oxford and Cambridge is less: now only eight, out of twenty-five, went to either university. Four went to Irish or Scottish universities, but thirteen went to no university. In schooling, four went to national grammar schools, eight to local English grammar schools, five to Scottish or Irish schools, and three (including two women) were educated at home (the third is Cobbett, who was really self-educated). Some distinctly new ways of thinking and feeling seem to enter with the greater representation from the peasants and craftsmen (Burns, Cobbett, Blake, Paine). In method of living, three were wholly independent. There was still some patronage, and some writers who went to national grammar schools made influential friends there, who later helped them in various ways. There was the usual reliance on other professional employment, in the church, law and medicine, and the importance of government posts made itself further felt. But the predominant impression of the period is one of the great poverty of writers, apparent in the preceding period but now affecting more men. There was just enough of a bookselling market, and associated hack work, to offer the possibility of living by writing, but those without any private income and with no influential friends, who tried it, were often exceptionally poor and exposed.

In the next period, 1780–1830, we are looking at the second generation of Romantic writers and at the early and mid-Victorians. The most decisive fact is that the expansion of the national literature, partly if unevenly resumed in the eighteenth century, is now very marked. In social origin, the largest single group of these writers came from professional families: twenty-five out of fifty-seven. One came from the nobility, and eight from the gentry. Nine came from the families of merchants. From the families of tradesmen, craftsmen, poor farmers and labourers came thirteen (five, five, two, one). In terms of new ways of thinking, mainly on social issues, the contribution of this last group was especially distinguished. The emergence of a significant number of important women writers is particularly notable.

Of the fifty-two for whom there is information on schooling, eighteen went to national grammar schools, fourteen to English local grammar schools, four to Scottish or Irish schools, and sixteen (including eight women) were educated, in many cases inadequately, at home. The importance of Oxford and Cambridge revived to some extent, with twenty-four entrants out of fifty-seven. Seven went to Scottish or Irish universities, one to London, and one to a French Catholic university. Looking over the whole list, it is noticeable that few writers follow any standardized route. Only ten of the fifty-seven went from the gentry or a professional family to a national grammar school and then Oxford or Cambridge. In method of life there was a marked change, due to improvements in the bookselling market and in particular to the greatly increased importance and stability of magazines. Where previously the Elizabethan theatre, or in a looser form the eighteenth-century coffeehouse, had served as institutions through which professional writers lived and made contact, there was now an evident concentration around magazines, in London and Edinburgh, and in particular the emergence of a new kind of established 'literary London'. Some nine of the fifty-seven were wholly independent in income, but many more became comfortably established as professional writers, not only through books, but through articles, reviewing, editing, travel-writing, and of course serial publication in the magazines. Far fewer writers, proportionately, were employed quite away from their work as writers. Of those who were, government service and education were the principal occupations, with some in the church and the law. For writers at home in the world of novels and magazines, the period was comfortable, but it is noticeable that the poets either had independent incomes or were dependent on help and patronage, or, if these failed, were as poor as their eighteenth-century predecessors. Among Victorian novelists, the contribution of women and of men from the poorer social groups is especially marked.

In the next period, 1830–1880, we are looking at writers of the late nineteenth and early twentieth centuries. The dominant impression is of a more highly organized upper-middle class making the major contribution. There are no writers listed from the nobility, but from the gentry and merchant and professional families, now commonly closely related, there are no less than forty-four out of fifty-three (seven, six, thirty-one). The remaining nine came from the families of tradesmen and craftsmen. This is a notably less varied social origin, to the disadvantage of the poorer groups, than in the earlier part of the nineteenth century. In schooling, nineteen went to national grammar schools, sixteen to English local grammar schools, seven to local Scottish and Irish schools, two to dissenting academies, and seven were otherwise educated (two women and two men adequately at home, the others inadequately). The relative importance of Oxford and Cambridge is maintained, with twenty-four out of the fifty-three listed. Nine went to Scottish or Irish universities, six to other English universities, and fourteen to no university. Six were independent in method of living, and eight were employed away from the work by which they are known. The vocational basis, either in the expanded market for books and magazines, or in relevant institutions such as universities, is very clear in the period. The imaginative writers are more varied in every respect than the philosophers and historians, who in majority follow a typical career of professional family, national grammar school, and Oxford or Cambridge.

In the final period, 1880–1930, we are looking mainly at the writers of the inter-war years, and at contemporary writers born before 1920. In social origins, the pattern is basically similar to that of the previous period, with one from the nobility, and thirty-nine out of fifty-three from the often closely related gentry and merchant and professional families (seven, two, thirty). The importance of professional families as the largest single source is marked as in earlier periods. From the families of tradesmen, farmers, craftsmen and labourers there are thirteen of the fifty-three listed (five, two, four and two). There are notable differences in the educational pattern, with the first modern majority from the national grammar (now 'public') schools: thirty-two out of fifty-three. Eight went to English local grammar schools, two to private schools, four to elementary schools only, and four (including two women) were educated at home. Thirty-two went to Oxford or Cambridge, one to an Irish university, four to other English universities, one to a German university, and fifteen to no university. The typical career, noted in the earlier period for historians and philosophers, is now more generally spread: professional family, public school, Oxford or Cambridge. Four of the fifty-three had substantial independent means, three were employed away from the work by which they are known, and the majority had a fairly clear vocational basis, in the world of books, magazines and related institutions.

We can at present take this factual inquiry no further, since there is no standard list for writers born since 1920. It has been generally assumed that there has been some shift in the years since 1945 from the regular majority pattern of the earlier period. A rough check, on the basis of a personal list of writers of this age who have attracted particular attention, indeed shows a more varied social origin (six out of twelve from the families of tradesmen and clerical and industrial workers), a different pattern of schooling (two public school, seven local grammar school, three other local authority schools), a continuing relative importance of Oxford and Cambridge (seven out of twelve), and a vocational pattern divided between full-time professional writing and university English teaching. Too much weight should not be given to these figures, since the list is necessarily highly selective, and covers writers who still have much of their work to do, while certainly neglecting others who must eventually be included. But so far as they go, they confirm the impression of some change.

II

The evidence of this whole inquiry is obviously limited in value, and will need to be checked and amplified by longer research. So far as it goes, however, I find it interesting, even when it only confirms general impressions of the writers of a period gained by other means. Looking through the body of detail, it is impossible to accept the extreme view, still held by some people, that the growth of a national literature is wholly autonomous, unaffected by variations in institutions, audiences, social and educational opportunity, and available methods of living. Indeed such a view is so unreasonable that it would probably not be held at all if the converse were not often stated in a similarly extreme and untenable way. Thus the social origins and educational history of writers clearly often influence their work, but to think primarily of social classes and institutions, and then of individuals as merely their representatives, is wholly misleading. Not only, in certain important cases, do individuals deviate from their group of origin, but also the whole process of individual growth is more complicated than any simple assignment to groups would indicate. Equally, however, since the individual grows in relation to a learned pattern, which is of social significance, the assumption of autonomous creation— the creative individual acting wholly freely—is misleading and naive.

It is worth looking briefly through the evidence to see

what kinds of correlation between a society and its literature are reasonable. The relation of Tudor literature to its social context seems quite clear, and the broadening into Elizabethan literature seems certainly connected with the greater social variety evidenced in its writers. It is difficult to say how far this should be taken, but there seems a possible relation between the majority origin of the Elizabethan dramatists in rising social groups, and the swing back from this in their Jacobean and Caroline successors. The change in the character of the drama over these years, the swingback from a popular drama to a more socially limited drama, follows this line. Moreover, the line is continued into the period of the frankly class-based Restoration theatre. Again, in the early eighteenth century, there is a clear correlation between the majority of writers from professional and trading families and the new forms and modes of what has often been described as a middle-class literature. The later eighteenth century shows no such simple correlation. It is socially a very varied period for writers, but the outstanding literary development, that of Romantic poetry, shows no consistent relation with the social history of its creators. Indeed it is a movement in which all social classes, educational patterns and methods of life are represented, often with marked individual variations from inherited social norms: perhaps the only factor that is significant, since this would certainly have a relation with part of the character of the movement. The importance of new social groups in much of the most original social thinking of the nineteenth century, and of these groups and of women in the major period of the Victorian novel, is a positive correlation. In the period between about 1870 and 1950 perhaps the most significant correlation is negative. It has been widely noted that an unusual proportion of the important imaginative literature of these years was written by people outside the majority English pattern. This had been true to some extent of the Victorian novel, but in these later years the relative importance of writers from abroad or from minority groups, as well as of women, is marked. Hardy, James, Shaw, Synge, Yeats, Eliot, Conrad, Lawrence, O'Casey, Joyce, Thomas compose a short list of some significance, not in the fact that, with the exception of the Irish, any particular minority is noticeable, but that difficult questions are raised about the majority pattern, the normal English mode, which certainly seems, in this period, relatively uncreative. Since judgements of quality are involved here, the analysis is not simple, but it seems to me there is some evidence of a social and imaginative narrowing which can be related to the emergence of a more standard social history of the principal contributors. The emergence of certain new elements in mood and content in more recent years might then be factually related to the limited variations which seem to have occurred in this standard pattern.

There is no single relation between the nature of a society and the character of its literature, but there are significant and possibly significant relations which seem to vary with the actual history. Since social origins have been factually related, in varying ways, both to educational opportunity and to methods of life which affect a writer's following his vocation, it can be said that this complex is of permanent significance, and has visibly affected parts of our literary development. Yet the emphasis should not fall only on origins. The character of literature is also visibly affected, in varying ways, by the nature of the communication system and by the changing character of audiences. When we see the important emergence of writers from a new social group, we must look not only at them, but at the new institutions and forms created by the wider social group to which they belong. The Elizabethan theatre is an exceptionally complex example, since as an institution it was largely created by individual middle-class speculators, and was supplied with plays by writers from largely middle-class and trading and artisan families, yet in fact was steadily opposed by the commercial middle class and, though serving popular audiences, survived through the protection of the court and the nobility. This very protection, later, steadily narrowed both drama and audiences, until in the Restoration a very narrow class was setting the dominant tone. The formation in the eighteenth century of an organized middle-class audience can be seen as in part due to certain writers from the same social group, but also, and perhaps mainly, as an independent formation which then drew these writers to it and gave them their opportunity. The expansion and further organization of this middle-class audience can be seen to have continued until the late nineteenth century, drawing in new writers from varied social origins but giving them, through its majority institutions, a general homogeneity. This general situation has persisted, but already in the nineteenth century there were signs of a break, with individuals deviating from the majority patterns, and, by the end of the century, a distinct and organized minority deviation. The social situation of literature in the twentieth century has been largely the interaction of continuing majority patterns, with an increasingly standard route into them, and this marked dissenting minority, which has tended to support and value writers from outside the majority pattern, and to provide an alternative outlet and affiliation for dissenting members of the majority groups. If we compare the social basis of literature between 1850 and 1870 and that between 1919 and 1939 we find in both cases an organized middle-class reading public as the major element, but whereas in the earlier period the literature was comparatively homogeneous, with most of its creators drawn from the same social group as the actual public, in the later period there is evidence of two publics, a majority and a minority, the former continuing the earlier type of relationship, the latter, while attracting individual dissenters, finding its major figures from outside, either from another culture or from other social groups. A large part of important modern literature—many novels, many plays, almost all poetry—has been communicated through the institutions of this minority public, in sharp contrast with the mid-Victorian situation, where the majority institutions were still closely related to the most important work of the time. The appearance of contributors from new social groups within the culture, which has attracted attention in recent years, has been normally through the institutions of this minority. Most of the new writers from the families of clerical and industrial workers are in fact being read not by the social groups from which they come, but by the dissident middle class. The expanding audience, for novels and plays, certainly includes members of new social groups, but in general they are simply being absorbed into the existing majority public. The danger of this situation is that the minority public may soon be the only identifiable group with an evident and particular social affiliation—defined largely through university education. There is some evidence that the separation of the majority public from its most creative members is leaving a cultural vacuum easily penetrated from outside. The rapid Americanization of most of the popular art-forms can be understood in these terms, at a time when so much of the best English art and thinking is closely related to an identifiable social minority which, with a limited educational system, most British people have no real chance of entering.

Thus the relations between literature and society can be seen to vary considerably, in changing historical situations. As a society changes, its literature changes, though often in unexpected ways, for it is a part of social growth and not simply its reflection. At times, a rising social group will create new institutions which, as it were, release its own writers. At other times, writers from new social groups will simply make their way into existing institutions, and work largely within their terms. This is the important theoretical context for the discussion of mobility, of which we have heard so much in our own generation. It is significant that mobility is now normally discussed primarily in individual terms and that the writer is so often taken as an example: he, like other artists, may be born anywhere, and can move, as an individual, very rapidly through the whole society. But in fact there are two major kinds of mobility: the individual career, which writers have often exemplified, and the rise of a whole social group, which creates new institutions and sometimes, as in the early eighteenth century, brings its writers with it. The problems of mobility can never be adequately discussed unless this distinction is made. Those affecting writers, in our own day, are primarily the result of a combination of individual mobility with the relative stability of institutions. This can be seen in the many literary works which take contemporary mobility as theme. At the end of the eighteenth century, Godwin, in *Caleb Williams*, produced an early example of such a career, with individual mobility very limited and with the institutions in relation to which it operated both powerful and harsh. Stendhal, in *Scarlet and Black*, took the same situation much further, ending with the individual being destroyed, first in character and then actually, instead of being merely hunted down to a compromise. The usual implication of Victorian treatments of this theme was (in default of one or other of the several magical solutions) that of control: the terms of origin must be basically respected, or the individual would degenerate. Hardy's protest, in *Jude the Obscure*, leaves the very effort hopeless. Lawrence introduced the new situation: the rapid if resentful rise, characteristically through art, into the dissident minority culture, but then, finally, into exile. In our own period, the characteristic pattern has been that of the more freely mobile individual mocking or raging at the institutions which are made available for him to join, or else, if he acquiesces, suffering rapid personal deterioration (cf. *Lucky Jim*, *Look Back in Anger*, *Room at the Top*). There is a continuing sense of deadlock, and much of the experience generated within it seems sterile. This is because the terms of mobility, thus conceived, are hopelessly limited. The combination of individual mobility with the stability of institutions and ways of thinking leads to this deadlock inevitably. And the experience of artists and intellectuals is then particularly misleading, for while such experience records particular local tensions, much of the real experience of mobility, in our own time, is that of whole social groups moving into new ways of life: not only the individual rising, but the society changing. This latter experience is, however, very difficult to negotiate while the institutions towards which writers and thinkers are attracted retain their limited social reference, and while new groups have been relatively unsuccessful in creating their own cultural institutions. There is an obvious danger of the advantage of individual writers drawn from more varied social origins being limited or nullified by their absorption into pre-existing standard patterns (as obviously now in the system of higher education) or by their concentration on fighting these patterns, rather than finding or helping to create new patterns. The problems of individual mobility have in fact been worked through to the point where the definition of mobility in individual terms can be plainly seen as inadequate. The whole society is moving, and the most urgent issue is the creation of new and relevant institutions.

The good writer may be born anywhere, and the evidence is that the pattern of his social development can be very varied, and that there may be danger in attempting to standardize it. But this does not mean that his development is autonomous or that what the society does, by way of institutions and forms of communication, will fail to affect him. What a society can properly do is revise and extend its institutions, first in education, second in means of communication, until these have an effective general relation with the real structure of the society, so that both writers and audiences can come through in their own terms. We are so far from this, in our own society, that we can say with certainty that the social history of writers which we have been tracing will continue to change.

SIX

The Social History of Dramatic Forms

WE are used to saying that drama is one of the most social of all art forms, and in certain obvious respects this is evidently true. The dramatist, like the poet or novelist, works in language to create a particular organization of experience, but the nature of the organization, in his case, is in terms of performance: the words he has arranged will be spoken and acted by other artists, the actors, in the normal process of communication. Already, by virtue of this, and in spite of the fact that the relation between text and performance, the literary work and the acted drama, varies greatly in different periods and societies, the extension from an individual creative activity to a social creative activity is clear. Again, whereas it is normal in the case of poems and novels for the work to be received, in the first instance, by temporarily isolated individuals, it is normal (though not universal) for drama to be received by a group, an actual audience. Thus not only in transmission but also in reception and response drama normally operates in an obvious social context, and this seems to be the reason why the social history of drama is in many ways easier to approach than the social history of some other arts. As a practical experiment in the possibility of this kind of inquiry, I propose to look briefly at the social history of English drama: partly as a way of describing actual changes in the relations between drama and society in the course of more general changes in the society as a whole; partly, also, as a way of approaching a much more difficult question, as to whether any relationship can be discovered between such social changes and actual changes in the forms of drama, changes of an artistic kind. We are used to the general idea that some relation must exist between social and artistic change, but in detail this is always very difficult to demonstrate, and because of the difficulty many people find good reasons for joining in the general retreat which would promote or relegate art to an autonomous area. If we can find certain demonstrable relations of this kind in drama, and if, where we cannot find them, we can look frankly at the difficulties as a way of revising the general idea, we may have made real progress in the whole field of these relations, of a kind useful in our inquiries into less obviously social arts.

I

The medieval period in English drama is, at first glance, a particularly clear case of an evident relation between social and dramatic forms. The earliest plays took their form from the liturgy, and were primarily a way of illustrating parts of the story of the scriptures to congregations few of whom could have understood this story when it was read in Latin. Thus the form of the little *Quem Quaeritis?* plays, showing the angel speaking to the women at the empty tomb of Jesus, is a clear example of direct dramatic reference to the purposes of a major social organization. Beginning as dramatic insets within the form of worship, the medieval religious drama moved out into a processional function: first the procession towards and within the church, later the procession through the town. As a social development, this is of considerable importance: the integration of dramatic performance, not only with the religious festivals but also with the life of the medieval town and the organization of trade and industry, became unusually close. The Corpus Christi processions, with their cycles of mystery and miracle plays, were not only official events in the life of the towns, but were organized through the trade guilds, each of which had a particular play as its continuing responsibility (as the Bakers, *The Last Supper*; the Tanners, *The Fall of Lucifer*; the Websters, *The Day of Judgement*). The form that had begun with the illustration of particular events in the Christian story, tying phrases of the liturgy to dramatic enactment, extended to a form of serial presentation of the whole story, from the Creation to the Ascension and the lives of the saints. The immediate form, in each episode, was determined by the primary illustrative function, but the whole form, as it developed, became a particular kind of episodic drama, determined by the fact of procession. This basic construction became a popular tradition, which was one of the many elements that later combined to make certain of the wholly new and characteristically English forms of the Elizabethan drama.

To this clear relation between a social function and method of organization and a particular dramatic form can be added the equally interesting relation between medieval society and the more sophisticated dramatic forms of the morality and its successor the interlude. The morality play takes its whole form and method from the pattern of feeling characteristic of medieval religion and society. It is unlike the mystery and miracle in that it is not dramatizing a religious narrative but the shape of a faith and a common human destiny. It is obviously only in certain societies, at certain stages of their development, that the idea of 'Everyman' can be deeply conceived. When there are true common meanings in the basic issues of life and death, and therefore when the sense of a truly universal destiny can be naturally felt, the form of the morality, with its abstract representative figures, and its dramatization of general human qualities and weaknesses that because they are felt as general need not be tied to individual human persons, takes organic shape. Yet this interesting form is not the whole form of the society. Even within the morality, we see the influence of other kinds of imaginative construction. *Everyman*'s House of Salvation is structurally related to the castle in *The Castell of Perseverance*, which has obvious affinities not only with the place of quest in the long tradition of magical folk stories which had been developed in the Christian romances, but also with real elements in the organization of society—the central place, church, castle, or hill, which in a practical way expresses the community's sense of itself (it is united and communicates in that place) and which is then a natural object of the search for value and security. Again, the development of the morality into the interlude shows in a very interesting way the interaction of a basic pattern and a slow social change. The interlude is differently based, socially, from the morality. Where the morality belonged in public places, in the towns, the interlude belonged in the halls of great houses, in the period when the medieval forms were beginning to change into those of Tudor society. The movement from popular religious drama to more sophisticated 'moral' drama takes in the morality as a stage, but is only completed in the interlude. At the same time, the characteristic interlude retains much of the impress of medieval social thinking; *The Four P's*, for example, is still the drama of men in their social functions, rather than of men as particular individuals.

The question of the relation between, on the one hand, figures in a religious story or in a religious or moral allegory, and, on the other hand, individualized human beings in a particular social context, is, while extremely complex, crucial in the subsequent development of English dramatic forms. It is noticeable in the miracles and mysteries that whereas the primary function is the reverent portrayal of figures who cannot be regarded as human in any ordinary sense, not only Jesus and his mother but the prophets and the saints, there is a powerful tendency to treat in a quite different way, first the figures to whom reverence need not be shown, such as Herod—the raging Herod, perhaps the most popular figure in this whole drama—and second, certain ancillary figures, as notably the shepherds at the nativity. It is perhaps best to see this whole matter as the interaction of the set roles of the traditional story with the living contemporary experience which they offered to interpret. There are then different degrees of interaction, and consequently different levels of individualization and contemporary realism. Even the great figures are contemporary in one sense: God the Father is watching this world, and Christ and the angels, Satan and the devils, are alive and moving in it. Figures like Noah think and talk in the medieval world, while retaining their traditional roles. Herod, in his raging authority, enters this contemporary world, going literally and dramatically down into the medieval street. And the shepherds in the Towneley *Secunda Pagina Pastorum* are Yorkshire shepherds, speaking their own dialect, dealing with their own problems, while also conceivable as the shepherds to whom the angel speaks and who go down reverently to worship Mary and Jesus.

It is significant to take this idea of levels of individualization and contemporary realism into the larger and more mature world of Elizabethan drama. Mingling with new elements, both the episodic construction of the processional drama and the figured pattern of the moralities had entered this world. So too, at a further stage of development, had this graded contemporaneity. In Elizabethan tragedy, the main figures (though heroically individualized, in terms we shall examine) retain the distancing element, of other places and other times, of the major figures of the medieval drama, yet, as has been often observed, are historical figures who are also, in certain radical ways, Elizabethans, alive in the drama's own time. Then, in rough grading, this process is carried further in the ancillary figures, until gravedigger and sexton in *Hamlet*, constable and headborough in *Much Ado*, and a host of similar figures, belong as frankly to the drama's own time as did the Towneley shepherds. This convention seems to embody a transitional attitude to the relation between dramatic pattern and social reality. The mixed form holds while a new society is evolving within the patterns of the old. While the old society stood firm, the single pattern sufficed. When the new society comes to full consciousness, the mixed pattern will be rationalized. Meanwhile, in the later medieval and Elizabethan drama, the mixed convention allows characters to function, with varying degrees of emphasis, both as individuals and as symbolic and social types. Much of the richness of Elizabethan drama, and in particular its ability to communicate at several different levels, can thus be related to a stage in consciousness corresponding to an historical stage in the development of society.

II

By the end of the fifteenth century, in different degrees in different parts of the country, the popular religious drama had in fact broken down, in its old universal forms. We can relate this, not only to changes in religious feeling, which were to erupt in radical changes in religious organization, but also to social changes directly connected with the drama. By Tudor times, the guilds, on which the main organization of the old drama had rested, had become very various in function, and in some cases had ceased altogether to be popular organizations, having been taken over by mercantile interests in a new economy in which the conflict between craftsman and trader was sharpening. Early Tudor drama shows some survivals of the old social organization, but shows also important developments of the new organization, with the growth of companies of touring actors, performing in inn-yards, and of performances of new kinds of play in schools, colleges, and great houses. Through these related channels, and especially through the close association of drama with places open to external influence, both of classical drama and the new drama of the Renaissance, major new directions were made possible, especially since the native popular drama had weakened. The decisive development occurred in the 1570s, when the first theatres began to be built. Typically, the organization of the drama passed into the hands of speculators, and the theatres were built on the edges of London, still growing as a trading centre, in part to attract audiences from travellers in and out of the capital. At the same time, the circumstances in which the theatres were built remind us of the growing tension between powerful social groups, which in the next century was to disrupt the drama both physically and socially. The new theatres, like the old touring companies, attracted the powerful opposition of the commercial middle class that had established its power in the towns. The drama was kept going, throughout the period of its Elizabethan greatness, by popular support certainly, but by a kind of popular support that would have been crushed if the court and the nobility had not extended its active patronage. The brevity of the great period is as remarkable as the greatness itself, and we can see both in terms of a remarkable but necessarily temporary fusion of many complex elements in the national life: elements which a little later were to fly apart. For this brief period, the colour and richness of the European Renaissance interacted with the vigour and realism of the popular tradition to create wholly new national forms. The most striking new element is a high consciousness of individual experience, which the medieval and early Tudor drama, set in markedly different social thought patterns, had so obviously lacked. In tragedy and romance, this new element, expressed in a new kind of rhetoric, raised the drama to unexampled intensity. Violent, rapid, and complicated action was the physical expression of these new modes of personal feeling, and the new dramatists, themselves characteristically uprooted and exposed, raised the language to comparable vitality and power. Yet these elements were in interaction with older ways of feeling. Where they were not, as in the different examples of Euphuism and the 'classical' drama associated with the Countess of Pembroke, the new influences ran away into meaningless display on the one hand, artificial refinement on the other. In the main body of popular Elizabethan drama it is clear that elements of an older tradition are present, not merely as survivals, but as equal factors in its power. The sense of symbolic function, within an ordered pattern of values, unites with the colour and richness of absolute individual expression, not only in the great tragedies, where the relation between these modes is again and again the essential theme, but also in the high comedy of the later Shakespeare and Jonson. And then both the individual aspiration and the immanent pattern take vigorous life, through the language, from the actual life of the times, until it seems that for this brief period all that is creative in the national life finds expression in this bewilderingly various and surprising drama.

It is customary to see this exciting development cut off by the growth to power of a new 'Puritan' element, marked by the closing of the theatres in 1642. Yet the disintegration of this national drama, the flying apart of the elements which had composed it, had begun much earlier. For perhaps the last fifteen years of the reign of Elizabeth, and the first few years of the reign of James, the conditions existed for the drama to express the mainstream of the national life, at a high tension corresponding to the conflicts which were soon to break out in the overtly political field. Already, at the beginning of the new century, we see the beginnings of the movement to a class drama, which had been incipient in earlier Tudor developments. The 'private theatres', though in fact open to the public, began to depend on an actually narrower audience. Where previously the court had protected a popular drama against the commercial middle class, now increasingly, with the growing alienation of the court from decisive elements in the national life, the drama itself began to change in character. On the one hand, there was an increasing tendency to elaboration and spectacle as formal elements to be consumed and enjoyed, rather than as elements in the dramatic experience itself. On the other hand, and especially in comedy, there is a steady movement through Middleton and Massinger, Beaumont and Fletcher, to Shirley and Brome, in the direction of new interests and new standards, leading naturally to the Restoration comedy of manners. As Dryden later observed, Fletcher 'understood and imitated the conversation of gentlemen' much better than Shakespeare, and this development is only one mark of the increasing preoccupation with social intrigue, with shifting class relations, and with fashion, as the drama narrows towards identification with a single class, in a changing and disintegrating society. Both the national element, which had been so vital in the drama of the 1590s, and the traditional patterns embodying the values of an older kind of society, slowly disappeared. In comedy the movement was towards the excitements of fashion and appetite, which produced the form of the comedy of manners, gaining in sophistication as it lost in general human reference. In tragedy the movement was towards the abstraction of impulses, in particular the abstraction of 'honour' from a social function to a mark of breeding: so that from a man confronting a destiny both particular and universal, and from a hero expressing (as in the developed chronicle plays) a national spirit, there was a decline to the posture of honour and destiny, within an artificial social context primarily motivated by intrigue, of the 'heroic drama'. Signs of these developments can be traced back to the great period, but with the narrowing of the social base they became much more evident, as many of the old interests faded. By the time of the closing of the theatres, in 1642, the national drama had become a class drama, as the manner of its restoration was to make obvious.

III

Restoration drama was based on the two 'Patent Theatres', authorized by Charles II in 1660. The theatres were of a new kind, with stages half-way from the Elizabethan platform to the modern picture-stage. As the theatres were under court patronage, the audiences were virtually limited to courtiers and their adherents, and there was continual difficulty in maintaining the theatres as successful enterprises on so narrow a base. In form, there was at first a development of the emphasis on music and spectacle—with more elaborate theatre scenery—which had first been evident in the Jacobean private theatres and then in masques and operas. D'Avenant, who directed one of the two new theatres, had not only written an early 'heroic play'—*Love and Honour*—in 1634, but during the closing of the theatres had produced an opera, *The Siege of Rhodes*, which blended the heroic play with the development of music and spectacle, itself influenced by French and Italian example. To follow the development of heroic drama is to see what I have called the abstraction of impulses (the increasing formalization of conventions of honour and innocence) transforming the style of tragedy into an elaborate mannerism. The reduction of mature Elizabethan and Jacobean blank verse, with its closeness to forms of ordinary speech, either into the heroic couplet, or into the stilted Restoration blank verse, is a central mark of the general change. Yet, even after these changes, the form of heroic drama, and of the revived blank-verse tragedy which succeeded it, bears little substantial relation even to the narrowed life which the theatres offered to serve. The true growth of the period was in the developed comedy of manners, which had a genuine correspondence with the narrow society on which it was based.

We must distinguish two periods of Restoration comedy, which correspond interestingly with actual periods in the theatre's fortunes. From 1666, after the Plague and the Fire, to the renewed political crisis in 1679, the true Restoration theatre, with its strictly limited audience, supported, as its best representatives, Etherege and Wycherley, in whom this direct relation between form and audience is most obvious. The actress, new to the stage with the Restoration, is crucial in this form, which is an elaborate illustration of the rules of the fashionable sex-game. The very fact that comedy of this kind was withdrawn, by its context, from other social groups and their alternative feelings and values, permitted a unity of feeling and style which, in its own terms, is a marked advance on earlier intrigue-comedies still complicated by a consciousness of other standards. Even when, as in Etherege and early Wycherley, the plays are simply flattering reflections of the lives of their audiences, the certainty of relation produces a characteristic spontaneity and liveliness. To criticize these plays on general moral grounds may well be necessary, as a next stage of judgement, but it is foolish to allow this to obscure the temporary success of the form on its own terms. Yet already in Wycherley's *Plain Dealer* (1676) the morality of the code itself is being questioned: his attack on personal betrayal and selfishness is difficult to contain within a form which at its simplest reduced all questions of behaviour to a correct if brittle gaiety. In the 1680s, in the mounting political crisis which saw the middle class successfully reaching for the first stages of power, the theatres were in difficulties, and relapsed to revivals as a dominant policy. After 1695, a new theatrical tradition is obvious, with the rise of the actor-manager who was often also the playwright. Yet then, in a brief period from 1693 to 1705, at a time when the true Restoration period was over, when citizens and their ladies were beginning to attend the theatres more frequently, and when non-aristocratic authors were increasingly in evidence, the second and more brilliant phase of what we call Restoration comedy flared and died. Vanbrugh and early Farquhar are a curious survival of the modes of Etherege and Wycherley, but Congreve, at such a time, succeeds in *The Way of the World* in taking the comedy of manners to its highest point. Yet when first produced, the play was not successful, and the whole episode is a curious example of the complex relationship between audiences and forms. In later Farquhar we can see the influence of new modes of feeling, consonant with the 'sentimental comedy' which we can also date from the 1690s. But of Congreve's *Way of the World* we must note the curious fact of a form finding its finest expression at a time when its social basis, if not broken up, was rapidly disappearing. It sometimes happens, in the history of an art, that a form reaches its highest point of development when its essential conditions are already vanishing, but given the unevenness of social and individual development this need not be surprising. The maturity and poise of *The Way of the World* seem, in retrospect, related to the fact that this was as far as the Restoration form of the comedy of manners could be taken: the complete understanding of its patterns is also, in effect, a concluding and valuing summary of them.

When an art-form changes, as the direct result of changes in society, we meet a very difficult problem in criticism, for it quite often happens that a local judgement will show a form that has been brought to a high level of skill and maturity being replaced by forms that are relatively crude and unsuccessful. With the ending of a Restoration drama based on an aristocratic and fashionable audience, and its replacement by a very mixed middle-class drama based on a wider social group, we see one of the clearest and most famous of these cases. Most critics have been natural Cavaliers, and have represented the change as a disaster for the drama. Yet it is surely necessary to take a longer view. The limited character of Restoration drama, and the disintegration of a general audience which had preceded it, were also damaging. Again, while the early products of eighteenth-century middle-class culture were regarded (often with justice) as vulgar, we must, to tell the whole story, follow the development down, to the points where the 'vulgar' novel became a major literary form, and where the despised forms of 'bourgeois tragedy' and 'sentimental comedy' served, in their maturity, a wide area of our modern drama. The development of middle-class drama is in fact one of the most interesting cases we have of a changing society leading directly to radical innovations in form.

IV

Opposition to the theatre, by the commercial middle class, can be traced back to the sixteenth century, and the renewed wave of criticism, from the 1690s, which effectively broke the Restoration dramatic spirit, in one way contains little that is new. Behind the criticism of Collier (*A Short View of the Immorality and Profaneness of the English Stage*, 1698), with its itemized complaint against the licentiousness of current comedies, the old hostility to the theatre as such can be detected. But now, with the court changed in character, and no longer actively protecting the theatre, middle-class opposition had to be taken more seriously, and while a Vanbrugh replied in kind, Farquhar and a new school of dramatists consciously reformed the drama to meet the immediate objections. The complexity of any adequate judgement of eighteenth-century drama follows from the fact that in some cases forms were changed reluctantly or superficially in response to the new moral tone; in other cases, new forms were made, by extension or discovery, as a positive expression of the new spirit. This mixed result is understandable in terms of the actual change in audiences. From the 1680s, merchants and their wives had begun to attend the theatres, and in the eighteenth century this element in the audience grew steadily. Yet there was no sudden changeover from a dissolute court audience to a respectable middle-class audience; indeed it was not until Victorian times that the audiences of ordinary theatres became 'respectable' in this way. The real situation, in the eighteenth century, is that of elements of the rising middle-class joining a still fashionable theatre public, at a time when the public tone of the court and aristocracy had itself been modified. Many authors began to be drawn from the commercial middle-class public; this is a period in which the 'one-play author' is a characteristic figure. It is fair to say that an important part of eighteenth-century drama offered a conscious image of the middle class and its virtues, but the creative possibilities of this new consciousness were very uneven, and in the drama, particularly, they were further limited. The uncertainty in dramatic forms combined with the strong fashionable element in the audience to produce a concentration of interest on actors as such. Whenever this happens, and plays, in consequence, are valued primarily as vehicles for particular acting talents, the drama tends to become mixed and eclectic. Thus one finds, in eighteenth-century drama, a characteristic interest in theatrical effect for its own sake, and it is in this context that the new forms had to make their limited way.

Sentimental comedy is the least attractive of the new forms, though it has continued to hold the stage, as a majority form of English drama, to our own day. We can trace its conscious development from Cibber's *Love's Last Shift* (1696) and *The Careless Husband* (1705), and Steele's *The Lying Lover* (1704). Elements of its particular consciousness can indeed be traced from much earlier in the century, but the direct application to contemporary behaviour is now much more obvious. A passage from Steele's preface to *The Lying Lover* clearly shows the new emphasis:

> He makes false love, gets drunk, and kills his man, but in the fifth act awakens from his debauch with the compunction and remorse which is suitable to a man's finding himself in a gaol. . . . The anguish he there expresses, and the mutual sorrow between an only child and a tender father in that distress are, perhaps, an injury to the rules of comedy, but I am sure they are a justice to those of morality: and passages of such a nature being so frequently applauded on the stage, it is high time we should no longer draw occasions of mirth from those images which the religion of our country tells us we ought to tremble at with horror.

The essential point here, as a description of the new form, is the mixture of comedy and pathos, with an explicit moral reference, that led to the alternative descriptions of 'weeping comedy' or the 'comedy of sentiments' (moral opinions)— the two elements uniting in the complicated history of the word 'sentimental'. Yet we must note also the curious way in which the 'compunction and remorse' are approached, for this element of 'fifth-act reform', after all the excitements of customary dramatic intrigue, became the basis of continued charges of hypocrisy and sentimentality: 'enjoy it while it lasts, then say you're sorry'. Goldsmith had this in mind, when in attacking sentimental comedy he wrote:

> If they happen to have faults or foibles, the spectator is taught, not only to pardon, but to applaud them, in consideration of the goodness of their hearts.

This criticism reaches home, in many such plays, and this aspect of sentimental comedy has been so persistent that Goldsmith's words could be transferred, as they stand, to a considerable part of modern drama. He continues:

> But there is one argument in favour of sentimental comedy, which will keep it on the stage, in spite of all that can be said against it.

It is, of all others, the most easily written. Those abilities that can hammer out a novel are fully sufficient for the production of a sentimental comedy. It is only sufficient to raise the characters a little; to deck out the hero with a riband, or give the heroine a title; then to put an insipid dialogue, without character or humour, into their mouths, give them mighty good hearts, very fine clothes, furnish a new set of scenes, make a pathetic scene or two, with a sprinkling of tender melancholy conversation through the whole, and there is no doubt but all the ladies will cry, and all the gentlemen applaud.

This again is just, but the casual dismissal of the novel should make us pause. Both novels and sentimental comedies were often, certainly, confections of this kind, and Goldsmith despised them by reference to older standards (his attack on mixing comedy and pathos was in classicist terms, as a confusion of the old distinct kinds). Yet, while the bad examples multiplied, the feelings which they exhibited were part of the new consciousness, and could not in fact be summarily dismissed. The ability to take a judgement right through, as in traditional tragedy and comedy, showing sin leading to disintegration and disaster, vice and error to thorough ridicule, rested on a more absolute morality, based either on religious sanctions or the strict standards of an established society, than the new middle class actually had. Already in Elizabethan drama, and certainly in some seventeenth-century developments, we see the traditional kinds, and their basic attitudes, often confused, and their modes of judgement muted, for similar reasons. Romantic comedy had pioneered the way of sentimental comedy, and 'fifth-act reform', where in spite of everything a happy ending must be contrived, is evident from Shakespeare. Restoration comedy contains these elements, but gains a measure of unity of feeling by confident judgements with reference to a very limited social scale: to offend against polite society was to be driven out of it, and that was that; but equally to offend against God and man, while respecting the polite code, was forgivable. At different levels, and for some good reasons, the new middle-class drama tried to go beyond this, to a new kind of judgement. Certainly, like its predecessors, it contrived happy endings, and padded the lash of the old comedy, often on sentimental grounds. But also, in dealing with contemporary life, it necessarily challenged the temporary certainties of the Restoration comedy of manners, offering as absolute virtues the sanctity of marriage, the life of the family, and the care of the weak. These had been neglected, or made ridiculous, in Restoration comedy, simply because the class which it served was parasitic: the true consequences of behaviour had never to be fully lived out. Narrow as the new bourgeois morality was, it at least referred to a society in which consequence was actual, and in which there was more to do than keep up with the modes of an artificially protected class. When we speak of the 'sentimentality' of appeals to these values, and of the 'smugness' of what we think we can dismiss as merely 'domestic virtues', we should be quite sure where we stand ourselves. The identification which some critics seem to make, in phantasy, between themselves and the insouciance of Cavalier rakes and whores, is usually ridiculous, if one goes on to ask to what moral tradition they themselves practically belong. Nor is this the only respect in which, if we are honest, we shall confess ourselves the heirs of the eighteenth-century bourgeois. The wider basis of sentimental comedy, and of a main tradition in the novel, was that particular kind of humanitarian feeling, the strong if inarticulate appeal to a fundamental 'goodness of heart'; the sense of every individual's closeness to vice and folly, so that pity for their exemplars is the most relevant emotion, and recovery and rehabilitation must be believed in; the sense, finally, that there are few absolute values, and that tolerance and kindness are major virtues. In rebuking the sentimental comedy, as in both its early examples and its subsequent history it seems necessary to do, we should be prepared to recognize that in the point of moral assumptions, and of a whole consequent feeling about life, most of us are its blood relations.

Sentimental comedy failed, and continues to fail, because it never works through, to any point of intensity, the conflict between the belief that certain social virtues are paramount and yet that good men can offend against them. Its history is an evasion of this conflict by artificial solutions or 'a sprinkling of tender melancholy'. It is significant that while in respect of real personal relationships the new bourgeois form was a failure, in respect of certain property relationships—the basis of early bourgeois tragedy—it succeeded. The thief, the dishonest apprentice, the murderer or seducer for gain, went straight to a firm and absolute judgement. Nevertheless, even here, the form includes a characteristic pathos; pity is possible, and real, so long as the judgement is executed. In Lillo's *The London Merchant* (1731) the apprentice Barnwell, led on to theft and murder by his seducer Mistress Millwood, goes with her to the gallows in an atmosphere that combines the certainties of an old morality—

> Unless we mark what drew their ruin on,
> And, by avoiding that—prevent our own

with the new pathos—

> With bleeding hearts and weeping eyes we show
> A human, gen'rous sense of others' woe.

The pity, here, is 'in vain' without the judgement and its lesson, and the feelings are thus integrated with the action in a way that was not ordinarily possible in sentimental comedy.

The rise of bourgeois tragedy is very important. There had been Elizabethan 'domestic tragedies', but it was still felt, in the early eighteenth century, that real tragedy was necessarily confined to persons of high social rank. Now, insistently, the claim was made that tragic feeling was a general human property, and that in the ordinary and the everyday a serious tragic drama could be based:

> Stripp'd of Regal Pomp, and glaring Show,
> His Muse reports a Tale of Private Woe,
> Works up Distress from Common Scenes in Life,
> A Treach'rous Brother, and an Injur'd Wife.

Yet the claim had to be urged; it could not be assumed:

> From lower life we draw our Scene's Distress:
> —Let not your Equals move your Pity less.

This development, narrow as at first it was, is an obvious and necessary basis for all serious modern drama. If the recognition of tragic situations in ordinary lives was at first confined to certain social categories—the consequences of debt, extravagance, false dealing, greed—still the advance is real. The range of Elizabethan tragedy is one of major human aspirations lived out in terms of a whole natural order, and its tension grew from the very scale and intensity of the aspirations, which the medieval drama had not known. But these heights had already been lost by the time when heroic drama held the field, and the pseudo-classical tragedy of Restoration and Augustan writers shows a similar decline. Bourgeois tragedy is an attempt to begin again, and it is a more relevant creative activity than the heroic and pseudo-classical exercises. It is social tragedy, often narrow and crude in its terms, but universal tragedy had already gone, more than a century before this bourgeois attempt began. *The London Merchant* is one of the few creative works in English eighteenth-century drama, and its essential superiority to works in the older manner, like *Cato* and *Douglas*, is evident.

The third interesting new form of this period is the ballad-opera, and this again is a conscious middle-class challenge to aristocratic taste. The extraordinary success of the ballad-operas was short-lived, but one principal reason for this was that a large part of their impulse was political satire, and this was cut off by the Licensing Act of 1737. As a native challenge to the fashionable taste for Italian opera, which had begun in 1705, *The Beggar's Opera* (1728) and its successors are genuinely creative in style and feeling, and the loss of this tradition was very damaging.

The curious fact about eighteenth-century drama as a whole is that a creative response, in bourgeois tragedy and ballad-opera, was in fact made, in this early period of middle-class culture, yet then in effect this was lost. (There is a similar case of challenge and relapse in Hogarth and the subsequent tradition.) The development of bourgeois tragedy passed to France and Germany, and England did not get it back, at any serious level, until late in the nineteenth century, when Ibsen was raising it to a major form. The ballad-opera disappeared, and the weaker tradition of comic opera had again to serve England until our own century. The realist novel, a creative response of the same period and by the same class, was always much stronger, but it too went back, except for isolated examples, between 1750 and the 1830s. It is as if the middle class, having made its dramatic challenge, lacked, at least in the theatre, the organization to carry this through. The result as a whole was an expanding theatre, but one flooded by a variety of inferior forms. In 1600 there had been six successful theatres in London; in 1700, after the narrowing of the Restoration, there were only two. By 1750, though the two Patent Theatres were still dominant, there were five other theatres and an opera-house, and at least five theatres in fashionable provincial centres. By 1800, the position in London was little improved, but there were now about forty theatres in the provinces. By 1850, there were twenty-one theatres in London, and about seventy-five in the provinces. By 1900, after the period of real expansion, there were sixty-three theatres in London, forty music-halls, and more than three hundred theatres in the provinces. It looks from this as if there could, from 1750, have been a genuine dramatic expansion, at many different levels, but in fact the period from 1750 to 1850 is the most barren in our dramatic history, if it is work of any lasting value we are looking for. Only the brief revival of high comedy, by Goldsmith and Sheridan in the 1770s, stands out. The explanation of the paradox—an expanding theatre and a declining drama—lies in one crucial fact: that throughout this period, with the temporary exceptions of Goldsmith and Sheridan, the connection between the theatre and literature was virtually lost. The new class was served, in print, not only by new popular work, but by a developing literary tradition and a new tradition of serious journalism. In the theatre, although the creative response had been made, the major expansion was served at a very low level throughout: farce, pantomime, burlesque, spectacular shows, and then, from the beginning of the nineteenth century, melodrama. It is true that Shakespeare began to be played more often, in this same period, but not only were most such performances either adapted texts or simply occasions for spectacle and acting display; a further consequence was the cult of Shakespearean drama, as a literary model, which distracted attention from the possibility of new contemporary forms. By the early nineteenth century, the frequency of plays written only to be read bears discouraging witness to the separation of the theatre from literature which was everywhere the dominating factor. In such a situation, not only does the theatre lose a vital element, in the serious dramatist, but also dramatic literature suffers, as it turns from contemporary possibilities and tends to work in dead forms. The Romantic movement, as a whole, produced one line of great drama, from *Faust* to *Peer Gynt* and beyond, but also the useless form of the costume-intrigue which, while theatrically successful, was in fact a dead end.

The complicated nature of the relations between a new class and effective new forms is thus very evident, in the history of English middle-class drama. We can perhaps look again at the time-scale of such a development, discouraging as this is. The eighteenth-century middle class broke up the old forms, which rested on meanings and interests that had decayed. Alternative forms were created, but were relatively isolated or temporary in their success. Only much later, when the class had built its major social institutions, was there an effective turning towards the making of a distinctive cultural tradition at all levels of seriousness. In the theatre this was later than in print, mainly because of the theatre's continued association with the fringes of the class, rather than its centre. By the 1830s, the solid expansion, in newspapers, periodicals, books, and theatres, is clear, and it is in this generation, in a number of ways—Reform Bill 1832, Stamp Duty reduction 1836, Patent Theatre monopoly ended 1843, Stamp Duty abolished 1855—that the restrictions of older social forms are removed. Only from this period is there cultural advance over the whole field. In the theatre, certainly, this was to remain slow: though new and more serious audiences were now being gathered, it was not until the sixties, with Robertson, that the attempt begun by Lillo and Gay was seriously resumed, and at a level as crude as if there had been no precedents. Yet then, in a wave of theatre-building (27 new theatres in the West End between 1860 and 1900, together with rapid expansion in the suburbs and provinces) the revival moved quickly, and by the turn of the century England again had a serious and well-attended drama. Before we turn to this latest phase, we must glance also at the growth of the music-hall, from the 1840s. With the ending of the monopoly of the Patent Theatres, the minor theatres of London moved increasingly into 'legitimate' drama (they had previously been kept to 'illegitimate' forms because of the monopoly, although this was never absolute and the lines were not easily drawn). The music-halls, at first attached to taverns and then taking over or building new premises, sprang up as the old 'illegitimate' theatres went 'legitimate', and much that they did was a continuation of their traditions. It is common to make a sentimental valuation of the music-halls as expressing the spirit of 'Old England' (which is nonsense in that what they expressed was not old), or as signs of great cultural vitality. In fact the music-hall was a very mixed institution and there is a direct line from the chaos of the eighteenth-century theatre through the music-halls to the mass of material now on television and in the cinemas, which it is stupid to overlook. To complain of contemporary work of these kinds—from striptease shows to 'pop' singers—and to use the music-hall as an example of contrasting vitality or health, is to ignore the clear evidence that it was the illegitimate theatres and the music-halls which established these kinds of entertainment. If you don't like it in one century, you can't reasonably like it in another, and the attendant features of fashionable booms, fantastic salaries, and high-pressure publicity are all equally evident in music-hall history. What can be said, however, and what remains important in similar work today, is that alongside the Champagne Charlies and the plush-and-tinsel extravaganzas and the jingo spectacles and songs, there were some performers—W. G. Ross ('Sam Hall, Chimney Sweep'), Jenny Hill, Dan Leno, Albert Chevalier, Marie Lloyd and others—who brought to performance new kinds and areas of experience which the 'legitimate' drama neglected or unreasonably despised. The urban working class created in the Industrial Revolution found in these performers their most authentic voices, and this part of the music-hall tradition is certainly to be honoured. But, as in the eighteenth century, the creative response had to take its place in very mixed institutions, often pursuing quite different ends, so that it is easy either to overlook or to overvalue it. The quick of a new life is unmistakably there, but it could no more establish itself, in whole forms and institutions, than earlier responses in periods of comparable change.

v

The flood of farces, melodramas, and spectacles has never slackened, and indeed a large part of the history of modern drama, with the expansion of distribution through the cinema, wireless, and television, is simply a continuation of the eighteenth-century story. Further, the majority form of serious drama in England, resting on a steady middle-class audience, has been sentimental comedy—refined in many ways by the influence of the novel, which had taken this form of feeling to considerable levels of achievement; yet still, in play after play, the recognizable configuration of fashionable sentiments, tender melancholy, and good-hearted error. The serious revival is not here, but mainly in the maturing of bourgeois tragedy, and in certain revivals of the comedy of manners (Wilde) and social satire (Shaw).

Bourgeois tragedy has succeeded absolutely in one of its aims: the admission of ordinary contemporary experience to tragic status. Indeed, the success is such that 'bourgeois' can be dropped, and what we then have is the important modern form of 'social tragedy'. The distinction that matters, by comparison with Greek or Renaissance tragedy, is that the centre of interest, in the modern form, is in experience of a social and secular kind. The tragic hero is not a man caught in some universal pattern, but at odds with his society and its particular moral laws. The distinguishing feature of the best work in this form, from Ibsen to Miller, is the intense critical seriousness, usually in contact with major intellectual interests, that has been brought to the working-out of such experience. It is significant, also, that the form matured at a time when the values of bourgeois society, which early bourgeois drama had been created to demonstrate and ex-pound, were being radically criticized, in a new period of change. Social tragedy, with its offshoot the 'problem play', has been normally 'progressive' in this sense, that instead of showing (as bourgeois drama, on a narrow base, had shared with Greek and Renaissance tragedy in showing) a man judged by an absolute law, it has in large measure been concerned with the criticism of such laws, in the light of particular experience. It has been liberal in the important sense that it represents a new stage of individualism. Earlier tragedy had shown the height of individual aspirations, but had ended by vindicating the law which opposed them. The modern hero, in social tragedy, is characteristically a man who rebels against some law, in any of its possible forms: the heroism lies in the rebellion, and is vindicated even in defeat. In some work, further, the rebellion is generalized, in terms of alternative values and laws: the liberal hero becomes the hero as liberator.

In fact this work has rested on a particular kind of social support, with audiences drawn from groups committed to reform, or at least prepared to give it a hearing. The increase in such groups, in the last decades of the nineteenth century, was reflected in theatre audiences, in France, Germany, Russia, and England, and the new drama rested substantially on this tendency, which in its turn it strengthened. One notable social development is the growth of 'free theatres' and theatre-clubs, which dates from the 1870s, and which provided an effective alternative platform for the new work. We are still in this period, as the history of English drama and theatre in the 1950s (Theatre Workshop, Royal Court) makes clear. It rests, substantially, on an important growth of middle-class dissidence from the majority values of the society, and it has brought social tragedy, and also social satire, to their present strength. It has also, since 1918, extended the social scale of such drama to working-class life, though this, while growing, is still a minor element.

Thus, alongside the continuity of the majority middle-class theatre, an important new movement has realized many of the potentialities of the more serious earlier forms. Yet the actual history is not summed up by continuity and this one new movement. Indeed, the forms of social tragedy were still only being matured when they were already powerfully challenged. The centre of interest, in such forms, was ordinarily confined to the conflicts of an individual with a particular society. Yet the questioning of values, by dissident groups, was often in terms wider than ordinary social criticism. For certain kinds of experience, the development and refinement of old forms seemed inadequate, or the development was such that the old form was broken, and new elements, or new whole forms, were created. Sometimes, as in the Irish theatre, a particular national consciousness united, for a time, in a single movement, both the maturing of social drama and the development and creation of new kinds of play. The use of national legends or historical material followed from the romantic drama of *Faust* and *Peer Gynt*, which had hitherto been isolated examples of the transformation of such material (common enough in ordinary costume-intrigue) by its use as a dramatic basis for experience of a religious or philosophical kind, similar in reach to Greek or Renaissance tragedy. In the Irish theatre, for a time, this development, mainly by Yeats, found audiences, and therefore contact with the working theatre, because it was part of a general national dramatic movement. It has also found audiences elsewhere, particularly in France where the use of classical myth has been of great importance. In England, in its serious examples (for these must be distinguished from the use of historical or legendary material for sentimental comedy or other older forms) it has been less successful in finding a social basis. It has depended, in fact, on two kinds of audience: first, one associated with the church, which in some cases has sponsored such work, and which was the effective basis for the introduction of Eliot's *Murder in the Cathedral*; second, particularly with classical material, a limited public with some classical education, usually served by minority broadcasting rather than by theatres. A considerable part of serious modern drama has been in this tradition, but it has been limited, and at times virtually halted, by the tenuity of its links with the working theatre and by the necessarily limited nature of its natural audiences.

At the same time, the forms of social drama were being extended and sometimes broken, by the pressure of actual experience. In early bourgeois tragedy, in spite of the certainty of its narrow assumptions, an element of apparently non-social experience was evident: an element best defined as fate. This ordinarily operated, it is true, to ensure by coincidence the working-out of certain laws; but they were not divine laws, they were fate not providence, and at the stage then reached they supported rather than challenged the form. In the work of Ibsen, even his most obviously social plays, this element of fate, while sometimes used in the old way to enforce an action determined on other grounds, must be seen, finally, in a quite different light. Fate is used to define kinds of experience which the social action of the drama will not admit. It is this pressure, of other kinds of experience, which led to the transformation, by a number of writers, of the ordinary social forms. By the use of non-realistic elements, within a realist framework, the drama was extended in directions ultimately similar to those of the developed romantic drama. Whether the action was formally contemporary and social, or historical and legendary, the experience now handled was not confined to the sphere of individual-and-society relationships for which the form had been originally devised. In Ibsen particularly, this development is clear and important, and the new drama—of an essentially 'symbolic' and universal character, whatever its immediate grounds—had important advantages in that it started from conventions with which audiences were familiar.

Yet the pressure continued, in other directions. The style of bourgeois drama, with its essentially conversational prose, had been adequate for the ends first proposed, but seemed inadequate for these farther purposes. Naturalism, as the style had come to be called, rested essentially on the original assumptions: that in the apparent action of everyday life the essential values could be demonstrated. The revolt against naturalism is, essentially, a growing disbelief that this is in fact possible. The importance of 'unconscious' and in any case unexpressed experience is one factor in this. Another factor, clearly, is the growing conviction that human values cannot be adequately considered in terms of existing social values: this indeed was part of the original revolt which brought social drama to its maturity. Thus the bases of the old form, in language and in action, were increasingly rejected.

Two new forms, of considerable importance, have emerged from this rejection. One is the modern verse drama, which, while accepting a framework of naturalist action, has used the greater range of dramatic verse as a way of expressing experience which the action, in its ordinary terms, could not express. This has led to some valuable drama, but the tendency to dissociate the language from the action, inherent in the attempt, has led to certain very difficult problems in creating a genuinely unified form. The other new form is the 'expressionist' play, which has consciously broken up the naturalist framework of action, and seeks to articulate these farther ranges of experience by devising scenes which refer primarily to the activity of the mind, whether or not these normally find expression in explicit and observable action. As the romantic drama uses myth, so the expressionist drama seeks to create myth, in the common sense of an action which expresses an area of universal experience. At times this has been an extremely individualist drama, expressing the action of a single mind at a level at which other persons have reality only in that mind's terms. In other examples, the method has been used to express changes and tensions of the kind which emerge when history is studied, or a society is analysed, but which are not necessarily apparent, in the details of local action, even when they may be radically affecting the common life. Thus we have 'personal expressionism' and 'social expressionism', at very different levels of consciousness. The success and influence of Brecht have made this line exceptionally important, in current dramatic experiment, yet much of Brecht's success is due to his late transformation of this always potentially opaque form by the application of a moral and intellectual system which is both generally powerful and individually distinguished.

Twentieth-century drama, for the first time since the Renaissance drama broke up, is a major activity, and one which has recovered, in certain areas, its vital links with literature and, through design, with other major arts. The revival of English opera, and the attempt to write serious contemporary musical plays, add to its growing importance. Drama today is more widely disseminated than ever before in history, though the theatres are often in difficulties since new media of performance, in cinemas, broadcasting, and television have been developed. Much of the increased distribution has simply expanded the older forms, but equally, the great flexibility of the new media has been an important element in the actual realization of the newer forms: verse drama in broadcasting, expressionism and serious romantic drama in all the media and particularly in the cinema, social drama of an expanded kind, again in all the media, have been greatly aided, in terms both of dramatic method and of audiences. It is never easy, in one's own generation, to see whether the situation is that of 1630 or 1735, with plenty of activity but on no lasting basis, or that of 1590 or 1890, at the beginning of a major movement. In terms of social history, the facts now are that drama of all kinds is regularly reaching the largest audiences in its history. Yet the confusion of forms, and in particular the separation, very evident at some points, between minority and majority drama, are seriously limiting factors. It is obvious that we are living through a revolutionary period in which the creative response through new forms is clear. At the same time these normally depend on minority social groups, and the emergence of a relatively unified audience, like the medieval or Elizabethan, seems unlikely in the theatre, though in the cinema and television it may be in process of formation. We cannot forecast what will happen, but one principle may be suggested. It is not merely the appearance of new audiences, but the creative discovery of new forms capable of expressing the meanings and values of substantial groups in these audiences, which determines dramatic history. The new audiences can come and not be served, at any important level, and there can be actual decadence within apparent expansion. The discovery of such forms is the work of creative individuals, but the necessary conventions and attitudes to ensure a form's survival depend on a degree of correspondence between the individual discovery and the new general consciousness. Of our current forms, the strength of social drama, of a generally naturalist kind, lies in its relevance to the lives of its expanded audience, in an art that has tended to restrict its content to a comparatively narrow area of society. The weakness of such drama may be its normal restriction, from the period of liberal revolt, to themes of the individual in conflict with his society, which, though rising at times to issues of general significance, can come to resemble the isolation and breakdown of some expressionist drama, serving a minority group but leaving other forms, even inferior forms, apparently nearer to general experience. Conflict of a different kind, between particular human values and certain established definitions of human scope and purpose, can, on the other hand, in the expanded social drama, in some romantic drama, and again in expressionism, reach out to and articulate a more general change in consciousness. I believe our crisis to be a social crisis, but its conditions are such that neither the simple liberalism, of the man who dissents, nor the set conflict, between an abuse and its remedy, an authority and its critics, seems able to express it. The more dynamic forms, capable of reaching out to inarticulate experience, and to possible common and universal references, seem to me more relevant, to our actual history. The weaknesses of such forms, hitherto, seem to me to have a social basis, in that the values ordinarily appealed to, especially in English verse drama and in some romantic drama, have been based, not on contemporary experience (which does not necessarily require explicit contemporary setting or reference) but on the preserved values of other societies and other drama, the groups supporting them being essentially opposed to the general directions of our society. Thus, while the socially reforming minority has fallen short of the true scale of the changes, the minority making wider reference has been limited by consistent reference to a past in which alone it tends to find value and meaning. Yet, from some directions, adequate forms seem to be coming into existence, with a common characteristic that they are capable of handling movement, and of reaching certain kinds of experience which dissolve the fixed categories of the individual and society as these have been ordinarily expressed. The dynamism of which film technique and the expressionist theatre have been masters, with the association of contemporary music, dance and a more varied dramatic language, seem to me the elements which correspond to our actual social history. We may be better able to consider them, and to grasp their connections with actual movements and ideas, on which they will undoubtedly depend, if we can accept the argument that dramatic forms have a real social history, in prospect as well as in retrospect. Though much is uncertain, in so wide and complex a field, it seems to me that we can accept the fact of such a history, from the real relations that I have examined. Complicated as it is by delay, by the unevenness of change, and by the natural variety of responses to change, only some of which achieve adequate communication, the outline surely exists, in which we can see drama, not only as a social art, but as a major and practical index of change and creator of consciousness.

SEVEN

Realism and the Contemporary Novel

T HE centenary of 'realism' as an English critical term occurred but was not celebrated in 1956. Its history, in this hundred years, has been so vast, so complicated and so bitter that any celebration would in fact have turned into a brawl. Yet realism is not an object, to be identified, pinned down, and appropriated. It is, rather, a way of describing certain methods and attitudes, and the descriptions, quite naturally, have varied, in the ordinary exchange and development of experience. Recently, I have been reconsidering these descriptions, as a possible way of defining and generalizing certain personal observations on the methods and substance of contemporary fiction. I now propose to set down: first, the existing variations in 'realism' as a descriptive term; second, my own view of the ways in which the modern novel has developed; third, a possible new meaning of realism.

There has, from the beginning, been a simple technical use of 'realism', to describe the precision and vividness of a rendering in art of some observed detail. In fact, as we shall see, this apparently simple use involves all the later complexities, but it seemed, initially, sufficiently accurate to distinguish one technique from others: realism as opposed to idealization or caricature. But, also from the beginning, this technical sense was flanked by a reference to content: certain kinds of subject were seen as realism, again by contrast with different kinds. The most ordinary definition was in terms of an ordinary, contemporary, everyday reality, as opposed to traditionally heroic, romantic, or legendary subjects. In the period since the Renaissance, the advocacy and support of this 'ordinary, everyday, contemporary reality' have been normally associated with the rising middle class, the bourgeoisie. Such material was called 'domestic' and 'bourgeois' before it was called 'realistic', and the connections are clear.

In literature the domestic drama and, above all, the novel, both developing in early eighteenth-century England with the rise of an independent middle class, have been the main vehicles of this new consciousness. Yet, when the 'realist' description arrived, a further development was taking place, both in content and in attitudes to it. A common adjective used with 'realism' was 'startling', and, within the mainstream of 'ordinary, contemporary, everyday reality' a particular current of attention to the unpleasant, the poor, and the sordid could be distinguished. Realism thus appeared as in part a revolt against the ordinary bourgeois view of the world; the realists were making a further selection of ordinary material which the majority of bourgeois artists preferred to ignore. Thus 'realism', as a watchword, passed over to the progressive and revolutionary movements.

This history is paralleled in the development of 'naturalism', which again had a simple technical sense, to describe a particular method of art, but which underwent the characteristic broadening to 'ordinary, everyday reality' and then, in particular relation to Zola, became the banner of a revolutionary school—what the *Daily News* in 1881 called 'that unnecessarily faithful portrayal of offensive incidents'.

Thus, entwined with technical descriptions, there were in the nineteenth-century meanings doctrinal affiliations. The most positive was Strindberg's definition of naturalism as the exclusion of God: naturalism as opposed to supernaturalism, according to the philosophical precedents. Already, however, before the end of the century, and with increasing clarity in our own, 'realism' and 'naturalism' were separated: naturalism in art was reserved to the simple technical reference, while realism, though retaining elements of this, was used to describe subjects and attitudes to subjects.

The main twentieth-century development has been curious. In the West, alongside the received uses, a use of 'realism' in the sense of 'fidelity to psychological reality' has been widely evident, the point being made that we can be convinced of the reality of an experience, of its essential realism, by many different kinds of artistic method, and with no necessary restriction of subject-matter to the ordinary, the contemporary, and the everyday. In the Soviet Union, on the other hand, the earlier definitions of realism have been maintained and extended, and the elements of 'socialist realism', as defined, may enable us to see the tradition more clearly. There are four of these elements: *narodnost, tipichnost, ideinost,* and *partiinost. Narodnost* is in effect technical, though also an expression of spirit: the requirement of popular simplicity and traditional clarity, as opposed to the difficulties of 'formalism'. *Ideinost* and *partiinost* refer to the ideological content and partisan affiliations of such realism, and just as *narodnost* is a restatement of an ordinary technical meaning of realism, so *ideinost* and *partiinost* are developments of the ideological and revolutionary attitudes already described. There is a perfectly simple sense in which 'socialist realism' can be distinguished from 'bourgeois realism', in relation to these changes in ideology and affiliation. Much Western popular literature is in fact 'bourgeois realism', with its own versions of *ideinost* and *partiinost*, and with its ordinary adherence to *narodnost*. It is in relation to the fourth element, *tipichnost*, that the problem broadens.

Engels defined 'realism' as 'typical characters in typical situations', which would pass in a quite ordinary sense, but which in this case has behind it the body of Marxist thinking. *Tipichnost* is a development of this definition, which radically affects the whole question of realism. For the 'typical', Soviet theorists tell us, 'must not be confused with that which is frequently encountered'; the truly typical is based on 'comprehension of the laws and perspectives of future social development'. Without now considering the application of this, in the particular case of Soviet literature, (the critical touchstone, here, is the excellence of Sholokhov, in *Tikhii Don* and *Virgin Soil Upturned*, as against the *external* pattern of Alexei Tolstoy's *Road to Calvary*), we can see that the concept of *tipichnost* alters 'realism' from its sense of the direct reproduction of observed reality: 'realism' becomes, instead, a principled and organized selection. If 'typical' is understood as the most deeply characteristic human experience, in an individual or in a society (and clearly Marxists think of it as this, in relation to their own deepest beliefs), then it is clearly not far from the developed sense of the 'convincingly real' criterion, now commonplace in the West in relation to works of many kinds, both realist and non-realist in technique. And it is not our business to pick from this complex story the one use that we favour, the one true 'realism'. Rather, we must receive the actual meanings, distinguish and clarify them, and see which, if any, may be useful in describing our actual responses to literature.

The major tradition of European fiction, in the nineteenth century, is commonly described as a tradition of 'realism', and it is equally assumed that, in the West at any rate, this particular tradition has ended. The realistic novel, it was said recently, went out with the hansom cab. Yet it is not at all easy, at first sight, to see what in practice this means. For clearly, in the overwhelming majority of modern novels, including those novels we continue to regard as literature, the ordinary criteria of realism still hold. It is not only that there is still a concentration on contemporary themes; in many ways elements of ordinary everyday experience are more evident in the modern novel than in the nineteenth-century novel, through the disappearance of certain taboos. Certainly nobody will complain of the modern novel that it lacks those startling or offensive elements which it was one of the purposes of the term 'realism' to describe. Most description is still realistic, in the sense that describing the object as it actually appears is a principle few novelists would dissent from. What we usually say is that the realistic novel has been replaced by the 'psychological novel', and it is obviously true that the direct study of certain states of consciousness, certain newly apprehended psychological states, has been a primary modern feature. Yet realism as an intention, in the description of these states, has not been widely abandoned. Is it merely that 'everyday, ordinary reality' is now differently conceived, and that new techniques have been developed to describe this new kind of reality, but still with wholly realistic intentions? The questions are obviously very difficult, but one way of approaching an answer to them may be to take this ordinary belief that we have abandoned (developed beyond) the realistic novel, and to set beside it my own feeling that there is a formal gap in modern fiction, which makes it incapable of expressing one kind of experience, a kind of experience which I find particularly important and for which, in my mind, the word 'realism' keeps suggesting itself.

Now the novel is not so much a literary form as a whole literature in itself. Within its wide boundaries, there is room for almost every kind of contemporary writing. Great harm is done to the tradition of fiction, and to the necessary critical discussion of it, if 'the novel' is equated with any one kind of prose work. It was such a wrong equation which made Tolstoy say of *War and Peace*: 'it is not a novel'. A form which in fact includes *Middlemarch* and *Auto-da-Fe*, *Wuthering Heights* and *Huckleberry Finn*, *The Rainbow* and *The Magic Mountain*, is indeed, as I have said, more like a whole literature. In drawing attention to what seems to me now a formal gap, I of course do not mean that this whole vast form should be directed to filling it. But because it is like a whole literature, any formal gap in the novel seems particularly important.

When I think of the realist tradition in fiction, I think of the kind of novel which creates and judges the quality of a whole way of life in terms of the qualities of persons. The balance involved in this achievement is perhaps the most important thing about it. It looks at first sight so general a thing, the sort of thing most novels do. It is what *War and Peace* does; what *Middlemarch* does; what *The Rainbow* does. Yet the distinction of this kind is that it offers a valuing of a whole way of life, a society that is larger than any of the individuals composing it, and at the same time valuing creations of human beings who, while belonging to and affected by and helping to define this way of life, are also, in their own terms, absolute ends in themselves. Neither element, neither the society nor the individual, is there as a priority. The society is not a background against which the personal relationships are studied, nor are the individuals merely illustrations of aspects of the way of life. Every aspect of personal life is radically affected by the quality of the general life, yet the general life is seen at its most important in completely personal terms. We attend with our whole senses to every aspect of the general life, yet the centre of value is always in the individual human person—not any one isolated person, but the many persons who are the reality of the general life. Tolstoy and George Eliot, in particular, often said, in much these terms, that it was this view they were trying to realize.

Within this realist tradition, there are of course wide variations of degree of success, but such a viewpoint, a particular apprehension of a relation between individuals and society, may be seen as a mode. It must be remembered that this viewpoint was itself the product of maturity; the history of the novel from the eighteenth century is essentially an exploration towards this position, with many preliminary failures. The eighteenth-century novel is formally most like our own, under comparable pressures and uncertainties, and it was in the deepening understanding of the relations between individuals and societies that the form actually matured. When it is put to me that the realist tradition has broken down, it is this mature viewpoint that I see as having been lost, under new pressures of particular experience. I do not mean that it is, or should be, tied to any particular style. The kind of realistic (or as we now say, naturalistic) description that 'went out with the hansom cab' is in no way essential to it; it was even, perhaps, in writers like Bennett, a substitute for it. Such a vision is not realized by detailed stocktaking descriptions of shops or back-parlours or station waiting-rooms. These may be used, as elements of the action, but they are not this essential realism. If they are put in, for the sake of description as such, they may in fact destroy the balance that is the essence of this method; they may, for example, transfer attention from the people to the things. It was actually this very feeling, that in this kind of fully-furnished novel everything was present but actual individual life, that led, in the 1920s, to the disrepute of 'realism'. The extreme reaction was in Virginia Woolf's *The Waves*, where all the furniture, and even the physical bodies, have gone out of the window, and we are left with voices and feelings, voices in the air—an equally damaging unbalance, as we can now see. It may indeed be possible to write the history of the modern novel in terms of a polarization of styles, object-realist and subject-impressionist, but the more essential polarization, which has mainly occurred since

1900, is the division of the realist novel, which had created the substance and quality of a way of life in terms of the substance and qualities of persons, into two separate traditions, the 'social' novel and the 'personal' novel. In the social novel there may be accurate observation and description of the general life, the aggregation; in the personal novel there may be accurate observation and description of persons, the units. But each lacks a dimension, for the way of life is neither aggregation nor unit, but a whole indivisible process.

We now commonly make this distinction between 'social' and 'personal' novels; indeed in one way we take this distinction of interest for granted. By looking at some examples, the substantial issue may be made clear. There are now two main kinds of 'social' novel. There is, first, the descriptive social novel, the documentary. This creates, as priority, a general way of life, a particular social or working community. Within this, of course, are characters, sometimes quite carefully drawn. But what we say about such novels is that if we want to know about life in a mining town, or in a university, or on a merchant ship, or on a patrol in Burma, this is the book. In fact many novels of this kind are valuable; the good documentary is usually interesting. It is right that novels of this kind should go on being written, and with the greatest possible variety of setting. Yet the dimension that we miss is obvious: the characters are miners, dons, soldiers first; illustrations of the way of life. It is not the emphasis I have been trying to describe, in which the persons are of absolute interest in themselves, and are yet seen as parts of a whole way of living. Of all current kinds of novel, this kind, at its best, is *apparently* nearest to what I am calling the realist novel, but the crucial distinction is quite apparent in reading: the social-descriptive function is in fact the shaping priority.

A very lively kind of social novel, quite different from this, is now significantly popular. The tenor, here, is not description, but the finding and materialization of a *formula* about society. A particular pattern is abstracted, from the sum of social experience, and a society is created from this pattern. The simplest examples are in the field of the future-story, where the 'future' device (usually only a device, for nearly always it is obviously contemporary society that is being written about; indeed this is becoming the main way of writing about social experience) removes the ordinary tension between the selected pattern and normal observation. *Brave New World*, *Nineteen Eighty-Four*, *Fahrenheit 451*, are powerful social fiction, in which a pattern taken from contemporary society is materialized, as a whole, in another time or place. Other examples are Golding's *Lord of the Flies* and *The Inheritors*, and nearly all serious 'science fiction'. Most of these are written to resemble realistic novels, and operate in the same essential terms. Most of them contain, fundamentally, a conception of the relation between individuals and society; ordinarily a virtuous individual, or small personal group, against a vile society. The action, normally, is a release of tensions in this personal-social complex, but I say release, and not working-out, because ordinarily the device subtly alters the tensions, places them in a preselected light, so that it is not so much that they are explored but indulged. The experience of isolation, of alienation, and of self-exile is an important part of the contemporary structure of feeling, and any contemporary realist novel would have to come to real terms with it. (It is ironic, incidentally, that it was come to terms with, and worked to a resolution very different from the contemporary formula of 'exile versus masses; stalemate', at several points in the realist tradition, notably in *Crime and Punishment* and, through Bezukhov, in *War and Peace*.) Our formula novels are lively, because they are about lively social feelings, but the obvious dimension they lack is that of a substantial society and correspondingly substantial persons. For the common life is an abstraction, and the personal lives are defined by their function in the formula.

The 'realist' novel divided into the 'social' and the 'personal', and the 'social novel', in our time, has further divided into social documentary and social formula. It is true that examples of these kinds can be found from earlier periods, but they were never, as now, the modes. The same point holds for the 'personal novel', and its corresponding division into documentary and formula. Some of the best novels of our time are those which describe, carefully and subtly, selected personal relationships. These are often very like *parts* of the realist novel as described, and there is a certain continuity of method and substance. Forster's *Passage to India* is a good example, with traces of the older balance still clearly visible, yet belonging, in a high place, in this divided kind, because of elements in the Indian society of the novel which romanticize the actual society to the needs of certain of the characters. This is quite common in this form: a society, a general way of living, is apparently there, but is in fact often a highly personalized landscape, to clarify or frame an individual portrait, rather than a country within which the individuals are actually contained. Graham Greene's social settings are obvious examples: his Brighton, West Africa, Mexico and Indo-China have major elements in common which relate not to their actual ways of life but to the needs of his characters and of his own emotional pattern. When this is frankly and absolutely done, as in Kafka, there is at least no confusion; but ordinarily, with a surface of realism, there is merely the familiar unbalance. There is a lack of dimension similar to that in the social-descriptive novel, but in a different direction. There the characters were aspects of the society; here the society is an aspect of the characters. The balance we remember is that in which both the general way of life and the individual persons are seen as there and absolute.

Of course, in many personal novels, often very good in their own terms, the general way of life does not appear even in this partial guise, but as a simple backcloth, of shopping and the outbreak of war and buses and odd minor characters from another social class. Society is outside the people, though at times, even violently, it breaks in on them. Now of course, where there is deliberate selection, deliberate concentration, such personal novels are valuable, since there is a vast field of significant experience, of a directly personal kind, which can be excitingly explored. But it seems to me that for every case of conscious selection (as in Proust, say, where the concentration is entirely justified and yet produces, obliquely, a master-portrait of a general way of life) there are perhaps a thousand cases where the restriction is simply a failure of consciousness, a failure to realize the extent to which the substance of a general way of life actively affects the closest personal experience. Of course if, to these writers, society has become the dull abstract thing of the social novel at its worst, it is not surprising that they do not see why it should concern them. They insist on the people as people first, and not as social units, and they are quite right to do so. What is missing, however, is that element of common substance which again and again the great realists seemed able to apprehend. Within the small group, personality is valued, but outside the group it is nothing. We are people, one sometimes hears between the lines; to *us* these things are important; but the strange case of the Virginia Woolf charwoman or village woman, with the sudden icy drop in the normally warm sensibility, symbolizes a common limitation. And this is not only social exclusiveness or snobbery, though it can be diagnosed in such ways, but also a failure to realize the nature of the general social element in *their own* lives. We are people (such novels say), people, just like that; the rest is the world or society or politics or something, dull things that are written about in the newspapers. But in fact we are people and people within a society: that whole view was at the centre of the realist novel.

In spite of its limitations, the personal-descriptive novel is often a substantial achievement, but the tendencies evident in it seem increasingly to be breaking it down into the other personal kind, the novel of the personal formula. Here, as in the novel of social formula, a particular pattern is abstracted from the sum of experience, and not now societies, but human individuals, are created from the pattern. This has been the method of powerful and in its own terms valid fiction, but it seems to me to be rapidly creating a new mode, the fiction of special pleading. We can say of novels in this class that they take only one person seriously, but then ordinarily very seriously indeed. Joyce's *Portrait of the Artist* is not only this, but contains it as a main emphasis. And to mention this remarkable work is to acknowledge the actual gain in intensity, the real development of fictional method, which this emphasis embodied. A world is actualized on one man's senses: not narrated, or held at arm's length, but taken as it is lived. Joyce showed the magnificent advantages of this method when in *Ulysses* he actualized a world not through one person but through three; there are three ways of seeing, three worlds, of Stephen, Bloom, and Molly, yet the three worlds, as in fact, compose one world, the whole world of the novel. *Ulysses* does not maintain this balance throughout; it is mainly in the first third of the book that the essential composition is done, with the last section as a coda. Yet here was the realist tradition in a new form, altered in technique but continuous in experience.

Since *Ulysses*, this achievement has been diluted, as the technique has also been diluted. Cary's *The Horse's Mouth* is an interesting example, for in it one way of seeing has been isolated, and the world fitted to that. This analysis is also the key to the popular new kind of novel represented by Amis's *That Uncertain Feeling* and Wain's *Living in the Present*. The paradox of these novels is that on the one hand they seem the most real kind of contemporary writing —they were welcomed because they recorded so many actual feelings—and yet on the other hand their final version of reality is parodic and farcical. This illustrates the general dilemma: these writers start with real personal feelings, but to sustain and substantiate them, in their given form, the world of action in which they operate has to be pressed, as it were inevitably, towards caricature. (This was also the process of Dickens, at the limits of what he could openly see or state, and caricature and sentimentality are in this sense opposite sides of the same coin, used to avoid the real negotiation.) To set these feelings in our actual world, rather than in this world farcically transformed at crisis, would be in fact to question the feelings, to go on from them to a very difficult questioning of reality. Instead of this real tension, what we get is a phantasy release: swearing on the telephone, giving a mock-lecture, finding a type-figure on which aggression can be concentrated. Because these are our liveliest writers, they illustrate our contemporary difficulty most clearly. The gap between our feelings and our social observation is dangerously wide.

The fiction of special pleading can be seen in its clearest form in those many contemporary novels which, taking one person's feelings and needs as absolute, create other persons in these sole terms. This flourishes in the significantly popular first-person narrative, which is normally used simply for this end. *Huckleberry Finn*, in its middle sections, creates a general reality within which the personal narrative gains breadth. Salinger's *Catcher in the Rye* has a saving irony, yet lacks this other dimension, a limitation increasingly obvious as the novel proceeds. Braine's *Room at the Top* breaks down altogether, because there is no other reality to refer to; we are left with the familiar interaction of crudity and self-pity, a negative moral gesture at best. Compare, for example, Carson McCullers' *Member of the Wedding*, which has its realist dimension, and in which the reality of personal feeling, growing into phantasy, interacts at the necessary tension with the world in which the feelings must be lived out. Or again, on the opposite side, there is Sagan's *Bonjour Tristesse*, where the persons are presented almost objectively, but are then made to act in accordance with the phantasy of the central character. A comparison of McCullers and Sagan is the comparison of realism and its breakdown. And it is the breakdown, unfortunately, of which we have most examples; the first-person narrative, on which so much technical brilliance has been lavished, is now ordinarily the mechanism of rationalizing this breakdown. The fiction of special pleading extends, however, into novels still formally resembling the realist kind. In Bowen's *Heat of the Day*, for example, the persons exist primarily as elements in the central character's emotional landscape, and are never seen or valued in any other terms, though there is no first-person narrative, and there is even some careful descriptive realism, to make the special pleading less stark. As it is now developing, the personal novel ends by denying the majority of persons. The reality of society is excluded, and this leads, inevitably, in the end, to the exclusion of all but a very few individual people. It is not surprising, in these circumstances, that so much of the personal feeling described should be in fact the experience of breakdown.

I offer this fourfold classification—social description, social formula, personal description, personal formula—as a way of beginning a general analysis of the contemporary novel, and of defining, by contrast, the realist tradition which, in various ways, these kinds have replaced. The question now is whether these kinds correspond to some altered reality, leaving the older tradition as really irrelevant as the hansom cab, or whether they are in fact the symptoms of some very deep crisis in experience, which throws up these talented works yet persists, unexplored, and leaves us essentially dissatisfied. I would certainly not say that the abandonment of the realist balance is in some way wilful; that these writers are deliberately turning away from a great tradition, with the perversity that many puzzled readers assign to them. The crisis, as I see it, is too deep for any simple, blaming explanation. But what then is this crisis, in its general nature?

There are certain immediate clarifying factors. The realist novel needs, obviously, a genuine community: a community of persons linked not merely by one kind of relationship—work or friendship or family—but by many, interlocking kinds. It is obviously difficult, in the twentieth century, to find a community of this sort. Where *Middlemarch* is a complex of personal, family and working relationships, and draws its whole strength from their interaction in an indivisible process, the links between persons in most contemporary novels are relatively single, temporary, discontinuous. And this was a change in society, at least in that part of society most nearly available to most novelists, before it was a change in literary form. Again, related to this, but affected by other powerful factors, the characteristic experience of our century is that of asserting and preserving an individuality, (again like much eighteenth-century experience) as compared with the characteristic nineteenth-century experience of finding a place and making a settlement. The ordinary Victorian novel ends, as every parodist knows, with a series of settlements, of new engagements and formal relationships, whereas the ordinary twentieth-century novel ends with a man going away on his own, having extricated himself from a dominating situation, and found himself in so doing. Again, this actually happened, before it became a common literary pattern. In a time of great change, this kind of extrication and discovery was a necessary and valuable movement; the recorded individual histories amount

286

to a common history. And while old establishments linger, and new establishments of a dominating kind are continually instituted, the breakaway has continually to be made, the personal assertion given form and substance, even to the point where it threatens to become the whole content of our literature. Since I know the pressures, I admit the responses, but my case is that we are reaching deadlock, and that to explore a new definition of realism may be the way to break out of the deadlock and find a creative direction.

The contemporary novel has both reflected and illuminated the crisis of our society, and of course we could fall back on the argument that only a different society could resolve our literary problems. Yet literature is committed to the detail of known experience, and any valuable social change would be the same kind of practical and responsible discipline. We begin by identifying our actual situation, and the critical point, as I see it, is precisely that separation of the individual and society into absolutes, which we have seen reflected in form. The truly creative effort of our time is the struggle for relationships, of a whole kind, and it is possible to see this as both personal and social: the practical learning of *extending* relationships. Realism, as embodied in its great tradition, is a touchstone in this, for it shows, in detail, that vital interpenetration, idea into feeling, person into community, change into settlement, which we need, as growing points, in our own divided time. In the highest realism, society is seen in fundamentally personal terms, and persons, through relationships, in fundamentally social terms. The integration is controlling, yet of course it is not to be achieved by an act of will. If it comes at all, it is a creative discovery, and can perhaps only be recorded within the structure and substance of the realist novel.

Yet, since it is discovery, and not recovery, since nostalgia and imitation are not only irrelevant but hindering, any new realism will be different from the tradition, and will comprehend the discoveries in personal realism which are the main twentieth-century achievement. The point can be put theoretically, in relation to modern discoveries in perception and communication. The old, naïve realism is in any case dead, for it depended on a theory of natural seeing which is now impossible. When we thought we had only to open our eyes to see a common world, we could suppose that realism was a simple recording process, from which any deviation was voluntary. We know now that we literally create the world we see, and that this human creation—a discovery of how we can live in the material world we inhabit—is necessarily dynamic and active; the old static realism of the passive observer is merely a hardened convention. When it was first discovered that man lives through his perceptual world, which is a human interpretation of the material world outside him, this was thought to be a basis for the rejection of realism; only a personal vision was possible. But art is more than perception; it is a particular kind of active response, and a part of all human communication. Reality, in our terms, is that which human beings make common, by work or language. Thus, in the very acts of perception and communication, this practical interaction of what is personally seen, interpreted and organized and what can be socially recognized, known and formed is richly and subtly manifested. It is very difficult to grasp this fundamental interaction, but here, undoubtedly, is the clue we seek, not only in our thinking about personal vision and social communication, but also in our thinking about the individual and society. The individual inherits an evolved brain, which gives him his common human basis. He learns to see, through this inheritance, and through the forms which his culture teaches. But, since the learning is active, and since the world he is watching is changing and being changed, new acts of perception, interpretation and organization are not only possible, but deeply necessary. This is human growth, in personal terms, but the essential growth is in the interaction which then can occur, in the individual's effort to communicate what he has learned, to match it with known reality and by work and language to make a new reality. Reality is continually established, by common effort, and art is one of the highest forms of this process. Yet the tension can be great, in the necessarily difficult struggle to establish reality, and many kinds of failure and breakdown are possible. It seems to me that in a period of exceptional growth, as ours has been and will continue to be, the tension will be exceptionally high, and certain kinds of failure and breakdown may become characteristic. The recording of creative effort, to explore such breakdowns, is not always easy to distinguish from the simple, often rawly exciting exploitation of breakdown. Or else there is a turning away, into known forms, which remind us of previously learned realities and seek, by this reminder, to establish probability of a kind. Thus the tension can either be lowered, as in the ordinary social novel, or played on, as in the ordinary personal novel. Either result is a departure from realism, in the sense that I am offering. For realism is precisely this living tension, achieved in a communicable form. Whether this is seen as a problem of the individual in society, or as a problem of the offered description and the known description, the creative challenge is similar. The achievement of realism is a continual achievement of balance, and the ordinary absence of balance, in the forms of the contemporary novel, can be seen as both a warning and a challenge. It is certain that any effort to achieve a contemporary balance will be complex and difficult, but the effort is necessary, a new realism is necessary, if we are to remain creative.

PART THREE

Britain in the 1960s

We have been trying to develop methods of analysis which, over a range from literature to social institutions, can articulate actual structures of feeling —the meanings and values which are lived in works and relationships—and clarify the processes of historical development through which these structures form and change. I shall attempt, in this part, a description of contemporary Britain in this sense: necessarily only in outline, needing expansion by other kinds of analysis and measurement, but offering an account of the essential language—the created and creative meanings—which our inherited reality teaches and through which new reality forms and is negotiated. The context I give to this particular description is the historical process which I have called the long revolution.

I

As we enter the 1960s, the effective historical patterns of British society seem reasonably clear. The industrial revolution, in an important technical phase, is continuing. The cultural expansion, again with new technical developments, also continues. In the democratic revolution, Britain has recently been mainly in a defensive position, as the colonial peoples move to emancipation. At home it is generally assumed that the democratic process has been essentially completed, with parliamentary and local government solidly established on universal suffrage, and with the class system apparently breaking up. Britain seems, from these patterns, a country with a fairly obvious future: industrially advanced, securely democratic, and with a steadily rising general level of education and culture.

There is substantial truth in this reading. It is not only the general consensus, but most attempts to challenge it seem unreasonable; even powerful local criticisms do not funda-

mentally disturb the sense of steady and general advance.
Yet in deeper ways, that have perhaps not yet been articu-
lated, this idea of a good society naturally unfolding itself
may be exceptionally misleading. It is perhaps an intuitive
sense of this that has given such emotional force to the total
denunciations, the sweeping rejections, so characteristic of
recent years, for even when these can be shown to be based
on selective evidence and particular minority tensions, the
experience they attest is still not easily set aside.

It seems to me that the first difficulty lies in the common
habit of supposing our society to be governed by single
patterns, arrived at by averaging the overall trends in
familiar categories of economic activity, political behaviour
and cultural development. As I see the situation, we need
quite different forms of analysis, which would enable us to
recognize the important contradictions within each of the
patterns described, and, even more crucially, the contradictions between different parts of the general process of change.
It is not only that the analysis should be more flexible, but
that new categories and descriptions are needed, if all the
facts are to be recognized. In particular fields we have made
some progress with these, but in our most general descriptions we are all still visibly fumbling, leaving an uncertainty
easily exploited by the blandest versions of a natural and
healthy evolution, and certainly not redeemed by such
general nostrums as the fight for socialism, which remains,
after all, in terms of this country, almost wholly undefined.

We have to observe, for example, that the ordinary
optimism about Britain's economic future can be reasonably seen as simple complacency. It is very far from certain
that on present evidence and given likely developments the
directions and rate of growth of the economy guarantee us,
over say fifty years, a steadily rising standard of living in this
economically exposed and crowded island. Both the rapid
rate of economic growth elsewhere, and the certainty of
steady industrialization of many areas now undeveloped,
seem ominous signs for a country so dependent on trade
and in fact given its prosperity by its early industrial start
(now being rapidly overtaken) and by its Empire (now
either disappearing or changing its character). Long-term

thinking of this kind is in fact beginning, but the gap between thinking and vigorous action to implement it seems no ordinary inertia, but the consequence of habits which, in other parts of our life, seem satisfactory and even admirable. The deep revulsion against general planning, which makes sense again and again in many details of our economic activity, may be really disabling in this long run. And this revulsion is itself in part a consequence of one aspect of the democratic revolution—the determination not to be regimented. Here is a substantial contradiction that I think now runs very deep. The very strong case for general planning, not simply to avoid waste but to promote essential development, research and reorganization, is practically nullified by a wholly creditable emotion: that we reject the idea of this kind of economic system controlling our lives. True, we are controlled now and will continue to be controlled by a quite different system, with its own denials and rigidities, but in the first place this is very much harder to identify, and secondly, by its very structure and ideology, it appears to offer, and in just enough places does offer, the feeling of freedom. It seems unlikely that the case for general planning will ever be widely accepted until not only do its forms seem sensible, but also its methods seem compatible with just this feeling of freedom. Democratic planning is an easy phrase, but nobody really knows how it would work, and the spectacular successes of economic planning elsewhere have after all not co-existed with any general democracy. This is the severe damage of the contradiction, because it is then easy to suppose that we have found good reasons for not planning, when in fact the need remains urgent and the problems will not disappear because on balance we find them too difficult to solve.

It remains very difficult, in fact, to think about our general economic activity at all. Both its successes and its failures remain obstinately local, and to this kind of description (particular successes announced by their makers, particular failures not announced until they erupt in crisis) the only ordinary alternative is an almost useless measurement of total production, as if some single thing were being produced. Economists have done a good deal to make these questions significant, but in ordinary thinking it is either this success and that failure, or this misleadingly simple general graph. We can only think in real terms if we know what real things are being produced, and ask relevant questions about need and quality. Some part of the production may be truly unnecessary, but the more likely situation is that the balance between various kinds of production will be wrong or even absurd. The usual answer to this kind of question is a particular description, the market, which supposedly regulates questions of need and quality. 'It is needed because it is bought; if it were not bought, it would not be made'. Of course this leaves out one major consideration: whether need and ability to buy are matched. But in any case the description is crude, because it leaves out too much. To match the block figure of production, we are offered another block figure, the consumer. The popularity of 'consumer' as a contemporary term deserves some attention. It is significant because, first, it unconsciously expresses a really very odd and partial version of the purpose of economic activity (the image is drawn from the furnace or the stomach, yet how many things there are we neither eat nor burn), and, second, it materializes as an individual figure (perhaps monstrous in size but individual in behaviour)—the person with needs which he goes to the market to supply.

Why 'consumer', to take the first point? We have to go back to the idea of a market, to get this clear. A market is an obviously sensible place where certain necessary goods are made available, but the image of the place lingers when the process of supply and demand has in fact been transformed. We used to go to markets and shops as customers; why are we regarded now as consumers? The radical change is that increasingly, in the development of large-scale industrial production, it is necessary to plan ahead and to know the market demand. What we now call market research was intended as a reasonable provision for this: demand is discovered so that production can be organized. But in fact, since production is not generally planned, but the result of the decisions of many competing firms, market research has inevitably become involved with advertising, which has itself changed from the process of notifying a given supply to a system of stimulating and directing demand. Sometimes this stimulation is towards this version of a product rather than that (*Mountain Brand is Best*), but frequently it is stimulation of a new demand (*You Need Pocket Radio*) or revival of a flagging demand (*Drinka Pinta Milka Day*). In these changing circumstances, the simple idea of a market has gone: the huckster stands level with the supplier. It is then clear why 'consumer', as a description, is so popular, for while a large part of our economic activity is obviously devoted to supplying known needs, a considerable and increasing part of it goes to ensuring that we consume what industry finds it convenient to produce. As this tendency strengthens, it becomes increasingly obvious that society is not controlling its economic life, but is in part being controlled by it. The weakening of purposive social thinking is a direct consequence of this powerful experience, which seeks to reduce human activity to predictable patterns of demand. If we were not consumers, but users, we might look at society very differently, for the concept of use involves general human judgements—we need to know how to use things and what we are using them for, and also the effects of particular uses on our general life—whereas consumption, with its crude hand-to-mouth patterns, tends to cancel these questions, replacing them by the stimulated and controlled absorption of the products of an external and autonomous system. We have not gone all the way with this new tendency, and are still in a position to reverse it, but its persuasive patterns have much of the power of our society behind them.

An equally important effect of the 'consumer' description is that, in materializing an individual figure, it prevents us thinking adequately about the true range of uses of our economic activity. There are many things, of major importance, which we do not use or consume individually, in the ordinary sense, but socially. It is a poor way of life in which we cannot think of social use as one criterion of our economic activity, yet it is towards this that we are being pushed by the 'consumer' emphasis, by the supposed laws of the market, and by the system of production and distribution from which these derive. It is beginning to be widely recognized, in Britain in 1960, that a serious state of unbalance between provision for social and individual needs now exists and seems likely to increase. It is easy to get a sense of plenty from the shop windows of contemporary Britain, but if we look at the schools, the hospitals, the roads, the libraries, we find chronic shortages far too often. Even when things are factually connected, in direct daily experience, as in the spectacular example of the flood of new cars and the ludicrous inadequacy of our road system, the spell of this divided thinking seems too powerful to break. Crises of this kind seem certain to dominate our economy in the years ahead, for even when late, very late, we begin thinking about the social consequences of our individual patterns of use, to say nothing about social purposes in their own right, we seem to find it very difficult to think about social provision in a genuinely social way. Thus we think of our individual patterns of use in the favourable terms of spending and satisfaction, but of our social patterns of use in the unfavourable terms of deprivation and taxation. It seems a fundamental defect of our society that social purposes are largely financed out of individual incomes, by a method of rates and taxes which makes it very easy for us to feel that society is a thing that continually deprives and limits us—without this system we could all be profitably spending. Who has not heard that impassioned cry of the modern barricade: *but it's my money you're spending on all this; leave my money alone*? And it doesn't help much to point out that hardly any of us could get any money, or even live for more than a few days, except in terms of a highly organized social system which we too easily take for granted. I remember a miner saying to me, of someone we were discussing: 'He's the sort of man who gets up in the morning and presses a switch and expects the light to come on'. We are all, to some extent, in this position, in that our modes of thinking habitually suppress large areas of our real relationships, including our real dependences on others. We think of my money, my light, in these naïve terms, because parts of our very idea of society are withered at root. We can hardly have any conception, in our present system, of the financing of social purposes from the social product, a method which would continually show us, in real terms, what our society is and does. In a society whose products depend almost entirely on intricate and continuous co-operation and social organization, we expect to consume as if we were isolated individuals, making our own way. We are then forced into the stupid comparison of individual consumption and social taxation—one desirable and to be extended, the other regrettably necessary and to be limited. From this kind of thinking the physical unbalance follows inevitably.

Unless we achieve some realistic sense of community, our true standard of living will continue to be distorted. As it is, to think about economic activity in the limited terms of the consumer and the market actually disguises what many of us are doing, and how the pattern of economic life is in any case changing. Even now, one person in four of the working population is engaged neither in production nor in distribution, but in public administration and various forms of general service. For a long time this proportion has been steadily rising, and it seems certain that it will continue to rise. Yet it is a kind of economic activity which cannot be explained, though it may be distorted, by such descriptions as the consumer and the market. A further one in thirteen work in transport, and it is significant that the ordinary argument about our transport systems, especially the railways, is unusually difficult and confused, as the problem of finding any criterion more adequate than consumption, any method of accounting more realistic than direct profit and loss in the market, inevitably shows through. As for administration and general services, from medicine and education to art, sport, and entertainment, the argument is almost hopelessly confused. The product of this kind of work, which one in four of us give our time to, is almost wholly in terms of life and experience, as opposed to things. What kind of accounting is adequate here, for who can measure the value of a life and an experience? Some parts of the process can be reduced to more familiar terms: medicine saves working days, education produces working skills, sport creates fitness, entertainment keeps up morale. But we all know that every one of these services is directed, in the end, to larger purposes: doctors work just as hard to save the life of a man past working age; every school teaches more than direct working skills, and so on. To impose an accounting in market terms is not only silly but in the end impossible: many of the results of such effort are not only long-term and indirect, but in any case have no discoverable exchange value. The most enlightened ordinary reaction is to put these activities into a margin called 'life' or 'leisure', which will be determined as to size by the shape of 'ordinary' economic activity. On the other hand, if we started not from the market but from the needs of persons, not only could we understand this part of our working activity more clearly, but also we should have a means of judging the 'ordinary' economic activity itself. Questions not only of balance in the distribution of effort and resources, but also of the effects of certain kinds of work both on users and producers, might then be adequately negotiated. The danger now, as has been widely if obscurely recognized, is of fitting human beings to a system, rather than a system to human beings. The obscurity shows itself in wrong identification of the causes of this error: criticism of industrial production, for example, when in fact we should starve without it; criticism of large-scale organization, when in fact this extension of communication is the substance of much of our growth; criticism, finally, of the pressures of society, when in fact it is precisely the lack of an adequate sense of society that is crippling us.

For my own part I am certain, as I review the evidence, that it is capitalism—a particular and temporary system of organizing the industrial process—which is in fact confusing us. Capitalism's version of society can only be the market, for its purpose is profit in particular activities rather than any general conception of social use, and its concentration of ownership in sections of the community makes most common decisions, beyond those of the market, limited or impossible. Many industrial jobs, as now organized, are boring or frustrating, but the system of wage-labour, inherent in capitalism, necessarily tends to the reduction of the meaning of work to its wages alone. It is interesting that the main unrest of our society—the running battle which compromises any picture of a mainly contented and united country—is in this field of wages. Whenever there is an important strike, or threat of a strike, we tend to react by defining a different conception of work—service to the community, responsibility to others, pulling together. The reaction is quite right: work ought to mean these things. But it is hypocritical to pretend that it now does, all the way through. While the light comes on when we press the switch, we take for granted just these qualities, but ordinarily fail to acknowledge, with any depth, the needs of the man who made the light possible. If we want to stop strikes, we have to carry the reaction right through, for this system of bargaining for labour necessarily includes, as a last resort, as in all other bargaining, the seller's refusal of his labour at the price offered. Strikes are an integral part of the market society, and if you want the advantages you must take the disadvantages, even to the point of dislocation and chaos. While we still talk of a labour market, as despite long protest many of us continue to do, we must expect the behaviour appropriate to it, and not try to smuggle in, when it becomes inconvenient, the quite different conception of common interest and responsibility. The moral disapproval of strikers is shallow and stupid while the system of work is based on the very grounds of particular profit which we there condemn.

What is happening to capitalism in contemporary Britain? We are told that it is changing, but while this is obviously true it can be argued that the patterns of thinking and behaviour it promotes have never been more strong. To the reduction of use to consumption, already discussed, we must add the widespread extension of the 'selling' ethic— what sells goes, and to sell a thing is to validate it—and also, I think, the visible moral decline of the labour movement. Both politically and industrially, some sections of the labour movement have gone over, almost completely, to ways of thinking which they still formally oppose. The main challenge to capitalism was socialism, but this has almost wholly lost any contemporary meaning, and it is not surprising that many people now see in the Labour Party merely an alternative power-group, and in the trade-union movement merely a set of men playing the market in very much the terms of the employers they oppose. Any such development is generally damaging, for the society is unlikely to be able to grow significantly if it has no real alternative patterns as the ground of choice. I remember that I surprised many people, in *Culture and Society*, by claiming that the institutions of the labour movement—the trade unions, the co-operatives, the Labour Party—were a great creative achievement of the working people and also the right basis for the whole organization of any good society of the future. Am I now withdrawing this claim, in speaking of moral decline? The point is, as I see it, that my claim rested on the new social patterns these institutions offered. I recognize that the motives for their foundation, and consequently their practice, must be seen as mixed. Sectional defence and sectional self-interest undoubtedly played their part. But also there was this steady offering and discovery of ways of living that could be extended to the whole society, which could quite reasonably be organized on a basis of collective democratic institutions and the substitution of co-operative equality for competition as the principle of social and economic policy. In the actual history, there has been a steady pressure, from the existing organization of society, to convert these institutions to aims and patterns which would not offer this kind of challenge. The co-operatives should be simply trading organizations, the trade unions simply industrial organizations with no other interests, each union keeping to its own sphere, and the Labour Party simply an alternative government in the present system—the country needs an effective opposition. This pressure could not have been as successful as it has if just these aims had not been part of the original impetus of the institutions: certain elements in their patterns have been encouraged, certain elements steadily opposed and weakened. And in every case, of course, to accept the proposed limitation of aims may lead to important short-run gains in practical efficiency; the men within these institutions who accept the limitation often make more immediate sense. But it is quite clear, as we enter the 1960s, that the point has been reached when each of these institutions is discovering that the place in existing society proposed for it, if it agrees to limit its aims, is essentially subordinate: the wide challenge has been drained out, and what is left can be absorbed within existing terms. For many reasons this has sapped the morale of the institutions, but also, fortunately, led to crisis and argument within them. The choice as it presents itself is between qualified acceptance in a subordinate capacity or the renewal of an apparently hopeless challenge. The practical benefits of the former have to be balanced against the profound loss of inspiration in the absence of the latter. If I seem eccentric in continuing to look to these institutions for effective alternative patterns, while seeing all too clearly their present limitations, I can only repeat that they can go either way, and that their crisis is not yet permanently resolved.

The situation is complicated by the fact that real changes have occurred in the society, through the pressure of these institutions aided by reforming elements within the existing patterns. The extension of social services, including education, is an undoubted gain of this kind, which must not be underestimated by those who have simply inherited it. But it remains true not only that the social services are limited to operation in the interstices of a private-ownership society, but also that in their actual operation they remain limited by assumptions and regulations belonging not to the new society but the old (a situation brilliantly described by Brian Abel-Smith in *Conviction*). The other substantial change, the nationalization of certain industries and services, has been even more deeply compromised. The old and valuable principle, of production for use and not for profit, has been fought to a standstill in just this field. The systems taken into public ownership were in fact those old systems no longer attractive in profit terms (coal, railways), new systems requiring heavy initial investment (airways) and systems formerly municipally or publicly developed (gas, electricity). Some of these systems have been much more successful than is generally allowed, but it remains true, first, that they have not only failed to alter the 'profit before use' emphasis in the general economy but have also been steadily themselves reduced to this old criterion; and, second, that they have reproduced, sometimes with appalling accuracy, the human patterns, in management and working relationships, of industries based on quite different social principles. The multiplication of such effects is indeed uninviting, and the easy identification of these institutions, as types of the supposed new society, has added to the general confusion. In being dragged back to the processes of the old system, yet at the same time offered as witnesses of the new, they have so deeply damaged any alternative principle in the economy as to have emptied British socialism of any effective meaning. The proposal to admit this formal vacuity, by detaching the Labour Party from any full commitment to socialism, then makes sense of a kind, the practical acknowledgement of an existing situation, until perhaps one remembers that the containment and eventual cancellation of any real challenge to capitalist society has been, for more than a century, the work of capitalist society itself.

These are major gains in capitalist ways of thinking, and it is easy to be overwhelmed by them. Meanwhile capitalism can point to its successes in expanding consumption, and to its extension of a huge system of consumer credit which, on its own terms, creates one kind of prosperity. With only the consumer in mind, as a point of economic reference, this is not easily challenged. Again, taking the point about restriction of ownership, capitalism has sought to extend ownership by promoting a wider holding of shares. This reply is characteristic, in that it misses the point of the criticism, and proposes reform in terms of the system criticized. The objection was only in part to restricted individual ownership (which in any case still holds); it was mainly to no social ownership. The extension of shareholding to about one in fifteen adults enables more of us to make money as a by-product of the system of satisfying our general needs (money made, in fact, out of the work of the other fourteen) but it does nothing to ensure that the needs are general or that the distribution of energy and resources is right in common terms. The latest device, of some limited control of this distribution by channelling public money into privately-owned systems, is only a further example of the way in which the very aspirations of the original challenge to capitalism are used as a means of strengthening it. Finally, capitalism (and its ex-socialist apologists) emphasizes the decline in control by shareholders (an ironic comment, of course, on the extension of shares, which is then not a new kind of ownership but simply an extension of playing the market), and the rise in importance of the managers and technicians. In fact the economy, while not controlled by ordinary shareholders, is not controlled by managers and technicians either, but by powerful interlocking private institutions that in fact command what some Labour politicians still wistfully call 'the commanding heights of the economy'. Even if the managerial revolution had occurred (and the real revolution is the passing of power to financial institutions and self-financing corporations) the original challenge would still be lost, for the direction of our common economic life would have been reduced to a series of technical decisions, without anything more than a market reference to the kind of society the economy should sustain.

The central point, in this contentious field, is that the concepts of the organized market and the consumer now determine our economic life, and with it much of the rest of our society, and that challenges to them have been so effectively confused that hardly any principled opposition remains, only the perpetual haggling and bitterness of the wage claim and the strike. It is difficult to believe that we shall remain satisfied by this situation, which is continually setting us against each other and very rapidly promoting patterns of crude economic cynicism, yet to which no clear and practical alternative exists. The challenge to create new meanings, and to substantiate them, will have to be met if that apparently obvious future is in fact to be realized.

II

The progress of democracy in Britain is deeply affected by what is happening in the economy, but also by other factors. The aspiration to control the general directions of our economic life is an essential element of democratic growth, but is still very far from being realized. Beyond this general control lies a further aspiration, now equally distant and confused. It is difficult to feel that we are really governing ourselves if in so central a part of our living as our work most of us have no share in decisions that immediately affect us. The difficulties of a procedural kind in ensuring this share are indeed severe, and because of the variety of institutions in which we work there is no single answer. Yet if the impulse is there, some ways can be found, and steadily improved from experience. I know from my own experience, in helping to work out such ways in my own job, some of the difficulties yet also some of the real gains. From practical experience alone, I agree with Burke that

> I have never yet seen any plan which has not been mended by the observations of those who were much inferior in understanding to the person who took the lead in the business.

Even the smallest human group produces leaders, though not always the same leaders for all projects. The difficulty lies in interpreting just what this leadership means. The majority patterns of our society, especially in work, offer an interpretation which not only fixes leaders, for all sorts of circumstances, but encourages them to believe that it is not only their right but their duty to make independent decisions and to be resolute in carrying them out. After all, a dog doesn't keep a man and then take the lead himself.

There are still many natural autocrats in our society, and the trouble they cause is beyond reckoning. More dangerous, perhaps, because less easily identified, are those skilled in what was called in the army 'man management'. The point here, as I remember, is that of course you have to command, but since a leader has to be followed he must be diligently attentive to the state of mind of those he is leading: must try to understand them, talk to them about their problems (not about his own, by the way), get a picture of their state of mind. Then, having taken these soundings, having really got the feel of his people, he will point the way forward.

I know few greater social pleasures, in contemporary Britain, than that of watching man-management, for indeed its practitioners are almost everywhere. It is true that they are usually very bad at it, although they invariably think themselves very good. The calmly appraising eyes (narrowed about an eighth of an inch; more would look suspicious), the gentle silences, the engaging process of drawing the man out: although I have watched these so often, I find them better than most plays. And these are the heroes of our public life, with a solid weight of mutual admiration behind them. An exceptionally large part of what passes for political commentary is now a public discussion of a party leader's command of this skill: how will the Prime Minister or the Leader of the Opposition 'handle' this or that 'awkward element'; how will he time his own intervention; if he says this, how can he avoid saying that? The really funny thing about this kind of commentary is that it is public; printed and distributed in millions of sheets; read by almost everybody, including the 'awkward elements'. The delicate art has become public myth, and it is rare to see it challenged. This, evidently, is what democratic leadership is supposed to be.

In fact, of course, it is the tactic of a defensive autocracy (and people do not have to be born into an autocracy to acquire its habits). The true process of democratic decision is that, with all the facts made available, the question is openly discussed and its resolution openly arrived at, either by simple majority vote or by a series of voluntary changes to arrive at a consensus. The skills of the good listener and the clarifier are indeed exceptionally necessary in such a process, but these are crucially different from the stance of the leader who is merely listening to the discussion to discover the terms in which he can get his own way. The intricate devices worked out by democratic organizations, to ensure the full record of facts, the freedom of general contribution, the true openness of decision, and the opportunity to review the ways in which decisions are executed, are indeed invaluable (some people thought I was joking when I mentioned committee procedure as part of our cultural heritage, but the joke is on them, if they are serious about democracy, for these are the means of its working). Yet just because they are intricate, they are easily abused by the man-managers: one even hears boasts about the ways in which this or that committee has been 'handled'. I would only say that I have never seen such handling, reputedly practised as a way of 'avoiding trouble', lead to anything but trouble. For once men are reasonably free, they will in the end assert their interests, and if these have not been truly involved in the decision (as opposed to collected and 'borne in mind') the real situation will eventually assert itself, often with a bitterness that shows how bad the man-managers really are. Our main trouble now is that we have many of the forms of democracy, but find these continually confused by the tactics of those who do not really believe in it, who are genuinely afraid of common decisions openly arrived at, and who have unfortunately partly succeeded in weakening the patterns of feeling of democracy which alone could substantiate the institutions.

We must add a note on the tones of contemporary discussion, if this situation is to be fully understood. Most people who pass through universities learn certain conventions of discussion which pass into the public process. The most important of these is a habit of tentative statement, characteristically introduced by such phrases as 'I should have thought that' or 'I don't know but it seems to me'. This manner is sometimes merely superficial, like the gambit of the Oxford lecturer who begins by saying that he knows practically nothing about the subject of the lecture, and in any case has forgotten his notes (I once saw this practised, by three lecturers running, on an audience of foreign graduates; they were not charmed, and indeed concluded that the lecturers were not quite as good as they supposed themselves to be—a 'not wholly inaccurate' diagnosis of a stance of modesty which in fact came through as insulting). These defects are evident, but elsewhere, for certain kinds of discussion, the conventions have their advantages. These can most easily be seen by contrast with the conventions of argument of many wage-earners (particularly manual workers, but not always trade union officers, who have sometimes learned tortuousness to a really amazing proficiency). At first, the bluntness of statement and assertion is refreshing after too long a course of 'I should have thought'. But one notices how easily, in such discussions, points of view become involved with the personal prestige of the speaker; the opinion cannot be attacked without attacking him as a man, and he cannot modify it without what looks like climbing down. I have listened in despair to many arguments of this kind, where in the end it would really be easier to adjourn and fight it out in the yard, all the signs of physical aggression and challenge being already more evident than the issues—except, of course, that tomorrow the discussion would only have to begin again. The value of the convention of tentative statement is that opinion can be reasonably detached from the personal prestige of the speaker, in a way that is ultimately necessary if a common opinion is to be arrived at. The frank speaking of the Labour movement has been, on balance, a great gain: the issues are forced into the open, away from the man-managers and the cupboarded autocrats. But at the same time the workings of democracy have been severely damaged by habits of aggressive assertion (personified in many a roaring old man at the rostrum) which must be seen quite clearly as pre-democratic: the language of unequals, shouting for their place in the world, and sometimes ensuring, by turning a common process into a series of personal demonstrations, that common improvement will not be got.

It is clear, on balance, that we do not get enough practice in the working of democracy, even where its forms exist. Most of us are not expected to be leaders, and are principally instructed, at school and elsewhere, in the values of discipline and loyalty, which are real values only if we share in the decisions to which they refer. Those who are expected to be leaders are mainly trained to the patterns of leadership I have been discussing, centred on the general development of confidence—but in fact that a leader should be self-confident enough to be capable of radical doubt is rarely mentioned and rarely taught. The necessary practice of the difficult processes of common decision and execution is left, on the whole, to hit or miss, and the result, not unexpectedly, is often both. A weakening of belief in the possibility of democracy is then inevitable, and we prefer to lament the 'general indiscipline' (trade-union leaders cannot control their members, party leaders are not firm enough; it is all sloppy discussion, endless talk, and then people behaving unreasonably) rather than nourishing and deepening the process to which in any case, in any probable future, we are committed.

The counterpart of this feeling, reinforced by the actual history of democratic institutions in this country, is an approach to government which in itself severely limits active democracy. A tightly organized party system and parliament seem to have converted the national franchise into the election of a court. As individuals we cast one national vote at intervals of several years, on a range of policies and particular decisions towards which it is virtually impossible to have one single attitude. From this necessarily crude process, a court of ministers emerges (in part drawn from people who have not been elected at all), and it is then very difficult for any of us to feel even the smallest direct share in the government of our affairs. Approaches through the party organizations, taking advantage of the fact that at least there are alternative courts, are more practicable, but not only is it generally true that inner-party democracy is exceptionally difficult in both large parties, it is also the case that the right not to be tied, not to be precisely committed, is increasingly claimed by both sets of leaders. The general influence of public opinion counts for something, since in the long run the court has to be re-elected. But the period is exceptionally long, given the rate and range of development in contemporary politics. In the four and a half years between the elections of 1955 and 1959 several wholly unforeseen major crises developed, and public opinion in fact violently fluctuated, to be met in general only by the bland confidence of the court in its own premises: that the duty of the government is to govern, for the Queen's government must be carried on. It is fair to say that this does not even sound like democracy, and we must be fair to our leaders, conceding them at least consistency, in their obvious assumption that direct popular government is not what democracy is about. It is true that any administration should have reasonable time to develop its policies, but this is not the same thing as the current uncritical belief in the importance of 'strong government': certainly one hopes that a good government will be strong, but a government that is both strong and bad (most people are agreed that we had such governments in the 1930s; I think we have had one or two since) is almost the worst possible public evil. I see no reason why two-year intervals of re-election of at least a substantial part of the House of Commons should not be our immediate objective, since it seems vital for the health of our democracy that more of us should feel directly involved in it. Such a change, coupled with working reforms now being canvassed in Parliament, and with an improvement of the democratic process within the parties, would be a substantial yet reasonable gain. The alternative is not only the rapid extension of man-management, monstrously magnified by the use of modern communications as its general device, but also the unpleasant development of organized pressure-groups, pushing into the anterooms of the court. One further necessary amendment seems to be a fixed date for the periodic elections, for to concede choice of this date to the court itself is psychologically quite wrong: we should not have to wait, within broad limits, for the court to ask our approval; the right of election is not theirs but ours.

These changes in themselves would make only a limited difference, but they would at least go some way towards altering the present atmosphere of British democracy, which seems increasingly formal and impersonal, and powered by little more than the belief that a choice of leaders should be periodically available. The next field of reform is obviously the electoral system, which seems designed to perpetuate the existing interpretations. Its most obvious characteristic is that it exaggerates, sometimes grossly, comparatively slight tendencies in opinion. Post-war electoral history suggests a violent fluctuation of opinion, from a very strong Labour to a very strong Conservative government. But actual opinion, reckoned in terms of people, has changed much less. What I notice most about current political commentary is that it is preoccupied by results at the level of the court, rather than by the registered opinion of actual persons; and this, however natural it may be to people who like living in anterooms, is quite undemocratic in spirit. It is ridiculous to talk of an overwhelming endorsement of Conservatism in the election of 1959, when less than half the people voting in fact voted Conservative, and when of adults entitled to vote only just over a third in fact approved the nevertheless very strong government to which all of us are committed for as long as five years. The same is true, of course, of previous 'overwhelming' Labour victories, and the mode of description suggests that we are not, in these terms, thinking about real people at all. I believe that the process of common decision, even as crudely registered by single occasional votes, must be carried through without such distortion into the formal process of government, if we are to have any honest democracy. The weight of conventional thinking by politicians is against this tendency, but such conventional thinking, when it is traced to its sources, is again the tactical wisdom of a defensive autocracy, carried on, through inertia and lack of challenge, into what is claimed to be a very different society. It is difficult, as we look over this whole field, to assent even in passing to the ordinary proposition that the democratic revolution is virtually complete.

At this critical point, the relative absence of democracy in other large areas of our lives is especially relevant. The situation can be held as it is, not only because democracy has been limited at the national level to the process of electing a court, but also because our social organization elsewhere is continually offering non-democratic patterns of decision. This is the real power of institutions, that they actively teach particular ways of feeling, and it is at once evident that we have not nearly enough institutions which practically teach democracy. The crucial area is in work, where in spite of limited experiments in 'joint consultation', the ordinary decision process is rooted in an exceptionally rigid and finely-scaled hierarchy, to which the only possible ordinary responses, of the great majority of us who are in no position to share in decisions, are apathy, the making of respectful petitions, or revolt. If we see a considerable number of strikes, as the evidence suggests, as revolts in this sense, we can see more clearly the stage of development we have reached. The defensive tactic, once again, is man-management, now more grandly renamed personnel management. This is an advance on simple autocracy, but as an

answer to the problems of human relations at work only
shows again how weakly the democratic impulse still runs.
It seems obvious that industrial democracy is deeply related
to questions of ownership; the argument against the
political vote was always that the new people voting, 'the
masses', had no stake in the country. The development of
new forms of ownership then seemed an essential part of any
democratic advance, although in fact the political suffrage
eventually broke ahead of this. The idea of public ownership
seemed to be a solution, but there is some truth in the argument that little is gained by substituting a series of still
largely authoritarian state monopolies for a series of private
monopolies (something is gained, however, to the extent that
the state is itself democratically directed). It is obvious that
in a complex large-scale economy, many central decisions
will have to be taken, and that their machinery easily becomes bureaucratic and protected from general control. At
this level there can be no doubt that the separate democratic
management of industry is unworkable. The true line of
advance is making this machinery directly responsible to the
elected government, probably through intermediate boards
which combine representation of the industry or service
with elected political representatives. With this framework
set, as for example it is to some extent set in educational
administration, the development of direct participation in the
local decisions of particular enterprises could be attempted.
The difficulties are severe, and there is no single solution. It
seems to me that a government which was serious about this
would initiate a series of varied experiments, in different
kinds of concern, ranging from conventional methods such
as the reform of company law, promoting actual and con-
tractual membership, with definite investments and rights
in the concern, to methods that would be possible in concerns already publicly owned, in which elected councils,
either from a common roll or at first representing interests
in an agreed proportion, would have powers of decision
within the accepted national framework. It is commonly
objected that modern work is too technical to be subjected
to the democratic process, but it is significant that in certain
fields, notably education and medicine, the necessarily

complicated processes of involving members in self-government are already much further advanced than in work where the 'service' criterion is not accepted, though in fact it is claimed. Education and medicine are not less technical or specialized, but they have a less obvious class structure, which is undoubtedly important. The necessary principle is that workers of all kinds, including managers, should be guaranteed the necessary conditions, including both security and freedom, of their actual work, in precise ways that are perfectly compatible with general decisions about the overall direction of the enterprise. Boards of directors elected by shareholders now give such directions, ordinarily with less security and freedom for all kinds of workers, since these are not represented. In publicly owned industries and services, and in reformed companies, the principle of boards elected by the members of the industry or service, to operate within the agreed national framework, is surely not difficult. There would be a long and continuous process of setting-up and improving such machinery, and many serious and largely unforeseen problems would undoubtedly arise. But the basis of the whole argument for democracy is that the substance of these problems would in any case exist, and that participation in the processes of decision leads to more rational and responsible solutions than the old swing between apathy, concession, and revolt.

One other field in which the growth of democracy seems urgently necessary is the ordinary process of decision about the development of our communities. This has been approached, but is still very muddled, and it is unfortunately true that there is even more dissatisfaction, and consequent apathy, about local government than about the national court. Authoritarian patterns at the centre seem to be widely reproduced in our local councils, where much more of the process is in the open and within our ordinary experience, unfortunately in its ordinary course giving far too much evidence of how easily democracy is distorted. Still, the problems here are quite widely understood, and the active struggle against distortion is encouraging. More seriously, behind this struggle is a familiar inertia of old social forms. Housing is an excellent example, because the common provision of homes and estates is so obviously sensible, in principle, and is already extending beyond the mere relief of exceptional need. Why then does such an extension, or further extension, leave many of us quite cold? One answer, certainly, is the way such houses and estates are commonly managed, by supposedly democratic authorities. I have seen letters to tenants from council housing officials that almost made my hair stand on end, and the arbitrary and illiberal regulation of many such estates is justly notorious. While this can still be fairly said even of Labour authorities, it is difficult to feel that the spirit of democracy has been very deeply or widely learned. Why should a public official, often a perfectly pleasant man to meet, transform himself so often into the jack-in-office who has done extraordinary harm to the whole development of social provision? Partly, I suppose, because he sees so many jacks-in-office above him. More generally, I think, because the patterns and tones of leadership and administration are still pre-democratic. The businessman, dealing with customers, has learned to be pleasant; so, usually, has the public official, at that level. But there are public officials who regard such people as council-house tenants as natural inferiors, and they speak and write accordingly. The remedy, of course, is not to teach them man-management, but to try to develop democratic forms within these areas of public provision. Why should the management of a housing estate not be vested in a joint committee of representatives of the elected authority and elected representatives of the people who live on it? While general financial policy obviously rests with the whole community, there is a wide area of decision, on the way the houses are used and maintained, on estate facilities, and on any necessary regulations, which could be negotiated through such channels more amicably and I think more efficiently. If this experiment has been tried, we should know more about it and consider extending it. If it has not been tried, here is an immediate field in which the working of democratic participation could be tested. Labour councils, in particular, ought continually to be thinking in these ways, for there is great danger to the popular movement if its organizations are persistently defensive and negative (as in the ordinary Tenants' Association), and it is Labour which has most to lose if it allows democracy to dwindle to a series of defensive associations and the minimal machinery of a single elected administration. The pressure has been to define democracy as 'the right to vote', 'the right to free speech', and so on, in a pattern of feeling which is really that of the 'liberty of the subject' within an established authority. The pressure now, in a wide area of our social life, should be towards a participating democracy, in which the ways and means of involving people much more closely in the process of self-government can be learned and extended.

III

Behind any description of the patterns of our economy and of our political and social life lie ways of thinking about 'class', which in Britain in the 1960s seem exceptionally uncertain and confused. Here, as a matter of urgency, we must go back from our ordinary meanings to our experience.

I showed in *Culture and Society* that 'class', as a social term, came into ordinary English usage in the period of the effective beginning of the Industrial Revolution.[1] Shaped by this particular history, it had from the first a confused reference, pointing to both social and economic facts in ways characteristic of a period of important transition. This confusion, unfortunately, has remained, and we are still not sure whether the determining factor, in our membership of a social class, is our birth or our adult work. 'Working class' has traditionally described the great body of wage-earners who came together in relation to the new methods of production. In much economic theory, this class is naturally contrasted with the propertied classes: people who own land, or other means of production, and employ wage-labour. Thus, on the one hand the working class could be contrasted with the land-owning aristocracy; on the other hand, and more usually, with the class of capitalists. But then who,

[1] Since writing *Culture and Society*, I have discovered a use of 'class', in its modern sense, from 1743. I have also discovered an isolated modern use of 'culture' from 1721. These amendments should be noted, though the examples seem exceptional, and the effective social history of a meaning must always be in terms of its passing into normal usage.

socially, were the capitalists, since they were usually not aristocrats? And to what social class did small independent employers, shopkeepers, small farmers, and professional men belong? From these two questions came one answer: the 'middling classes', later settled as the 'middle classes'. But there were obviously very wide variations here, from the large employer to the small shopkeeper, and from the successful professional man to the humble independent craftsman. Eventually, then, the middle class went into 'upper' and 'lower' divisions, but the upper division, as it became richer, was increasingly involved and mingled with the old aristocracy or 'upper' class. And movement between the working class and the lower-middle class was also fairly common, apart from the difficulty, as the character of work changed and many wage-earning jobs that were not in the old sense 'manual' were created, of drawing any clear line between the 'workers' and these 'lower-middle-class' wage-earners. These difficulties and complexities are all still with us today, and anyone who is used to either professional or amateur attempts at social classification will know how intricate it has all become. The question we need to ask however—and it is only very rarely asked—is what all this classification is for, what actual purposes in the society it serves. Some people look forward to increasing accuracy in classification, and propose new formulas. Others speak of amending the old class descriptions to bring them into line with 'modern experience'. My own position is that we might get rid of most of this classification, and save ourselves much needless trouble, if we looked rigorously at what it is there to do.

Most people in Britain now think of themselves as 'middle class' or 'working class'. But the first point to make is that these are not true alternatives. The alternatives to 'middle' are 'lower' and 'upper'; the alternative to 'working' is 'independent' or 'propertied'. The wonderful muddle we are now in springs mainly from this confusion, that one term has a primarily social, the other a primarily economic reference. When people are asked if they belong to the working class many of them agree; when they are asked if they belong to the lower class many less agree. Yet the persistent suggestion of 'middle' is that the working class is 'lower', and it is hardly surprising that many wage-earners want to think of themselves as 'middle class' if 'lower' is explicitly or implicitly the alternative description. Again, many 'middle class' people are indignant at the suggestion or implication that they do not work because they do not belong to the 'working classes'. They are quite right to be indignant, but they have only themselves to blame if they have contributed in any way to the confusion between the economic description—the wage-earning 'working classes', and the social implication that these people are the 'lower' class. It seems that we have to ask not only what purposes are served by the classification, but also what purposes are served by so persistent a confusion.

The fact is that we are still in a stage of transition from a social stratification based on birth to one based on money and actual position. The drive towards the latter kind of society is very strong; it is both built into our economic system and continually stimulated by it. But we do not have to look far, in Britain, to find older ways of thinking. The principal function of the otherwise insignificant 'upper' class is to keep distinction by birth and family alive. A simple description of power in Britain might show the irrelevance of this, but there are still, after all, the monarchy, the House of Lords, and a system of honours involving change of family name and status. So far from these systems being regarded as merely the vestiges of an older society, they are now so intensively propagated that their practical effect is still considerable. By their very removal from the harsh and controversial open exercise of power, their social prestige is even enhanced. But why is this so, in a changing society? The intense propaganda of monarchy (by a shrewd mixture of magnificence and ordinariness which in its central incompatibility bears all the signs of functional magic) seems a conscious procedure against radical change. The emphasis on the unity, loyalty and family atmosphere of the Queen's subjects is not easy to reconcile with the facts of British life, but as an ideal, though silly, it catches just enough real desires, and just sufficiently confuses consciousness of real obstacles, to be a powerful reserve of feeling in favour of things as they are. This mellow dusk then spreads over the ancillary power system, still important in many areas of actual decision, in which people chosen by family status and not by the democratic process carry on in a special position, whether in the House of Lords or as chairmen of many official and unofficial but influential committees (a process still curiously known as voluntary public work, in which if the practitioners are discovered to have the common touch the magic is even more potent).

This could hardly have happened if the rising middle class had remained independent, or retained any real confidence in itself. Somewhere in the nineteenth century (though there are earlier signs) the English middle class lost its nerve, socially, and thoroughly compromised with the class it had virtually defeated. Directed personally towards the old system of family status, it adopted as its social ideal a definite class system, blurred at the top but clear below itself. The distinction of public schools from grammar schools led to a series of compromises: in the curriculum, where just enough new subjects were introduced to serve middle-class training, but just enough old subjects kept to preserve the older cultivation of gentlemen; and in social character, where just enough emphasis on the superiority of the whole class was shrewdly mixed with a rigorous training in concepts of authority and service, so that a formal system could be manned and yet not disturbed. The principal difficulty, in preserving this system, was that new middle-class groups kept rising behind those who had made their peace. However closely the grammar schools imitated those few of their number that had been renamed public schools, it was necessary for distances to be kept, and 'grammar school', in some ears, soon sounded like 'soup kitchen'. The principal tension, in recent English social life, has been between the fixed character of the arrived middle class, with its carefully conditioned ways of speaking and behaving, and the later arrivals or those still struggling to arrive. The worst snobberies still come, with an extraordinary self-revealing brashness, from people who, if family were really the social criterion, would be negligible. The compromise takes care of that, for it had included (what the aristocracy was not unwilling to learn) the accolade of respectability on work and especially the making of money by work. This enabled the pattern to be kept mobile, without altering its character. It is true now, as Mr Ralph Samuel has argued, that the captain of industry has become the social hero, but distinctively, in Britain, the captain of industry provides himself with a family title and status expressing prestige in older terms. And since honours are easy, in the sense that they can be continually created and extended, it has been possible to work out a system whereby the results of individual effort and merit can be confirmed in terms of hereditary values. There is even a very nice grading, quite formalized in the public service, in which the particular point reached in climbing the bourgeois-democratic ladder is magically transformed into a particular feudal grade: a Prime Minister equals an Earl, a Permanent Secretary a Knight and so on. This fundamental class system, with the force of the rising middle class right behind it, requires a 'lower' class if it is to retain any social meaning. The people cast for this lower rôle keep turning round, it is true, and pointing the same finger at those below them. This is the basic unreality of the 'middle class' in Britain, and also the explanation of its vagueness. I remember sitting with a group of small shopkeepers who were trying to explain to me how you could never trust 'that class of people' (shop assistants): it seemed, in the most colourful phrase, that they always had their fingers in the toffees. The particular climax of this discussion, for me, was a description of the group, by one of its members, as 'tip-top business men'; this went down very well. Here, in fact, was a solid assumption of middle-class membership and distinction by a group of people who if they moved only a little way up this same middle class would at once be placed and despised, much as the shop assistants were placed and despised (they would probably call the waitress 'Miss', which as the normal mode of address to a young unmarried woman by the eighteenth century gentry is of course now obviously 'low'). But so long as a group can find another group to turn round and point at, the contradictions seem hardly to be noticed. All class distinction in Britain is downward, under the mellow dusk from the very top. And it seems very doubtful if it will simply wither away, for the confusion noted earlier, between social and economic description, has, as explained, been built into the system. The drive for money, power and position, which might have created the separate ideal of self-made prestige, has been neatly directed into the older system, at a cost in confusion which we are all still paying.

In this respect, I belong to the awkward squad who have been discussed a good deal since the war. Many people have told us that the reason for our interest in class is that we are frustrated to find that educational mobility is not quite social mobility; that however far we have gone we still find an older system above us. This is a very revealing account of the class-feeling of someone born just too far down in the middle class but still accepting its ethos. That sense of differential mobility is just the confusion that many middle-class groups encounter, if they are thinking in their own class terms. I can only say for myself that I have never felt my own mobility in terms of a 'rise in the social scale', and certainly I have never felt that I wanted to go on climbing, resentful of old barriers in my way: where else is there to go, but into my own life? At the same time, the particular history of going from a wage-earning family to one of the old universities takes one on a very rapid traverse of this same social scale, which seems largely to survive with the confusions it now has because really, when it comes to it, movement along it is normally quite limited, and the divisions are quite carefully kept. It is then less the injustice of the British class system than its stupidity that really strikes one. People like to be respected, but this natural desire is now principally achieved by a system which defines respect in terms of despising someone else, and then in turn being inevitably despised. In my own traverse, I have seen so much of this, aware of the standards of one group while watching another, in a truly endless series, that I should have to be very odd indeed to be bitter: the predominant feeling is of pathos. The more widely this is experienced the better; we might even get back our nerve. But then we cannot stop at this stage of the analysis; we have still to look at what the system is for, in the actual running of our kind of society.

In part, as noted, it is for respect, though in making this respect differential it is often self-defeating. Still, as we move around in our own country, the operation of differential respect is evident enough to tempt some people into accepting the scale so long as they can improve their own position on it. Anyone who wants to experience the reality of the differential has only to put himself, physically, at a point on the scale other than that he is used to, changing some of the signals by which the ordinary exchange is operated, and he will feel the difference quickly enough. Let any middle-class man who thinks class distinction has died out put aside, if only for a day, his usual clothes, his car, his accent, and go to places where he is not known but where he knows how he would be normally received: he will learn the reality quickly enough. Let him go in the working clothes of a manual worker, but with his 'standard' accent, to a shop, an office, a pub, and watch the confusion as the contradictory signals are sorted out. In daily experience this complicated differential goes on, but we have to cross the borders to appreciate it fully, for we normally get used to the rate of respect our evident market value commands. Is this differential anything to worry about, though, in its patent hypocrisy? Not personally, of course, but it would be a change to have a community in which men and women were valued either as real individuals or, where that closeness is impossible, by a common general respect.

There are many signs that money, in the form of conspicuous possession of a range of objects of prestige, is rapidly driving out other forms of class distinction, and it is this change which is behind the argument that class distinction is diminishing. This is a simple confusion of meanings, for it is the reality of differential treatment, rather than the particular forms through which it operates, that makes a class system. The point is particularly important in that the money we earn, to set the differential system going, is itself subject to built-in differentials of an especially complicated kind. The differential for extra skill and extra responsibility is part of this system, but only part, and all arguments about pay become hopelessly confused if this basis of differential is assumed to be the only one generally operative. There is the first obvious fact that a radical differential is imposed by the general financial position of the industry or service in which a man is working. The teacher and the engine-driver start on different total scales, in services where money is short, from the copywriter or the car-assembly worker, where money is easier. And if standing in the community is increasingly assessed in straight money terms, this situation is a very serious distortion from the outset. The next radical differential is more closely tied to class. Most of us live by selling our labour, but in some cases the pay is called salary, in other cases a wage. In practice this is much more than a verbal difference: we hear of wage demands from one kind of man, but of requests for a review of remuneration from another. Public indignation, or what passes as such in the newspapers, is quite regularly reserved for the 'wage demands', while much larger 'adjustments' in the pay of salaried men pass with little comment. When workers in one industry agitate for more pay, there is too little comparison with the whole range of pay, and too much with other workers no better off. Or one reads the public discussions, in some minority newspapers, of the level of percentage increase which wages can be confined to in a given year. In the same year quite different and much larger percentage increases are discussed in relation to salaries, but hardly ever within the same terms of reference. It is difficult to know what else to call this but a practical class system.

Many of the lower-salaried workers are in practice treated as wage-earners: there is great confusion at that point in the scale. But at a certain level a whole world of difference begins, not only in straight money, but in such critical factors as an automatic incremental scale, a contract of service conferring important rights in such things as payment in sickness and protection against dismissal, and differential facilities in many things from cups to carpets. The system is almost infinitely graded within itself, but the class-line, below which these benefits are not available, is ordinarily quite clear.

Once again, however, it is misleading to confine such analysis to comparison between salaried and wage-earning employment. Many salaried people consider themselves unjustly treated, in such matters as tax-relief for expenses, by comparison with salary-earners or employers in different parts of the economy. Between all these groups there is enough resentment to ensure a cynical community for generations. I support those economists who believe that in spite of the immense difficulties the attempt to establish some general principle of equity, to which particular arguments about pay can be referred, must be made. The present resentments, and the crude ways in which they are fought out, are more than a healthy community can afford.

Meanwhile, to finance the system of conspicuous expenditure, an extraordinary credit network has been set up, which, when considered, reveals much of our real class situation, and the ways in which it is changing. The earners of wages and salaries are alike in this, that most of them become quickly involved in a system of usury which spreads until it is virtually inescapable. How many supposedly middle-class people really own their houses, or their furniture, or their cars? Most of them are as radically unpropertied as the traditional working class, who are now increasingly involved in the same process of usury. In part it is the old exaction, by the propertied, from the needs of the unpropertied, and the ordinary middle-class talk of the property and independence which make them substantial citizens is an increasingly pathetic illusion. One factor in maintaining the illusion is that much of the capital needed to finance the ordinary buyer comes from his own pocket, through insurance and the like, and this can be made to look like the sensible process of accumulating social capital. What is not usually noticed is that established along the line of this process are a group of people using its complications to make substantial profit out of their neighbours' social needs. The ordinary salary-earner, thinking of himself as middle class because of the differences between himself and the wage-earners already noted, fails to notice this real class beyond him, by whom he is factually and continually exploited. Seeing class-distinction only in the limited terms of the open differential, he is acquiescing in the loss of his own freedom and even, by the usual upward identification with which the struggling middle class has always been trapped, underwriting his real exposure, as one of the unpropertied, as if it were his system and his pride.

As we move into this characteristic contemporary world, we can see the supposed new phenomenon of classlessness as simply a failure of consciousness. The public discussion is all at the level of the open differential and its complicated games, but if this were eventually resolved, into a more apparent equity, there would still be no real classlessness; indeed there can be none until social capital is socially owned.

It is in this context that the distinction between middle class and working class must always be considered. The line between them, always difficult to draw, is now blurred at many more points by a common involvement which the remaining distinctions not only disguise but in part are meant to disguise. Is the working class becoming middle class, as its conditions improve? It could as reasonably be said that most of the middle class have become working class, in the sense that they depend on selling their labour and are characteristically unpropertied in any important sense. The true description is one that recognises that the traditional definitions have broken down, and that the resulting confusion is a serious diminution of consciousness. New kinds of work, new forms of capital, new systems of ownership require new descriptions of men in their relations to them. Our true condition is that in relation to a complicated economic and social organization which we have not learned to control, most of us are factually servants, allowed the ordinary grades of upper, middle, and lower, insistent on the marks of these grades or resentful of them, but, like most servants, taking the general establishment for granted and keeping our bickering within its terms.

This situation is clearly reflected in contemporary politics. The Conservative Party is still basically the party of the propertied and the controllers, with an old and natural genuflection to the mellow dusk in which these processes are blurred. But it is felt to be the party of most of those who still anxiously call themselves 'middle class', preoccupied as always with the upward identification and the downward keeping-in-place, the latter now fortunately expressible in precise wage percentages. The Labour Party, with vestigial ideas of a different system, offers little alternative to this structure of feeling, and upward identification, it is now learning, can spread a long way down. This is no sudden and dramatic change, though particular voting results may appear dramatically to reveal it. It is part of the logic of a particular system of society, which will operate so long as there is no adequate rise and extension of consciousness of what the system is and does.

Such consciousness is not helped by the ordinary kind of discussion which has followed Labour's third electoral defeat in 1959. The most popular formula has been that the defeat was inevitable because Labour is identified with the proletariat and the proletariat is breaking up. This is extremely doubtful. It is true, of course, that modern houses, modern furniture, television sets and washing machines and, in some cases, cars, are increasingly available to many wage-earners. But what is meant by calling this process 'deproletarianization', as the *Economist*, following E. M. Durbin and others, has done? If the electoral decline of Labour in the 1950s is evidence of this, what are we to make of the fact that when working-class standards were low, as in the inter-war depression, and so when more 'proletarian' conditions might have been supposed to exist, many less people than now in fact voted Labour. Thus the Labour vote in 1959, in its third defeat, was nearly half as much again as it was in the worst periods of poverty and depression. In 1924 the Labour vote was $5\frac{1}{2}$ million, in 1929 $8\frac{1}{2}$ million, in 1931 $6\frac{1}{2}$ million, in 1935 $8\frac{1}{2}$ million. In the famous victory of 1945, the Labour vote rose to 12 million, and a slump in the Conservative vote brought Labour a large parliamentary majority. After this peak, according to the popular formula, Labour lost electoral support because its first measures towards socialism were disliked. How curious, then, that in 1950 the Labour vote was 13,235,610, and in 1951 the highest figure ever polled by a British party, 13,949,105. The 'proletarian' situation of the depression had produced a maximum of

$8\frac{1}{2}$ million votes, the full-employment situation of 1951 nearly
14 million. And what of the elections since then, with more
consumer goods and consumer credit, breaking up this
'proletariat' of the past? In 1955, on a lower total poll,
12,405,246 Labour votes. In 1959, on a poll still much
lower than 1951, 12,216,166. The loss in voters in the last
two elections is marked. In 1955 it was blamed on bad
polling weather, internal dissensions (these were also
serious in 1951), and 'apathy'. In 1959, the weather was
perfect, the dissension was less, and the election received
more publicity, through television, than ever before. Yet the
vote went down again, and, most significantly, the total poll
was still some 5 per cent lower than in 1951. It is a difficult
situation to analyse, but we need not be hindered by myths of
a 'proletariat' and 'deproletarianization'. In the whole
'proletarian' period up to 1939, Labour never got more than
38% of the total votes cast. In the 'deproletarian' period since
1945 it has never got less than 43%. These facts reduce the
usual analysis to nonsense.

The British working class, in the traditional sense of the
great body of wage-earners and their families, has in fact
never voted solidly Labour, as anyone who grew up in a
wage-earning family would know without being told. If
Labour had ever got a regular 70 per cent of these wage-
earning voters, it would have been permanently in power. It
is an extraordinary misunderstanding of politics to suppose
that a man necessarily votes for a proletarian party because
he was born in a proletarian position. The building of the
labour movement, both industrially and politically, has been
a continuous struggle to create a particular political and social
consciousness. To the ordinary difficulties of education and
propaganda has been added a continuous campaign, by other
social groups, to check and confuse and sidetrack this
movement. At times hardly any headway has been made;
at times there have been real defeats; at times, again, important advances. Consider only, on the negative side, these
statements:

Propose to a working man any great measure affecting the whole
body, and he immediately asks himself the question, What am I to

get by it? meaning, what at this instant am I to have in my hand or in my pocket? There he sticks.

Lancashire working men were in rags by thousands, and many of them lacked food. But their intelligence was demonstrated wherever you went. You would see them in groups discussing the great doctrines of political justice . . . or they were in earnest dispute respecting the teachings of socialism. *Now* you will see no such groups in Lancashire. But you will hear well-dressed working men talking, as they walk with their hands in their pockets, of Coops . . . and their shares in them or in building societies.

The difficulty of persuading workmen to listen to anything which does not concern pleasure or profit has long been acknowledged, and is, I think, even stronger than it used to be.

The people have all been busy getting on, some too busy to think of anything except their work, some too set on the pleasures now opened to them to care for knowledge.

Any of these statements might be made now, in the fashionable exposition of the 'I'm all right Jack' ideology of the workers. But their dates, respectively, are 1835, 1870, 1882, and 1900: spanning the years in which the labour movement's foundations were built. The ragged groups of our own century, discussing socialism, may have been similarly replaced by 'well-dressed working men talking of their shares', but this is no new phenomenon: the fluctuations are the real historical process, and in fact, as we have seen, there are more Labour voters in our own well-dressed times than in the days of the ragged groups of the 1930s. The fact is that there is no simple rising graph, for the process does not take place in a vacuum. It is profoundly affected by changing political conditions and by phases of change in the society as a whole. This is the real historical context from which any serious contemporary analysis must begin.

My own view of the political fluctuations since the war can be briefly stated. The Labour victory of 1945 was outstandingly an expression of determination not to return to pre-war conditions, with which the Conservatives were widely identified. The very low Conservative vote in that year (8½ million) is as significant as the Labour increase.

Between 1945 and 1951, the evidence of opinion polls shows a loss by Labour of much of the support from salary-earners which had helped it in 1945. Yet in 1950 and 1951 Labour's vote increased, which can only mean that more and more wage-earning voters had turned to its positive support. The huge vote of 1951, still in conditions of post-war austerity and planning, was the most conscious working-class determination ever recorded in Britain, to reject the conditions of pre-war society and go on with the new system. But by 1951, the Conservative Party had been significantly reorganised, not only technically but in terms of policy. It was identified now, not with a return to the 1930s, but with basic acceptance of the Welfare State and with the relaxation of austerity and controls. The Conservative Party could not beat Labour in 1951, in real votes, but by the vagaries of the electoral system (huge Labour majorities piling up and wasting in the heavy industrial areas) it regained parliamentary power. Millions of salary-earning voters had come back to it, and its traditional wage-earning vote had at least survived. And then, in government, it remained reasonably faithful to its new identity. There were incidental cuts in the social services, and redistributions of taxation favouring the better-off, but all in the context of a more visibly prosperous economy and a general reduction in taxation. The dread of the return to the 1930s lifted; the Welfare State was not dismantled; earnings—with full employment, overtime, and an increasing number of wives working—rose, and there was plenty to buy. If the Conservatives did as little as they could to redress poverty and basic inequality, still a given minimum—what one Conservative MP has called 'Butler Socialism'—was the evident price of power, and they were able and willing to pay it. In such conditions, with each new election preceded by a boom in spending power, the Labour Party's permanent task of creating a new kind of social consciousness was just too difficult.

Drawing back from this detail of immediate politics, what can we learn, from such evidence, about the general development of the society? We have already rejected the ordinary explanation, of 'deproletarianization': a proletariat

329

may be factually created by an industrial system, but it is only politically created by political action, and in Britain this has never been fully achieved. Millions of wage-earners and their wives voted Conservative in 1959, as in previous elections. The significant questions are what kinds of people these were, and whether there are any new and permanent social patterns shaping them. It is difficult to answer these questions with any certainty, but one fact stands out. The division of votes by sex cuts right across the usual analysis by class, introducing questions which cannot be negotiated within our ordinary political categories. Thus, in the 1959 election, when the British people is supposed to have decisively endorsed conservatism, the votes of all men (according to poll analysis) resulted in a narrow majority for Labour. The figures were 51% Labour against 49% Conservative among men; 55% Conservative against 45% Labour among women. This male Labour majority has been normal since the war, though it is also significant that it narrowed during the fifties, and that the Conservative majority among women has also been narrowing. The reasons, in each case, are still speculative, but at least it is impossible to analyse the distribution of the wage-earning vote without serious allowance for this difference by sex. In 1955, for example, the wage-earning vote split 55½% to Labour, 40½% to Conservatives, while all men split 50% Labour to 45½% Conservative, all women 54% Conservative to 42% Labour. It is then highly probable that in addition to wage-earning Conservative families, there were many Conservative wives of Labour husbands. Given actual trends, it is very difficult to see any radically new pattern in this complex, especially if we are rid of the 'proletarian' myth that before 1939 almost all wage-earners and their wives voted Labour as a matter of course. Labour gets a higher percentage of the total vote in the period of washing-machines and television than in the period of high unemployment, and the adjustments within this are obviously too complicated for any single explanation.

Another possible line of approach is in terms of new kinds of community. If we look at a political map of Britain, over the century, we see an important relation between kinds of community and political representation, and this seems a real clue to understanding contemporary change. A map of Labour representation is virtually a map of the coalfields and the great towns, with the significant exception of some of the 'Celtic' areas, where English social patterns are less marked and where Labour can win even in scattered rural constituencies. Conservatism is strong in almost all the English counties, some Scottish counties, Northern Ireland (where English politics are confused by questions of religion and partition) and the smaller English towns. This diversity is the reality, which is masked by overall counts and the exaggerations of the present electoral system. In 'Conservative Britain', in 1960, Wales is strongly Labour, Scotland has a Labour majority for the first time, and, to take only the outstanding cases, there is a Labour London, a Labour Birmingham, a Labour Manchester, and a Labour Glasgow. Thus in the heavy industrial areas and in the great towns the wage-earning identification with Labour remains high, though in no sense total or even nearly so. Similarly, in other easily identified communities, such as the English rural counties, and the traditional 'residential' resorts, popular support of the Conservatives is high, as it has traditionally been. It is in other kinds of community, between these extremes, that the difficult social analysis begins.

We think of the new housing-estates, the new suburbs and the new towns as characteristic of the new Britain, and on the whole it is in these areas that Labour hopes are now most regularly disappointed. This is the living-space of that other popular figure of contemporary analysis, the 'semi-detached proletariat'. But in fact people of many different kinds live in these places, which also between themselves have important differences. Attention has been concentrated on the break-up of old community patterns, by such physical removal, but this needs discriminating description. There is social variation, all the way from the estate still mainly serving a single works to the new town wholly mixed in origins and centres of work. There is also historical variation, from the first-generation estate in which social relations are still at the level of casual neighbourly contact, to the second-generation estate on which people have been born, grown up and married. The disruption of extended families noted in some removals is in itself a temporary phenomenon: all first-generation estates will become second and third-generation, though not necessarily with exactly the same family patterns. We cannot be sure what will happen, but it would be rash to assume that all former patterns are permanently gone. The old working-class communities grew, over a century, from a situation of removal and exposure fully comparable in effect to the present phase. When the temporary and artificial nature of the newest communities has been allowed for, and when we have overcome the simple determinism of supposing that things (whether houses or washing-machines) shape men, we shall perhaps be more cautious in assuming that there are wholly new permanent patterns, and in particular that we know what these are. All that can reasonably be noted at the present stage is that these communities were not planned by the people who live in them, but by others with their own versions of what these people needed and what a society or a community is. Again there is variation, but in many places certain patterns of thinking are now on the ground—as they were in the terrace-barracks of the first industrial towns—and these, characteristically, are a cheap version of recent middle-class provision for itself. Thus the houses or flats have more space around them, which is a gain, and have hardly any social buildings ancillary to them, which I think is a loss. A social pattern of a particular kind is thus built into the provision of better housing; you take the one with the other, and the housing, given previous conditions, you must take. At the same time, new communication systems, built on old social patterns but on a very wide scale, are immediately accessible: the cheap national newspaper, the woman's magazine, television. It is not that these external systems are new in kind, though certainly in scale. It is that their growth interlocks with the uncertainties of the general transition, among which there is less to countervail. A new and uncertain factor, in those new communities where work is very mixed, is the degree of interaction between social consciousness gained at work—a classic centre of the growth of Labour consciousness—and social consciousness gained in the community. It is too early to say anything definite about this, since both elements in the interaction are themselves changing, but I am interested in some evidence of a split between trade-union consciousness (the simplest thing learned at work) and Labour consciousness in the wider sense, which has to be in terms of a mixed community and a whole society. Since it is in some groups' interests to encourage this split we must not take such signs of it as there are as an act of God (the 'American future', which this is also sometimes called, would be very much an act of men). At the same time, the conditions for this kind of change exist, indeed have been created. Caught in these many currents, the men and women of the newer communities are living out, explicitly, a pattern of learning and response which is also involving the society as a whole. I am not greatly surprised that contemporary Conservatism, in part directing just this complex, makes sense as an interpretation of it to very many people. For at just this point, Labour seems to have very little to offer. A different version of community, a pattern of new consciousness, it has not been able to give. Its compromise policies combine the two irrelevant elements of appeal to old and fading habits and memories, and of cultural adjustment to the present social confusion. Old Left and New Right in the Labour Party are unconscious allies in delaying any relevant analysis and challenge. The invocation of old habits, which to some extent people are bound to change and reject, combines with the rejection of socialism as a radically different human order, to leave the ruling interpretations and directions essentially unchallenged. Thus the complex and uneven growth of consciousness, most marked in the new communities but present almost everywhere in the society, is left with too few channels through it which can be politically expressed. This cannot be a permanent situation. Men and women do not wait for ever on established systems. New learning, new response, will work through, perhaps in forms we cannot yet envisage (already the Aldermaston marches seem to me new in spirit, whatever their final implications). For the one absolute fact about the men and women of the new communities, as of the new kinds of society everywhere in the world, is that they are created in a human image, and not in the image of anybody's version of them. The 'telly-glued masses' do not exist; they are the bad fiction of our second-rate social analysts. What the masses, old or new, might do is anybody's guess. But the actual men and women, under permanent kinds of difficulty, will observe and learn, and I do not think that in the long run they will be anybody's windfall.

The received descriptions of social classes have been at their most confusing, in just this new situation. How is anyone to know, in a new town or on a new housing estate, if he or she belongs to the 'working' or the 'middle' class? The traditional meanings that come through are not in economic terms (where, as we have seen, the working class-middle class description is very difficult to draw) but in terms of style of life and behaviour. 'Working class', for very many people, is simply a memory of poverty, bad housing, and exposure, while 'middle class' is a name for money to spend, better housing, and a more furnished and controllable life. Since the styles of living of the whole society are in any case changing, this contrast very easily becomes one between past and present: 'working class' is the old style, that people are steadily moving away from; 'middle class' is the new 'contemporary' style. It is easy to point out that by this time these terms have lost any relevant meaning, as descriptions of actual social organization, but their emotional charge is no less powerful for that. 'Working class and proud of it' may last in the older communities, and in some politically active individuals, but in most cases it is now deeply confused: on the one hand, 'I work for my living' (which almost everyone does); on the other hand, the strong social sense of 'working' = 'lower' class, with inferiorities and deprivations to which nobody in his senses wants to return. I have the impression that when socialists speak now of the working class, they attract to themselves natural resentments against the whole idea of class and inferiority. In its social sense, most people only talk about class when they are anxious, and often want to get rid of the feeling that there are these kinds of distinctions between people. I think this desire should be respected, for it is an exceptionally valuable piece of social growth and maturity. But the point has been reached where the growing feeling that class is out of date and doesn't matter is being used to ratify a social system which in other terms than those now visibly breaking down is still essentially based on economic classes.

To perpetuate the present confusion is to guarantee a minimal social consciousness. We have instead to concentrate on two general facts: the open differential, and the ownership and control of social capital. If the open differential, which still gives some reality, though confused and confusing, to the working class-middle class distinction, is discussed on its own, the society cannot be understood. The differential is merely an operative function of a particular kind of society, and to promote an even more tense competition within it, setting one kind of worker against another, has the effect of directing social consciousness into forms that simply perpetuate the overall system. It is certainly my view that the differential will have to be revised, but the only possible basis for this is a real feeling of community— the true knowledge that we are working for ourselves and for each other—which, though present now as an ideal, is continually confused and in some cases cancelled by the plain fact that most of us do not own or control the means and the product of our work. In an industrial economy, social production will either be owned or controlled by the whole society, or by a part of it which then employs the rest. The decision between these alternatives is the critical decision about class, and if we are serious about ending the class system we must clear away the survivals, the irrelevancies, and the confusion of other kinds of distinction, until we see the hard economic centre which finally sustains them. With that basic inequality isolated we could stop the irrelevant discussion of class, of which most of us are truly sick and tired, and let through the more interesting discussion of human differences, between real people and real communities living in their valuably various ways.

IV

The extension of culture has to be considered within the real social context of our economic and political life. My studies of the growth of particular cultural institutions showed a real expansion, which of course is continuing, but showed also the extent to which this was affected or determined by other facts in the society. In the 1960s, the rate of growth seems promising, and we are busy with plans to maintain and increase it. Yet here, very clearly, is a major contradiction easily overlooked by following a simple rising graph, for while real art and argument are being more widely enjoyed, the distribution of a bewildering variety of bad art and bad argument is increasing even more rapidly. We are reaching the point where the contradiction between these different lines and rates of growth is serious and inescapable, yet even those who see this situation feel particularly uncertain about what can be done.

We must look first at a particular and local contradiction which can quickly confuse any such discussion. If someone proposes ways of extending good art and argument, and of diminishing their worst counterparts, someone else usually answers that we mustn't be snobs: that football, after all, is as good as chess; that jazz is a real musical form; that gardening and homemaking are also important. Who exactly is someone like this arguing with, since it is usually obvious that he is not really arguing with the man to whom he replies? Unfortunately he is arguing with actual people and a familiar way of feeling. It is true that certain cultural forms have been used as a way of asserting social distinction, and that much wholesale condemnation of new forms has been a way of demonstrating the inferiority of those two groups who have regularly to be put in their (lower) place: the masses and the young. This habit has to be resisted, but there is equal danger in a popular form of demagogy which, by the use of selective examples, succeeds in avoiding the problem of bad culture altogether. Can we agree, perhaps, before passing to the more difficult questions, that football is indeed a wonderful game, that jazz is a real musical form and that gardening and homemaking are indeed important? Can we also agree, though, that the horror-film, the rape-novel, the Sunday strip-paper and the latest Tin-Pan drool are not exactly in the same world, and that the nice magazine romance, the manly adventure story (straight to the point of the jaw) and the pretty, clever television advertisement are not in it either? The argument against these things, and the immense profits gained by their calculated dissemination, cannot afford to be confused by the collateral point that a good living culture is various and changing, that the need for sport and entertainment is as real as the need for art, and that the public display of 'taste', as a form of social distinction, is merely vulgar.

In a rapidly changing and therefore confused society, in which cultural forms will in any case change but in which little is done by way of education to deepen and refine the capacity for significant response, the problems that confront us are inevitably difficult.

Two parallel efforts are necessary: on the one hand the maximum encouragement of artists who are seriously trying to create new forms or do significant work in traditional forms; on the other hand, the steady offering and discussion of this work, including real criticism and therefore its distinction at least from calculated and indifferent manipulation. It would be wrong to say that these efforts are not being made: some help, though still inadequate, is being given to the arts; some responsible offering and discussion are publicly underwritten. These policies fall within the evolutionary conception: a steady encouragement of elements of valuable growth. But while supporting them, and certainly wishing to see them extended, I find it difficult to feel that they go to the root of the problem. For it is usually not recognized that inferior and destructive elements are being much more actively propagated: that more is spent, for example, on advertising a new soap, and imprinting a jingle attached to it, than on supporting an orchestra or a picture gallery; and that in launching two new magazines, one trying to do a serious new job, the other simply competing to capture a share of a known popular market, the ratio of comparative investment is ludicrous, for hardly anything is behind the former, while huge sums of money are poured out on the latter. The condition of cultural growth must be that varying elements are at least equally available, and that new and unfamiliar things must be offered steadily over a long period, if they are to have a reasonable chance of acceptance. Policies of this degree of responsibility seem impossible in our present cultural organization. The encouragement of valuable elements is restricted to what is little more than a defensive holding operation, which of course is better than nothing but which is hardly likely to make any general change. The rest of the field is left to the market, and not even to the free play of the market, for the amounts of capital involved in financing our major cultural institutions restrict entry to a comparatively few powerful groups, so that both production and distribution are effectively in very few hands. The serious new magazine referred to, usually the result of a major voluntary effort by a group of dedicated people, is unlikely to be even available for buying, in the sense of lying ready on the average bookstall where somebody might try it, while the new commercial magazine will be so widely displayed that it can hardly be avoided. It is then stupid and even vicious, when it is clear that no real competition exists, to use the evidence of immediate results as proof of the unalterable vulgarity of the public. Instead of the ritual indignation and despair at the cultural condition of 'the masses' (now increasingly uttered even by their supposed friends) it is necessary to break through to the central fact that most of our cultural institutions are in the hands of speculators, interested not in the health and growth of the society, but in the quick profits that can be made by exploiting inexperience. True, under attack, these speculators, or some of them, will concede limited policies of a different kind, which they significantly call 'prestige'; that is to say, enough to preserve a limited public respectability so that they will be allowed to continue to operate. But the real question is whether a society can afford to leave its cultural apparatus in such irresponsible hands.

Now I think many people feel the strength of this question, but feel even more strongly the difficulties of any possible alternative. Steady and particular encouragement, in the obvious limited fields, is quite widely approved, but any attempt to tackle the whole situation runs into major difficulties. For it is obvious that the amount of capital and effort required, to make any substantial change, can come only from public sources, and to this there are two objections. The first is the question whether such resources are really available, on the scale required. This goes back to the difficulty discussed earlier: that we find it almost impossible to conceive the financing of social policy out of the social product, and have never learned a system of accounting which would make this possible or even visible. For it is true, of course, that the present investment comes from the society and economy as a whole. The supply of advertising money (the contemporary equivalent of manna) can only come in the end from us, as workers and buyers, though it is now routed through channels that give control of this social capital to very limited groups. If we can realize that we are paying for the existing cultural system, by one kind of organization of the economy, we need not be frightened by the scale of resources required, since that organization is in fact subject to change. We should be much clearer about these cultural questions if we saw them as a consequence of a basically capitalist organization, and I at least know no better reason for capitalism to be ended. It is significant that the liveliest revolt against the existing system, particularly among the new young generation, is in precisely these cultural terms.

But then the second objection is deeply involved with this point. What is the alternative to capitalism? Socialism. What is a socialist culture? State control. There are many good liberals, and many anxious socialists, who draw back if this is the prospect. Better even the speculators, they say, than the inevitable horde of bureaucrats, official bodies, and quite probably censorship.

This difficulty has a representative significance. It is not only in cultural questions, but in the whole area of thinking about change in our society, that this knot is tied. Here is the deepest difficulty in the whole development of our democracy: that we seem reduced to a choice between speculator and bureaucrat, and while we do not like the speculator, the bureaucrat is not exactly inviting either. In such a situation, energy is sapped, hope weakens, and of course the present compromise between the speculators and the bureaucrats remains unchallenged.

Democratic policies are made by open discussion and open voting. In relatively small bodies, contact between members and policies can be close, though even here some responsibility for decisions will be passed to elected representatives rather than to members as a whole, and where much administrative work is necessary will also be passed to officials. The principle of the official in a democratic organization is quite clear: he administers within an elected policy, and is responsible to the membership for his actions. The practice, we all know, can be otherwise, but given an adequate constitution and genuine equality of membership it is still the best and most responsible system known.

There are strong arguments for the national organization of the means of cultural exchange, but the persistent danger, even in a democratic country, is that too large an organization becomes rigid and in a sense impenetrable. Any adequate cultural organization must be open, flexible and committed to genuine variety of expression. It would seem simple to say that the best people to run the various cultural organizations are those who use them for the production of their own work, for here is the deepest and most practical interest in keeping the organization flexible and open. Yet it is equally clear that the actual producers of cultural work cannot, from their own resources, command the ownership of any but the simplest means. Where indeed they can do so, no change is necessary. But in the press, in broadcasting and television, in the cinema and theatre it is obvious that this simple co-operative ownership is impossible. This ought not then to mean, however, that the control of these expensive means should be made available to the highest bidder, especially when he is not even particularly interested in the actual work but mainly in its financial possibilities. The signs are, in contemporary Britain, that this worst of all arrangements is becoming normal, with a dominant policy criterion of profit and with the producers turned into employees within this emphasis. In press and television this is especially the case, and powerful interests are working to extend the same system to broadcasting. It is urgent to define the alternative principle, which I think can only be that when the producers cannot themselves own the means of their work, these must be owned by the community in trust for the producers, and an administration set up which is capable of maintaining this trust. The difficulties here are obvious, but all administration and constitution-making in fact proceed from an emphasis of what is desirable, and I believe that if we can agree that this end is desirable, no society is better qualified from experience to devise adequate practical methods.

In the drama, for example, it would be possible for most theatres to be publicly owned, preferably by local authorities though perhaps with a small national network in addition, and then licensed to companies of actors. It would then be possible for these companies, through open regional and national organizations which they would be free to join or not as they decided, to pursue reasonably long-term policies on the guarantee that a particular production would go to a series of theatres, when financially necessary. Similar arrangements could be made, through permanent and regular liaison, with the broadcasting and television services. The advantages to the drama of permanent companies creating their own varying traditions, in a context of adequate professional security, would undoubtedly be great: almost all the good work we now have in the theatre comes from such companies, which are left, though, to struggle on as best they can with the hope of being eventually hired by the speculators who control the big national theatres. If we are serious about freedom in the arts, we can give it, in this way, to actual artists.

In the cinema, a related system is possible. As things now are, the makers of films are almost wholly in the hands of the distributors, who decide, by certain crude tests, whether a film is worth making before it is made. This is the freedom of the artist which our liberals so complacently defend. It is clear that the number of cinemas is in any case going to decline. The opportunity this presents of a sensible reorganization ought not to be missed. The cinemas should become publicly owned and vested in an independent public authority. There should be at least two or three circuits, including one specialized circuit, to ensure alternatives. Production should be in the hands of independent permanent companies, which as in the case of the theatre would have to satisfy the public authority of their professional competence. Public money should then be made available to these companies, for the making of films which would be guaranteed exhibition on one of the circuits. The more independent companies there are the better, and it would be encouraging to see some links between some of these and the theatre companies already referred to. A possible organization of the independent authority would be joint representation between officers appointed by and responsible to Parliament and representatives elected by the permanent companies.

In the case of books, we already have a good range of independent publishers, though the pressures on them to surrender independent policies are severe. A rapid process of amalgamation (often retaining apparently independent imprints) seems to be under way, and new kinds of owner, often little concerned with literature, are becoming more common. With high costs, and the wide opportunities of the 'paperback revolution', it seems that a stage has been reached very similar to that in newspapers at the turn of the century. The quantitative thinking that can follow from such a system would be disastrous to publishing, past a certain point, and I think the time has come for an inquiry into the facts of recent changes and possible courses of action. Meanwhile it is of vital importance that publishers who pursue, as now, responsible and therefore varying policies should be given all possible help. This can probably best be done in the now chaotic field of distribution. It is a standing disgrace that there should be hundreds of towns without anything that can be called a decent bookshop. The good independent bookseller performs an especially valuable service, but unless he is lucky in his locality he will often go under. The existing chain shops apply to books and periodicals simple tests of quantity: below a certain figure they do not consider particular items worth handling. Is this any kind of freedom, or free availability? I think we could set up a Books Council, representative on the one hand of publishers, booksellers and authors, on the other hand of Parliament, which would have the duty of ensuring the continued independence of publication, and at the same time the best possible distribution of books and periodicals here and overseas. The pressure to reduce publications to a limited number of standard items, easily sold in quantity, should be resisted as a matter of public policy. Such a Council could review existing bookselling arrangements, and wherever it found (as it would now widely find) that the real range of books and periodicals is not offered, it would have power to establish and guarantee independent enterprises committed to the policy outlined. It is very odd that we have accepted this principle, in the public library service, for the borrowing of books, but are still so far short of it in terms of books that readers can buy and keep.

In the case of newspapers and magazines, we have to deal with a situation in which control is passing into fewer and fewer hands, within a policy dedicated not to the quality of newspapers and magazines but to their profitability. The criterion of profitability is being raised to absurd levels, in which for example a daily newspaper may have to cease publication if less than a million people buy it, and in which a steady decline in the number of newspapers and magazines seems assured. Again, is this freedom, or free availability? The quality of newspapers is unlikely to be raised either by exhortation or censorship. Experience in all other fields suggests that standards in a profession rise when they are in the control of members of that profession. Such professional responsibility is now virtually impossible, as a permanent and consistent policy, since the whole organization of the press (like the organization of the cinema and the theatre) creates a different atmosphere, in which standards are set by the controllers, on an estimate of likely profit, and the actual producers instead of feeling a common responsibility to their work are encouraged, in far too many cases, to compete with each other in supplying a predetermined article. Personal standards will always vary, but it is a poor society which creates institutions that give success to the least scrupulous and the least concerned. Any attempt to reform these institutions, though, is met with prolonged abuse and misrepresentation. Obviously we do not want a state-owned press, but I think we have reached the point where we need a new Press Council, including public and elected journalist representatives, charged with the maintenance and extension of genuinely independent newspapers and magazines. We need in particular to ensure the survival of local newspapers, and I think it is essential that these should become locally owned and managed, as very few of them now are. There are serious objections to involving local authorities in the ownership of local newspapers, though in certain cases this might be done. More generally, the guarantee of independence, and any necessary provision of capital, should be accepted as a public service at national level, through a Press Council including, as defined, journalist representatives. The same public service principle should be applied to magazines, on terms guaranteeing independence to professionally recognized editorial bodies. With experience, this principle could be extended to the national press. I do not see why the editorial bodies of any newspaper or magazine should not be free, by their own democratic decision, to apply to such a Press Council to be recognized as an independent enterprise, which would then be guaranteed freedom from any external private financial control. The terms on which this recognition and support would be granted would be the producers' own definition of policy. There might be cases when the Council, including public and professional representatives, would be unwilling to underwrite a particular policy proposed, but in such cases we should be no worse off than we are now: such a policy could be tried on the market, or financed much as now, for of course there can be no question of any newspaper or magazine being forbidden to publish. I think that with experience and goodwill a majority of professionally responsible independent papers could be built up, and even if we did not achieve a majority, we should at least have ensured that no newspaper or magazine could be killed by a financial organization indifferent to quality and interested only in immediate profit. Reform can only come from within, in such a field, if it is publicly supported.

In broadcasting and television we see an imperfect but still generally responsible public authority, the BBC, powerfully challenged by new kinds of organization. It is obvious, as these services extend, that we need the continual extension of choice, but it is doubtful if we shall get this, on any responsible basis, if we construe independence as the possession of working capital from elsewhere (mainly, as now, from advertising). There might well be two or more public authorities owning the technical means of distribution, but the same principle holds as before: policy can be generally defined by the public authorities, but the provision of actual work must be in the hands of the real producers. Practical networks exist, and their wide use is clearly desirable, but what one would like to see serving them is a variety of independent groups, with genuine local affiliations and alternative policies. The existing programme companies, in commercial television, are hardly ever of this kind, but are essentially a congeries of financial interests employing the real producers. It should be a matter of public policy to encourage the formation of professional companies to whom the technical means of distribution would be made available by the public authorities. The core of such groups would be the professional broadcasting and television producers, who would work out means of association with other professional companies in the theatre, the cinema and the press, with orchestras and other similar institutions of their region, and preferably with wider local organizations, including education committees and the great voluntary societies. In this way the dangers both of a central monopoly and of simple surrender to the speculators could be avoided.

I am very much aware, in putting forward these outline proposals, that much remains to be done, in detailed planning and in improvement, by discussion between all those with relevant experience. I do not suppose that any of these measures of reorganization would be easy, but I do claim, emphatically, that we can envisage a cultural organization which would greatly extend the freedom of the cultural producers, by the sensible application of public resources to cut out their present dependence on dominant but essentially functionless financial groups, and by forms of contract which while preserving responsibility in the spending of public money would give the producers control over their actual work. This is surely a hopeful way forward, and constitutions can in fact always be devised if there is substantial agreement on principles.

The matter is now urgent, for while some liberals still shy away from reform in the name of the freedom of the artist, or argue that culture in any case can never be organized (the spirit bloweth where it listeth), a very rapid reorganization of a different kind is in fact going on, with the area of real ownership and independence shrinking in every part of our culture, and seeming certain to continue to do so. I must plainly ask such liberals what they are really defending, for there seems little in common between the freedom they value and the actual freedom described recently by an owner of a television service and a great chain of newspapers as 'a licence to print your own money'. We have reached a crisis in which freedom and independence can only be saved if they are publicly assured and guaranteed, and the ways I propose seem a working basis for this, taking care as they do to avoid or minimize the real dangers of bureaucracy and state control.

Would the quality of our cultural life be improved by such measures? I feel certain that it would, in the real energies that would be released, but I am not thinking in terms of any overnight transformation. I say only that the channels would be more open, that the pressure for quick profit would be lifted, and that a more genuine range of choices would be made available. My whole case about social change is, moreover, that the interdependence of elements which I described as a matter of theory is an argument for conceiving change on the widest possible front: the changes in emphasis in our economy, in our ordinary working relationships, in our democratic institutions, and in education are all relevant to cultural change in this more explicit field. I would repeat my emphasis on the overriding educational problem: the provision of new kinds of education for the now neglected majority between fifteen and twenty-one. The growth of adult education is also relevant: much more could be done to house this increasing work properly, at the centre of its communities, and to improve its connections with the wider cultural services.

A particular job is waiting in relation to information about the quality and use of the new range of goods now available. We are spending £400,000,000 annually on an advertising system which, instead of performing this rational service, lives in a world of suggestion and magic. The existing 'consumers' advice' associations should certainly be encouraged, but characteristically, like most existing encouragement of the arts, they serve only a limited public. Could we not then have a public research and information service, with adequate offices and showrooms in every town, where genuine choice could be made available to the ordinary buyer? This could be done on the present expenditure on the antiquated system of advertising, which is simply a pre-democratic form of manipulation of a public regarded as 'masses'. And the more all this new work could be brought together, so that these new kinds of community service could be seen as factually linked—buying and learning, using and appreciating, sharing and discriminating—the more likely a healthy cultural growth would be.

v

The human energy of the long revolution springs from the conviction that men can direct their own lives, by breaking through the pressures and restrictions of older forms of society, and by discovering new common institutions. This process necessarily includes both success and failure. If we look back over recent centuries, the successes are truly spectacular, and we ought to keep reminding ourselves of them, and of the incomprehension, the confusion, and the distaste with which the proposals for things now the most ordinary parts of reality were received. At the same time the failures are evident: not only the challenging failures, as new and unrealized complexities are revealed, but also the straight failures, as particular changes are dragged back into old systems, and as ways of thinking deeply learned in previous experience persist and limit the possibility of change. We tend to absorb the successes and then to be preoccupied by the hard knots of failure. Or as we approach the failures, to see if anything can be done, we are distracted by the chorus of success.

I am told by friends in the United States that in effect the revolution is halted: that my sense of possibility in its continued creative energy is a generous but misleading aspiration, for they in America are in touch with the future, and it does not work—the extension of industry, democracy and communications leads only to what is called the massification of society. A different stance is then required: not that of the revolutionary but of the dissenter who though he cannot reverse the trends keeps an alternative vision alive. I hear this also in Britain, where the same patterns are evident, and it is true that in a large part of recent Western literature this is the significant response: the society is doomed, or in any event damned, but by passion or irony the individual or the group may preserve a human enclave. Meanwhile I am told by friends in the Soviet Union that the decisive battle of the revolution has been won in nearly half the world, and that the communist future is evident. I listen to this with respect, but I think they have quite as much still to do as we have, and that a feeling that the revolution is over can be quite as disabling as the feeling that in any case it is pointless. To suppose that the ways have all been discovered, and that therefore one can give a simple affiliation to a system, is as difficult, as I see it, as to perform the comparable act of ingratiation in Western societies: either the majority formula of complacency, or the minority announcement (tough, hard, realistic) that we are heroically damned.

In the long revolution we are making our own scale, and the problem of expectations seems crucial in every society that has entered it. 'That's enough now' is the repeated whisper, and as we turn to identify the voice we see that it is not only that of the rich, the dominant and the powerful, who want change to stop or slow down, but also that of many others, who have no further bearings and are unwilling to risk their real gains. 'That's enough now; we've got rid of poverty, we've got the vote, every child can be educated.' And there it all is, for once these were all seemingly impossible expectations. Even to shape them took many men's lives, and to realize them took the work of many generations. 'But that's enough now; let's tidy up and consolidate.'

We have to distinguish three kinds of thinking by which the long revolution is continually limited and opposed. The first and most important, though it is often left unnoticed, is the steady resistance of privileged groups of many kinds to any extension of wealth, democracy, education or culture which would affect their exceptional status. In the early stages this is usually quite open, but later it becomes a very delicate strategy, using the advances that have been gained as reasons for doing no more, and above all creating the maximum of delay. It is because of the existence of this conscious and highly skilled opposition that the process is still as much a revolution, though in different forms, as when earlier expectations were met with open violence. Recent arguments and measures against African democracy are very similar to the history of early nineteenth-century Britain, but a further relation is even more important, that the arguments and measures against, say, the extension of education in Britain on any adequate scale are part of the same historical process. This strategy must obviously be defined and opposed at every stage.

Yet the privileged groups, again at all stages, find strange allies. The ordinary tactic of attaching the leaders of one phase to its achievements, and encouraging them to identify with the existing order, is extremely successful. The history of the labour movement is full of such cases, in which former leaders become determined opponents of further change, and give much of their energy to fighting new elements coming up through their own movement. This is still going on, in very much its old forms, though the reality of what such men are doing is usually not generally recognized until they are dead. In our own generation we have a new class of the same kind: the young men and women who have benefited by the extension of public education and who, in surprising numbers, identify with the world into which they have been admitted, and spend much of their time, to the applause of their new peers, expounding and documenting the hopeless vulgarity of the people they have left: the one thing that is necessary, now, to weaken belief in the practicability of further educational extension. They could find plenty of vulgarity and narrowness where they are, if they had the nerve to look, just as the knighted trade-union leader, indignant about shop-stewards and communists and all kinds of disruptive elements, could find plenty of arbitrary and ignorant power and conscious intrigue in the world in which he now moves. In our own period it is impossible to overlook this body of people who are effectively limiting and opposing the revolution by which they themselves have benefited.

The third kind of thinking which limits and opposes is much the most difficult to understand. What the Americans call the 'massification' of society can only happen, however hard the new élites may work, if a majority of the people whom they regard as 'the masses' accept this version of themselves. But then it is a fact that for long periods, given sufficient skill in the élites in confusing and flattering, such a majority can for practical purposes be got. I remember watching in a backstreet fish-and-chip shop, the man and his wife, obviously not well off, with obvious local accents, looking in, with what seemed pleasure, at a television play in which people like themselves and their customers, with the same local accent, were made nonsense of, as a class of obviously ignorant clowns. This is not an isolated example of a human version of ordinary people which is regularly and widely presented for the enjoyment of the very people whom the version misrepresents and insults. It is from evidence like this that some people resign themselves to 'massification': the masses will create themselves, take any inferior position that is offered them, and that is the end of any hope of change. I am conscious of the weight of the evidence, but I think it is ordinarily misinterpreted. There is a very skilful obliquity in all such versions: it is always other people who are inferior, the practical identification is never with oneself. While no significant version of other people is there as an alternative, the degrading version makes easy headway. But this version of other people is, precisely, a social expectation. The version of ordinary people as masses is not only the conscious creation of the élites (who work very hard at it, by the way). It is also a conclusion from actual experience within the forms of a society which requires the existence of masses. The framing of different expectations of others has to be carried out, always, against the pressures of an existing culture which is teaching, often very deeply, incompatible patterns. A good example of this is the popularity of 'I'm all right, Jack' as an interpretation of our majority social feelings. Whatever moral notes may be added on the selfishness of this attitude, the fact is that this is a version of ordinary people which the terms of our society need people to accept: if everyone is only out for himself, why bother about social change? Very few people, however, would accept this attitude as an adequate description of their *own* feelings. It is how the others are, and the irony is that some real behaviour in the society, against which there might otherwise be principled protest, feeds in to this cynical version to promote and confirm the safe attitudes it embodies.

The central problem is that of expectations. I do not think the 'I'm all right, Jack' attitude correctly describes our majority social feelings; it is, rather, a skilful stabilization of achieved expectations. Facing real contradictions, which cannot be argued away but need long and difficult effort for any solution, it makes sense to very many of us to concentrate on an area of immediate living where the relation between desire and achievement is straight and practical. If you accept your place and work hard at your job, you *can* make a big improvement in your life, as things now are. Any alternative effort will not only make less visible progress, but it is by no means clear what in fact the effort would be for. The main pressure of the last three generations of social criticism has been towards the abolition of individual poverty, and the point has now been reached where the social conditions for this have been largely achieved, and can then be taken for granted, the immediate climb from poverty seeming now an individual effort. And the point is not so much to remind ourselves that unless the social effort had been made the individual effort, as in the past, would have been normally fruitless. Most people, understandably, will not take much notice of the past. The point is always to frame new expectations, in terms of a continuing version of what life could be. Thus the crucial definition, in the coming generation, is that of social poverty, which in overcrowded hospitals and classrooms, inadequate and dangerous roads, ugly and dirty towns, is as evident in a supposedly prosperous Britain as were the rags and hunger we have abolished. But it is characteristic of all cultural growth that the intensity with which the old patterns have been learned is itself a barrier to the communication of new patterns. Everything will in any case be done, by those opposed to social change, to keep the old patterns alive, even if originally these were bitterly opposed in their turn. And since these patterns are not abstractions, but deeply learned ways of thinking and feeling and forms of behaviour, it is not surprising that for some time a majority in their favour can usually be got. The long effort to communicate new patterns must continue, but it can be cut short and weakened if, falling into old types of despair, those who wish to communicate them dismiss other people, who are under real pressures, as the ignorant and selfish masses who are deliberately prolonging their own condition.

The definition of social poverty, and the revolt against it, have in fact already begun. Parallel definitions of cultural poverty and of inadequate democracy are also being actively shaped. These ways of thinking require not only new kinds of analysis of the society, but also new versions of relationship and new feelings in human expectation. Characteristically, much of the first phase of this growth of consciousness has been negative. The new feelings of the middle 1950s were not in themselves creative; they were a stage of dissent from old formulations, and contempt, sickness and anger were the predominant impressions. These feelings, rooted in a brittle boredom, were indeed strange counterparts of the more general reasoned catalogues of an achieved Utopia. It was comparatively easy to isolate this kind of protest, and to discount it as the expression of an eccentric minority out of touch with the mood of a society which had gathered its energies to a pattern of known expectations. Yet the patterns of real communication in a society are always changing, and people thinking in the old ways suddenly found that a generation had grown up behind them which was similarly isolated, and which found little meaning in the achieved patterns that had seemed so satisfactory. The new feelings, if still only at the stage of disbelief, boredom and contempt, were getting through with surprising speed. New areas of feeling and expectation were being actively reached, if only in the sense of the touching of an exposed nerve. As this was realized, the old kind of attempt to dilute, contain and direct the new feelings was hurriedly made. 'Youth' became a problem, and the more this was said the more contemptuous and insulted most young people felt: 'Can't they see that they're a problem too?' A process very familiar to any historian of cultural change emerged with unusual clarity. People tied to the old definitions and expectations assumed, as always, that the new feelings were either irresponsible or a misunderstanding. 'Perhaps we ought to explain to them that people are earning good wages, that every child gets his chance in education, that we all have the right to vote. Men struggled for these things, so can't these young people show a bit of respect?' 'Or if we trained them more carefully, some wiser investment in qualified leadership perhaps, until they share our values.' But this kind of reaction, characteristically passed through many committees, is in fact useless. Consciousness really does change, and new experience finds new interpretations: this is the permanent creative process. If the existing meanings and values could serve the new energies, there would be no problem. The widespread dissent, and growing revolt, of the new young generation are in fact the growth of the society, and no reaction is relevant unless conceived in these terms. The most useful service already performed by the new generation is its challenge to the society to compare its ideals and its practice. This comparison, as we saw earlier, is the first stage of new learning. People get a sense of reality, and of their own attitudes to it, from what they learn of a whole environment. It is one thing to offer certain meanings and values and ask people to consider and if possible accept them. Yet we all naturally look, not only at the meanings and values, but at their real context. If, for example, we are to be co-operative, responsible, non-violent, where exactly, in our actual world, are we expected to live? Is the economy co-operative, is the culture responsible, are the politics non-violent? If these questions are not honestly answered,

353

propagation of the values as such will have little effect. The degree of evasion will be matched by a degree of contempt, and this can as easily degenerate into cynical apathy as grow into protest and new construction. The only useful social argument is that which follows the meanings and values through to the point where real contradictions are disturbing or denying them. Then, with the real situation admitted, the stage of contemptuous comparison and dissent may pass into constructive energy. For my own part, I see the present situation as a very critical phase in the long revolution, because it is by no means certain, in the short run, whether the new and constructive stage will be reached in time. There are many warning signs of dissent and boredom being capitalized, as a new kind of distraction. The cult of the criminal, the racketeer, the outsider, as relevant heroes of our society, is exceptionally dangerous, because it catches up just enough real feelings to make the heroism seem substantial, yet channels them towards those parodies of revolution often achieved in modern history in the delinquent gang or even in fascism. These destructive expressions can only occur when, in the widest sense, the society is in a revolutionary phase. It is not time then for the reasoned catalogues of sober achievement, but for new creative definitions. The contradiction between an apparently contented society and a deep current of discontent emerging mainly in irrational and ugly ways is our immediate and inescapable challenge.

A growing number of people, in recent years, have been trying to describe new approaches and to make them practical. They have, of course, been widely dismissed as utopians or extremists. But how did they seem at the time, those men we look back to who 'in opposition to the public opinion of the day', 'outraging their contemporaries', 'challenging the general complacency', somehow live with us and even seem tame and 'limited by their period'? Working for something new, a writer or thinker easily identifies with these men, and of course may be wholly wrong: not everything new is in fact communicated and lived. But the reasonable man, tolerantly docketing the extremists of his day: who is he exactly? For he too identifies with these figures from the past; it is usually where he learned to be reasonable. And then who is left for that broad empty margin, the 'public opinion of the day'?

I think we are all in this margin: it is what we have learned and where we live. But unevenly, tentatively, we get a sense of movement, and the meanings and values extend. I have tried to describe some possible ways forward, and ask only for these to be considered and improved. But what I mainly offer is this sense of the process: what I have called the long revolution. Here, if the meaning communicates, is the ratifying sense of movement, and the necessary sense of direction. The nature of the process indicates a perhaps unusual revolutionary activity: open discussion, extending relationships, the practical shaping of institutions. But it indicates also a necessary strength: against arbitrary power whether of arms or of money, against all conscious confusion and weakening of this long and difficult human effort, and for and with the people who in many different ways are keeping the revolution going.

BOOK LIST

Principal texts, sources and authorities, with a selection of secondary material:

1; i.

ARISTOTLE	Poetics
PLATO	Republic; Ion
VALLA	Elegantiae Linguae Latinae
POLITIAN	Letter to Paolo Cortesi
VIVES	De Ratione Dicendi
CASTELVETRO	Theory of Poetry
WILSON	Arte of Rhetorique
WILLIS	De Re Poetica Disputatio
SIDNEY	Apologie for Poetrie
REYNOLDS	Mythomystes
YOUNG	Conjectures on Original Composition
WORDSWORTH	1815 Preface
COLERIDGE	Biographia Literaria; Notebooks
SHELLEY	Defence of Poetry
CROCE	Aesthetic
COLLINGWOOD	Principles of Art
BERENSON	Seeing and Knowing
BELL	Art
RICHARDS	Principles of Literary Criticism
LANGER	Philosophy in a New Key; Feeling and Form; Problems of Art.
FREUD	Introductory Lectures; New Introductory Lectures
JUNG	Modern Man in Search of a Soul
READ	Art and Society
CAUDWELL	Illusion and Reality; Further Studies in a Dying Culture
LERNER	The Truest Poetry
ATKINS	Literary Criticism of the Renaissance
YOUNG	Doubt and Certainty in Science

BRAIN	The Nature of Experience; Mind, Perception and Science.
GHISELIN (ed)	The Creative Process

1; ii.

KROBER AND KLUCKHOHN	Culture, a Critical Review of Concepts and Definitions
BENEDICT	Patterns of Culture
SOROKIN	Social and Cultural Dynamics
FROMM	The Fear of Freedom; The Sane Society
MANNHEIM	Essays in the Sociology of Culture
ELIOT	Notes towards the definition of Culture
COWELL	Culture in Public and Private Life
WILLIAMS	Culture and Society
TILLOTSON	Novels of the 1840s
DALZIEL	Popular Fiction a Hundred Years Ago

1; iii and iv.

HOBBES	Leviathan
LOCKE	Two Treatises of Government
ROUSSEAU	The Social Contract and Discourses
BURKE	Reflections on the Revolution in France
HEGEL	Philosophy of Right
TOCQUEVILLE	Democracy in America
MARX	Critique of Political Economy; 1844 mss.
MILL	Liberty
GREEN	Political Obligation
PLEKHANOV	Rôle of the Individual in History
LINTON	Cultural Background of Personality
SPROTT	Human Groups
SARTRE	Existentialism and Humanism
CAMUS	The Rebel
RIESMAN	The Lonely Crowd
ARENDT	The Human Condition

See also Benedict, Fromm, Sorokin, Freud, Jung, Caudwell above.

2; i.

BOLGAR	The Classical Heritage
ADAMSON	The Illiterate Anglo-Saxon

357

SMITH	Origins of English Culture
MORE	Utopia
ASCHAM	Scholemaster
ELYOT	Governour
CURTIS AND BOULTWOOD	Short History of Educational Ideas
JUDGES	Pioneers of English Education
SMITH	History of English Elementary Education
JONES	Charity School Movement
HANS	Comparative Education; New Trends in Education in C18
KAY-SHUTTLEWORTH	Four Periods of English Education
DE MONTMORENCY	State Intervention in English Education
DOBBS	Education and Social Movements
BINNS	A Century of Education
BIRCHENOUGH	History of Elementary Education in England and Wales
MORLEY	Studies in Board Schools
ADAMSON	English Education, 1789-1902
PETERSON	A Hundred Years of Education
CONNELL	Educational Thought and Influence of M. Arnold
BIBBY	T. H. Huxley
OTTAWAY	Education and Society
CLARKE	Education and Social Change
JAMES	Essay on the Content of Education
VERNON	*in* Bearings of Recent Advances in Psychology on Educational Problems
FLOUD, HALSEY AND MARTIN	Social Class and Educational Opportunity
SIMON	Studies in the History of Education, 1780-1870

English Historical Documents: Vols. VIII, X, XI, XII

2; ii.

PLANT	The Book Trade
ALTICK	English Common Reader
LEAVIS	Fiction and the Reading Public

BOOK LIST

WATT	Rise of the Novel
BELJAME	Men of Letters and the English Public
STEPHEN	English Literature & Society in C18
TOMPKINS	Popular Novel in England, 1700-1800
CRUSE	Victorians and their Books
SADLEIR	C19 Fiction; Collecting Yellowbacks
WEBB	British Working Class Reader
HOGGART	Uses of Literacy
HART	The Popular Book
The Bookseller	

2; iii.

History of *The Times*

HINDLE	The *Morning Post*, 1772-1937
BURNHAM	Peterborough Court
MORISON	The English Newspaper
WILLIAMS	Dangerous Estate
HERD	March of Journalism
ASPINALL	Politics and the Press, 1780-1850
WADSWORTH	Newspaper Circulations, 1800-1954
KELLETT	*in* Early Victorian England
ENSOR	England, 1870-1914
JONES	Fleet St. and Downing St.
RYAN	Northcliffe
SCOTT	Making of the *Manchester Guardian*
PEP	Report on the British Press; Planning 383, 384, 388.

Report of the Royal Commission on the Press, 1947-9
General Council of the Press: annual reports from 1954
Audit Bureau of Circulations: official handbook
Hulton Readership Surveys
IPA Readership Surveys
(Pamphlet): *The People* and the Mass-Sale Sunday Press
Oxford History of Technology, Volume V

2; iv.

JESPERSEN	Language, its Nature, Development and Origin; Mankind, Nation and Individual; Growth and Structure of the English Language

359

SAPIR	Language, an Introduction to the Study of Speech
WYLD	Historical Study of the Mother Tongue; A History of Modern Colloquial English (3rd edn.)
BRADLEY	The Making of English
SKEAT	English Dialects
BAUGH	History of the English Language
ROBERTSON	Development of Modern English
SMITH	The English Language
WEEKLEY	The English Language
WRENN	The English Language
POTTER	Our Language
VALLINS	The Pattern of English
DOBSON	English Pronunciation, 1500-1700
McKNIGHT AND EMSLEY	Modern English in the Making
LEONARD	Doctrine of Correctness in English Usage, 1700-1800
DAVIS	English Pronunciation from C15 to C18
STRAUMANN	Newspaper Headlines, a study in linguistic method

2; v.

Dictionary of National Biography

2; vi.

CHAMBERS	Mediaeval Stage; Elizabethan Stage
YOUNG	Drama of the Mediaeval Church
DAVIDSON	Studies in English Mystery Plays
BOAS	Tudor Drama
KNIGHTS	Drama and Society in the age of Jonson
HARBAGE	Shakespeare's Audience
CHASE	The English Heroic Play
NETTLETON	English Drama of the Restoration and C18
NICOLL	History of Restoration Drama
DOBREE	Restoration Tragedy; Restoration Comedy
KRUTCH	Comedy & Conscience after the Restoration
BATESON	English Comic Drama, 1700-1750
BERNBAUM	The Drama of Sensibility

NOLTE	Early Middle-Class Drama
NICOLL	English Drama
REYNOLDS	Early Victorian Drama
WILLIAMS	Drama from Ibsen to Eliot; Drama in Performance
KITTO	Form and Meaning in Drama
PEACOCK	The Art of Drama
DONOGHUE	The Third Voice

2; vii.

| LUKACS | Studies in European Realism |

3.

BUTLER	The Electoral System in Great Britain, 1918–1951
NICHOLAS	The British General Election of 1950
BUTLER	The British General Election of 1951; The British General Election of 1955
BUTLER AND ROSE	The British General Election of 1959

Sources of quotations on pp. 327–8 are, respectively:
Place MSS. 27827
Cooper, Life of Thomas, by himself (392)
Toynbee (Cooperative Congress, 1882)
Toynbee Hall Report, 1899–1900
(See Dobbs, above)

Index

INDEX

INDEX

INDEX